T0386109

THE
JEFFERSONIAN
VISION,
1801–1815

Also by William Nester

The Revolutionary Years, 1775–1789:
The Art of American Power During the Early Republic

The Hamiltonian Vision, 1789–1800:
The Art of American Power During the Early Republic

THE JEFFERSONIAN VISION, 1801–1815

The Art of American Power During the Early Republic

WILLIAM NESTER

Potomac Books
Washington, D.C.

Maps by Chad Blevins.

Library of Congress Cataloging-in-Publication Data
Nester, William R., 1956–
  The Jeffersonian vision, 1801–1815 : the art of American power during the early republic / William Nester. — 1st ed.
    p. cm.
  Includes bibliographical references and index.
  ISBN 978-1-59797-676-3 (hardcover : alk. paper)
  ISBN 978-1-59797-895-8 (electronic)
  1. United States—Politics and government—1801–1809. 2. United States—Politics and government—1809–1817. 3. United States—Foreign relations—1801–1815. 4. United States—History—War of 1812. 5. Jefferson, Thomas, 1743–1826—Political and social views. 6. Madison, James, 1751–1836—Political and social views. I. Title.
  E331.N47 2013
  973.4—dc23

                                                                2012034678

Printed in the United States of America on acid-free paper that meets the American National Standards Institute Z39-48 Standard.

Potomac Books
22841 Quicksilver Drive
Dulles, Virginia 20166

First Edition

10 9 8 7 6 5 4 3 2 1

Contents

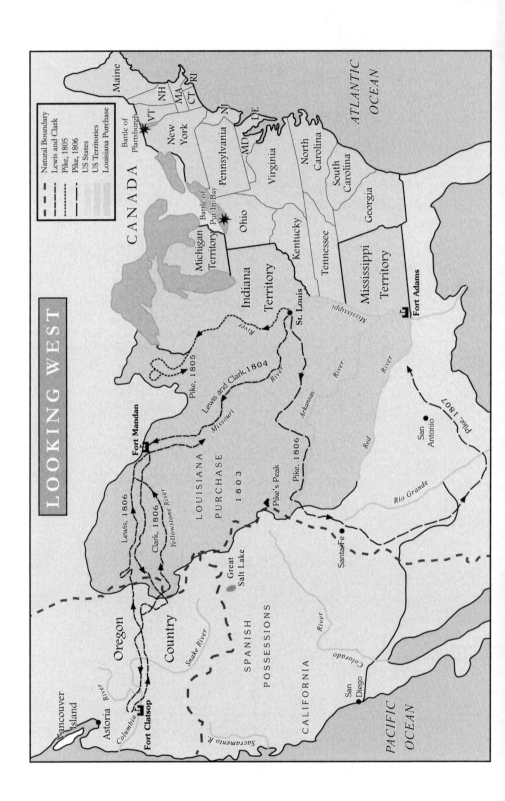

LOOKING WEST

Legend:
- Natural Boundary
- Lewis and Clark
- Pike, 1805
- Pike, 1806
- US States
- US Territories
- Louisiana Purchase

CANADA

ATLANTIC OCEAN

Maine

VT
NH
MA
CT
RI

New York

Pennsylvania

NJ
DE
MD

Virginia

North Carolina

South Carolina

Georgia

Battle of Plattsburgh

Battle of Put-In-Bay

Michigan Territory

Ohio

Kentucky

Tennessee

Indiana Territory

Mississippi Territory

Fort Adams

St. Louis

Mississippi River

Missouri River

Arkansas River

Red River

Pike, 1805

Lewis and Clark, 1804

Pike, 1806

Pike's Peak

Pike, 1807

San Antonio

Rio Grande

Santa Fe

Fort Mandan

Yellowstone River

Lewis, 1806

Clark, 1806

LOUISIANA PURCHASE 1803

Great Salt Lake

SPANISH POSSESSIONS

Snake River

Oregon Country

Vancouver Island

Astoria River

Columbia River

Fort Clatsop

CALIFORNIA

Colorado River

Sacramento R.

San Diego

PACIFIC OCEAN

American Naval Battles 1804–1815

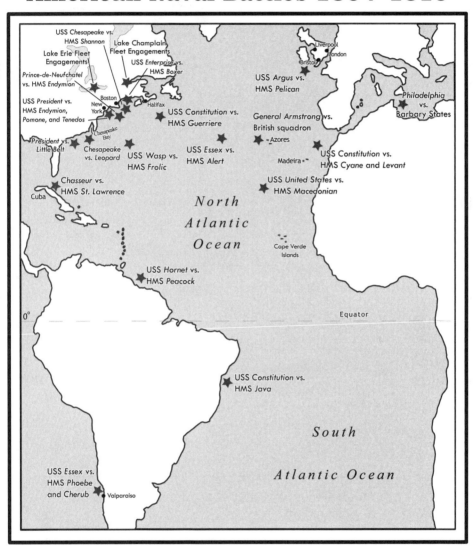

USS Chesapeake vs. HMS Shannon

Lake Champlain Fleet Engagements

Lake Erie Fleet Engagements

USS Enterprise vs. HMS Boxer

Prince-de-Neufchatel vs. HMS Endymion

USS President vs. HMS Endymion, Pomone, and Tenedos

Boston

New York

Halifax

USS Constitution vs. HMS Guerriere

USS Argus vs. HMS Pelican

Liverpool

Bristol

London

Philadelphia vs. Barbary States

President vs. Little Belt

Chesapeake Bay

Chesapeake vs. Leopard

USS Wasp vs. HMS Frolic

USS Essex vs. HMS Alert

General Armstrong vs. British squadron

Azores

Madeira

USS Constitution vs. HMS Cyane and Levant

Chasseur vs. HMS St. Lawrence

Cuba

USS United States vs. HMS Macedonian

North Atlantic Ocean

Cape Verde Islands

USS Hornet vs. HMS Peacock

0°

Equator

USS Constitution vs. HMS Java

South

Atlantic Ocean

USS Essex vs. HMS Phoebe and Cherub

Valparaiso

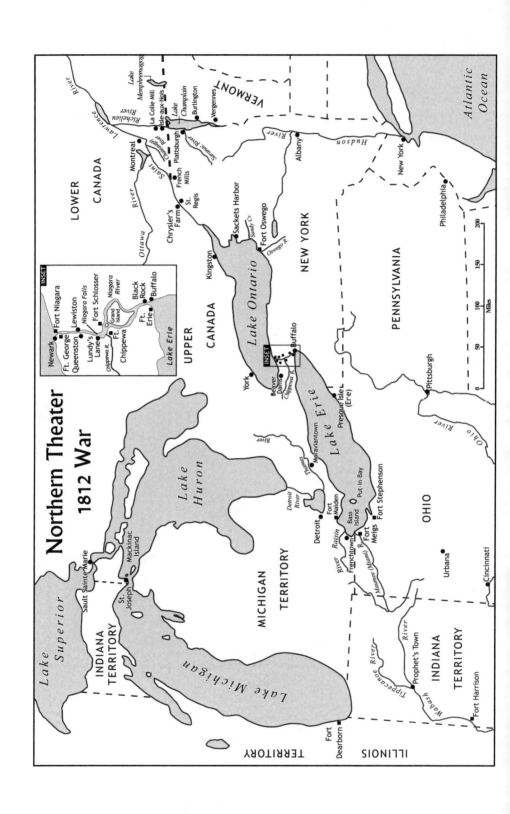

Northern Theater
1812 War

Lake Superior

Lake Huron

Lake Michigan

INDIANA TERRITORY

Sault Sainte Marie

Mackinac Island

St. Joseph

MICHIGAN TERRITORY

ILLINOIS TERRITORY

Fort Dearborn

Detroit

Fort Malden

Bass Island

Put-in-Bay

Frenchtown

River Raisin

Fort Meigs

Fort Stephenson

OHIO

Urbana

Cincinnati

Prophet's Town

Tippecanoe River

Wabash River

Vermilion River

Fort Harrison

INDIANA TERRITORY

Moraviantown

Thames River

Detroit River

Maumee (Miami) R.

Lake Erie

Presque Isle (Erie)

Beaver Dams

Chippewa R.

Buffalo

York

Kingston

Lake Ontario

Sackets Harbor

Sandy Cr.

Fort Oswego

Oswego R.

NEW YORK

UPPER CANADA

LOWER CANADA

Ottawa River

Saint Lawrence River

Montreal

St. Regis

Chrysler's Farm

French Mills

Plattsburgh

Chateaugay River

Saranac River

Richelieu River

La Colle Mill

Isle-aux-Noix

Lake Champlain

Burlington

Vergennes

Lake Memphremagog

VERMONT

Albany

Hudson River

New York

Philadelphia

PENNSYLVANIA

Pittsburgh

Ohio River

INSET

Newark

Ft. George

Queenston

Fort Niagara

Lewiston

Niagara Falls

Fort Schlosser

Lundy's Lane

Chippewa R.

Ft. Chippewa

Grand Island

Niagara River

Ft. Erie

Black Rock

Buffalo

Lake Erie

Miles

0   50   100   150   200

Atlantic Ocean

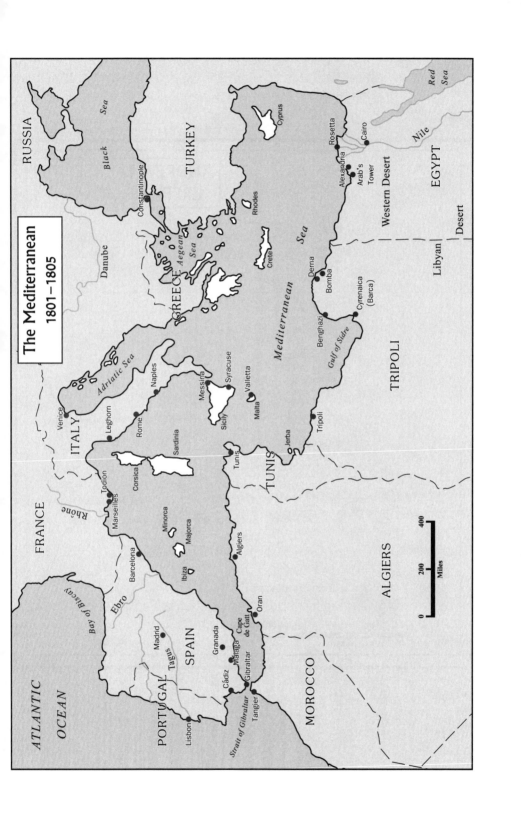

The Mediterranean
1801–1805

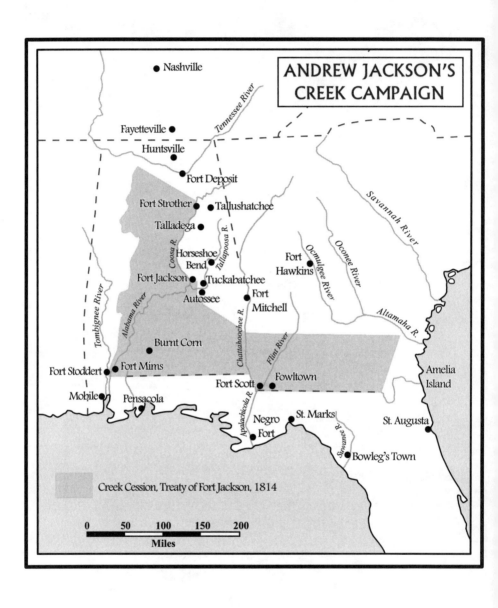

ANDREW JACKSON'S
CREEK CAMPAIGN

Nashville

Tennessee River

Fayetteville

Huntsville

Fort Deposit

Savannah River

Fort Strother   Tallushatchee

Talladega

Coosa R.

Tallapoosa R.

Horseshoe
Bend

Fort
Hawkins

Oconee River

Ocmulgee River

Fort Jackson   Tuckabatchee

Autossee   Fort
Mitchell

Alabama River

Chattahoochee R.

Flint River

Altamaha R.

Tombigbee River

Burnt Corn

Fort Mims

Amelia
Island

Fort Stoddert

Mobile   Pensacola

Fort Scott   Fowltown

Apalachicola R.

Negro
Fort   St. Marks

St. Augusta

Suwanee R.

Bowleg's Town

Creek Cession, Treaty of Fort Jackson, 1814

0   50   100   150   200

Miles

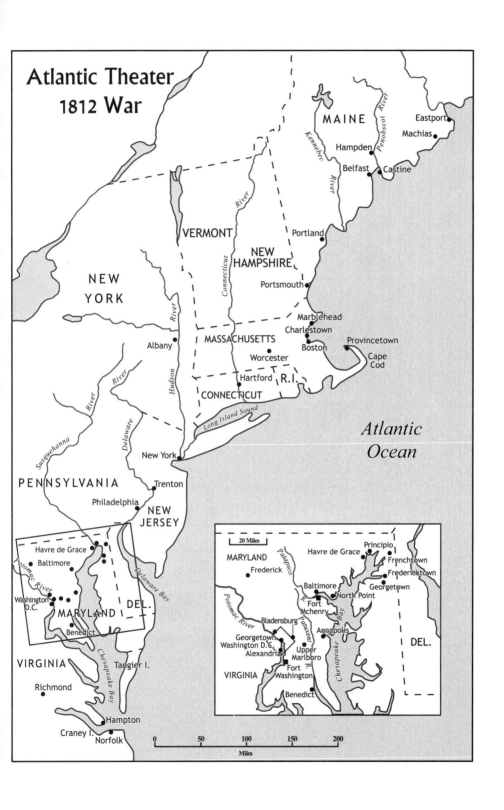

Atlantic Theater 1812 War

MAINE

Eastport
Machias

Penobscot River

Hampden
Belfast Castine

Kennebec River

Portland

VERMONT

NEW HAMPSHIRE

Connecticut River

Portsmouth

NEW YORK

Marblehead
Charlestown

River

Albany

MASSACHUSETTS

Boston

Provincetown

Cape Cod

Hudson River

Worcester

Hartford R.I.

CONNECTICUT

Long Island Sound

Atlantic Ocean

Susquehanna River

Delaware River

New York

PENNSYLVANIA

Trenton

Philadelphia

NEW JERSEY

Havre de Grace

Baltimore

Potomac River

Delaware Bay

DEL.

Washington D.C.

MARYLAND

Benedict

VIRGINIA

Tangier I.

Chesapeake Bay

Richmond

Hampton

Craney I.

Norfolk

20 Miles

MARYLAND

Patapsco

Havre de Grace Principio

Frenchtown

Fredericktown

Frederick

Georgetown

Baltimore

North Point

Potomac River

Fort McHenry

Chesapeake Bay

DEL.

Bladensburg

Georgetown
Washington D.C.
Alexandria

Annapolis

Patuxent R.

Upper Marlboro

VIRGINIA Fort Washington

Benedict

0   50   100   150   200

Miles

THE SOUTHERN THEATER

0   50   100   150
Miles

Ohio R.

Tennessee River

Nashville

Duck River

T E N N E S S E E

Mississippi River

River

Fort Strother ■   *River*
                    Tallushatchee

Coosa River

MISSISSIPPI

Talladega   *River*   *River*
          Emuckfau   Enotachopco

TERRITORY   Horseshoe Bend

River   *Tallapoosa*

Alabama   GEORGIA

Burnt Corn

Apalachicola

Natchez

Fort Mims ■

Plain of
Gentilly   *Perdido River*   WEST
                                FLORIDA
LOUISIANA   Mobile
Baton   *Lake*   *Lake*   Pensacola   EAST
Rouge   *Ponchartrain* *Borgne*   FLORIDA

Lake   ⌐ Cat Island   *Mobile Bay*
Barataria   ○ Pea   Fort
            Island   Bowyer
New
Orleans

■ Fort St. Philip

Gulf of Mexico

Acknowledgments

I cannot express enough my deep gratitude to Elizabeth Demers, senior editor at Potomac Books, first for wanting to publish my Art of American Power series and then for carefully editing each book. She made numerous corrections and wonderful suggestions that greatly strengthened my books. I also owe a great deal to Kathryn Owens, for her meticulous copyediting, Julie Kimmel, for her outstanding proofreading, and Aryana Hendrawan, the production editor. It is such a great pleasure to work with such wonderful people and outstanding professionals as Elizabeth, Kathryn, Julie, and Aryana.

Introduction
The Inauguration

When Thomas Jefferson was inaugurated as president on March 4, 1801, the builders of America's permanent capital had made only snail-like progress on realizing the vision of Pierre Charles L'Enfant, the man most responsible for designing the model city.[1] It had been over a decade since L'Enfant had unveiled his plan for grand neoclassical buildings, boulevards, and parks that would epitomize the budding republic.

So far members of the federal government had merely laid out a few of the broad avenues, the street-grid, and elegant circles, and new buildings stood in various stages of incompletion. The Executive Mansion had come the furthest, although most of the rooms lacked paint, plaster, and woodwork. That work largely ended when John and Abigail Adams had moved in the previous November, and it resumed only once they moved out. Jefferson would have to wait two weeks until those projects were finished and he could settle in. For passersby the Executive Mansion at least looked done, if forlorn, amid its vast lot shorn of trees or grass, with rutted paths leading to the doors. The Capitol, however, clearly had a long way to go. Although the Capitol's wings could respectively accommodate the then 107 representatives and 32 senators, they were joined by only a skeleton of frames and scaffolding. As for the rest of government, the Treasury Department's building was a mere brick shell, while the building that would house the State and War departments was nothing more than a foundation surrounded by piles of boards, cut stones, and bricks. Regardless of the project, slaves rather than freemen provided most of the literally backbreaking labor.

Money, or its want, explained why so little had been done. Although L'Enfant's blueprint had initially excited most members of Congress, they were loath to raise taxes to pay for its realization. Instead they insisted that the nation's capital be underwritten by auctioning off land in that ten-by-ten-mile square straddling the Potomac River, which had been donated by Maryland and Virginia. For years those sales, and thus construction, sputtered along as few people other than speculators saw any sense in transplanting themselves to what was falsely promoted as the "city" of Washington. A syndicate led by Robert Morris, who had served as the chief treasury officer and financier during the Revolution, bought six thousand lots in 1794, but the paucity of sales forced him to file for bankruptcy three years later. Most of the land reverted to the federal government, which once again had to find willing buyers with ready cash. The pace of sales picked up in the year before John Adams and Congress were scheduled to arrive in November 1800.

Quite likely after their first hard look at Washington City, most of those who had served in the previous capital fought the urge to turn tail and run back. Philadelphia was a prosperous, diverse, dynamic metropolis with its thirty thousand people, theaters, concert halls, museums, schools, learned societies, university, fire department, hospital, paved and lighted streets, newspapers, inventors, painters, essayists, poets, churches for every domination, synagogue, and countless shops piled with goods. The new capital was nothing more than a makeshift town with a scattering of shops, taverns, inns, and houses among pastures, swamps, and construction sites; the 1800 census counted 109 brick and 267 wooden houses inhabited by 2,464 whites, 623 slaves, and 123 free blacks. Not one church bell yet beckoned those who would have come from piety or propriety, nor did any school bell toll either for diligent students or those who preferred playing hooky. The demand for houses soared as more politicians, bureaucrats, lobbyists, and merchants set up their respective shops in the new capital. All but the wealthiest among them were forced to share not only rooms but often beds in drafty boarding houses. Sky-high prices only added injury to insult. Winds and traffic on the roads stirred small dust storms during dry spells; for days after a hard rain the muddy roads sucked deep boots, hoofs, and wheels. During the summer, swarms of malarial mosquitoes rose nightly to dine on the residents. Pigs rooted through the streets, fattening off the slop thrown by the residents. The prevailing entertainment was politics, often fueled by whiskey and occasionally enlivened by pistols at dawn when some hothead's "honor" was too grossly offended. Aside from the dueling grounds, politicians could blow off varying types of steam in the score or so drinking dens, or with prostitutes awaiting every taste in brothels or alleys.

Thomas Jefferson most likely paid no mind to the capital's deficiencies and raw pleasures. After all, perhaps no prominent leader of the early republic exceeded the new president as a visionary. He could gaze southwest to the Potomac's far shore and see with crystal clarity his beloved plantation of Monticello, about 120 miles and several long days on horseback beyond the horizon. Within view on all sides, he could envision a metropolis that would one day rival Philadelphia and New York in amenities, entertainment, high culture, and intellectual depth. Indeed, he could take ample pride in counting Washington City among his most notable progeny. It was Jefferson who had hosted that famous dinner at which his protégé, James Madison, grudgingly made a promise—with profound historic consequences for the United States—to his political nemesis Alexander Hamilton. Madison would withhold enough otherwise Republican nay votes to allow passage of a bill authorizing the Bank of the United States and the federal assumption of the states' debts in return for enough Federalist votes for a bill designating a southern capital.

As vice president, Jefferson had joined the exodus from Philadelphia for that new capital just across from his "country," Virginia. For the last four months he had resided in a small room of his own at Conrad's boarding house on New Jersey Avenue, a few blocks from the Capitol. With his official duties slight, he had plenty of leisure to contemplate the full spectrum of his visions, with ever more hours devoted to what he would do if he were president.

By ten o'clock on the morning of Jefferson's inauguration, congressional friends and allies, a small crowd of the curious, a militia company, and drummers and fifers stood impatiently outside Conrad's boarding house. Jefferson emerged, plain-dressed and hatless, his once sandy hair gray, his six-foot frame lean, his movements slightly gawky, his face still sharp and mostly unlined even after fifty-eight years, and his countenance imperturbable despite the significance of the day. As the musicians struck up the first of a medley of tunes, he joined his intimates. With the militia and musicians marching before them, and the rest of the crowd trailing behind, Jefferson and his coterie set off for the Capitol.

Awaiting them were hundreds of people, along with a cannon and gunners. Vice President Aaron Burr and Supreme Court Justice John Marshall stood before the entrance to the Capitol's skeleton core. The three men detested one another. Notably absent was outgoing president John Adams, who was so embittered at losing his bid for reelection that he slipped into a closed carriage in the dead of the previous night and was whisked away to Baltimore for the first leg of a long journey to his home in Braintree, Massachusetts.

The artillery officer barked a command. A gunner lowered a smoldering punk to the touchhole and ignited several pounds of gunpowder that exploded with a deafening roar. Jefferson and Marshall then turned to each other, and the Supreme Court justice asked the new president to raise his right hand. After repeating the oath, Jefferson, the other dignitaries, and as many others as could fit headed for the Senate chamber.

Most of the politicians and others who squeezed into the room did not expect to hear much of the inaugural address. With his soft voice and halting cadence, Jefferson won no laurels as an orator. Their feelings toward the man who stood awkwardly before them differed wildly. Depending on his political creed, each member of the audience either gazed reverently or glared contemptuously at the Republican leader. However, most of the spectators, Republican and Federalist alike, did share one perspective—they were confident that Jefferson's words would be eloquent, profound, and uplifting, whether they agreed with them or not.

In that Jefferson did not disappoint them. His first inaugural address is counted among the greatest expressions of "the American mind" and its vision of liberty, prosperity, unity, and empire.[2] Paraphrasing perhaps the key principle of Washington's farewell address, he called for "peace, commerce, and honest friendships with all nations—entangling alliances with none." That would nurture America as "a rising nation, spread over a wide and fruitful land, traversing all the seas with the rich productions of their industry engaged in commerce with nations who feel power and forget right, advancing rapidly to destinies beyond the reach of mortal eye." For those who feared that the Republicans, with their control over the Executive Mansion and Congress, would abuse their powers against the Federalists, he offered the reassurance that while "the will of the majority is in all cases to prevail, that will to be rightful must be reasonable; that the minority possess their equal rights, which equal law must protect"; he appealed for his countrymen "to restore to social intercourse that harmony and affection without which liberty and even life itself are but dreary things." Fulfilling these ambitions would forever strengthen America's title as "the world's best hope." What Americans then or since could disagree?

The Federalists did not support all that Jefferson said. As proponents of a muscular, problem-solving government that guided the nation's development, they scorned Jefferson's insistence on restricting its duties merely to "restrain men from injuring one another, [and] . . . leave them otherwise free to regulate their own pursuits."[3] But besides that the Federalists searched in vain for other specifics to fault.

In a powerful speech, one memorable and at first gratifying phase shone above all for a nation battered by years of vicious political squabbling capped by a deadlocked election. Jefferson insisted that "we are all republicans, we are all federalists."[4] It was a political inkblot test that had immediate appeal as each favorably interpreted it according to his own inclinations. Time would soon tell just what Thomas Jefferson meant.

Most Americans laud Jefferson's presidency for the purchase of the Louisiana Territory, which stretched the United States westward to the Rocky Mountains, and the launch of the Lewis and Clark expedition, which journeyed to the Pacific Ocean and back. But critics then and since have blasted Jefferson and his successor Madison for a series of ideologically driven blunders. Jefferson envisioned a largely autarkic nation with yeoman farmers making up its economic and political backbone. This idea was at odds with an America whose wealth was gleaned from foreign markets. The Republican policy of wielding partial or complete trade embargoes as a diplomatic weapon repeatedly backfired, inflicting grievous damage on America's economy and culminating with an unnecessary war with Britain that devastated American power and wealth, if not honor. Nonetheless, those debacles did not faze most American voters. The Republican Party, which would soon be renamed the Democratic Party, would dominate American politics for another half century.

The art of power is one's ability to get what one wants. *The Jeffersonian Vision, 1801–1815: The Art of American Power* reveals how well or poorly the nation's leaders understood and asserted power to defend or enhance their view of American interests from when Thomas Jefferson took the oath as the third president in 1801 to the last shots fired at the battle of New Orleans in January 1815.

PART 1

Jefferson, 1801–1805

We are all Republicans—we are all Federalists.

THOMAS JEFFERSON

*At headquarters a most visionary theory presides. . . . No army, no navy,
no active commerce; national defense, not by arms, but by embargoes, prohibitions
of trade; as little government as possible . . . these are the pernicious dreams which
as far and as fast as possible, will be attempted to be realized.*

ALEXANDER HAMILTON

*There is on the globe one single spot, the possessor of which is our
natural and habitual enemy. . . . It is New Orleans.*

THOMAS JEFFERSON

An insult unpunished is the parent of many others.

THOMAS JEFFERSON

*You have made a noble bargain for yourselves and I suppose
you will make the best of it.*

TALLEYRAND

Millions for defense, but not one cent for tribute!

(POPULAR SLOGAN)

My head or yours, Mustifa.

WILLIAM EATON

From this day the United States take their place among the powers of first rank.

ROBERT LIVINGSTON

1

The Revolution of 1801

Thomas Jefferson was fifty-eight years old when Supreme Court Chief Justice John Marshall swore him in as president of the United States on March 4, 1801. He would be the first president to spend his entire tenure in the new capital of Washington City and to live in the Executive Mansion, as they were then called. Most Americans undoubtedly respected him for penning the Declaration of Independence, as well as for serving successively as a representative to Virginia's House of Burgesses and then Congress, as Virginia's governor, as America's minister to France, as the country's first secretary of state, and as its second vice president.

But Jefferson was by no means universally admired, let alone loved. The Federalists reviled him for espousing a political philosophy that spurned commerce and manufacturing and celebrated farming as the nation's economic backbone, for being at once an apostle of liberty and a slave owner, and for his facade of public civility while secretly doing all he could to destroy his political foes. Hamilton captured the Federalist fear and loathing for Jefferson's ideal world as a realm where "a most visionary theory presides . . . no army, no navy, no active commerce; national defense, not by arms, but by embargoes, prohibitions of trade . . . as little government as possible within—these are pernicious dreams which as far and as fast as possible, will by attempted to be realized."[1]

Those were not the only Federalist nightmares that Jefferson and his fellow Republicans would realize. Although no one could have known it at the time, the 1800 election had broken the Federalist Party forever and suppressed its political philosophy for two generations. When Jefferson took office, the Republicans had an edge of 17 to 15 in the Senate and an overwhelming advantage of 68 to 38 in the House; however, eight years later, on the cusp of his retirement to Monticello, the Republicans outvoted the Federalists by 28 to 6 in the Senate and 116 to 26 in the House. The Federalist Party's wounds were largely self-inflicted. The party first alienated many Americans with the 1798 Sedition Act and then tore itself apart during the 1800 election in the battles of egos and issues between the Hamilton and Adams wings. Thereafter, those factions warred against one another as bitterly as they did against the Republicans. By 1815, the Federalists as a national party had ceased to exist with only a handful of politicians and pundits keeping its outlook alive. This would be disastrous for the development of American power.[2]

Jefferson may never have realized his dream of bringing harmony to the nation, but he proved to be an able head of an administration and a party.[3] Dumas Malone, Jefferson's wordiest biographer, declared that

> no presidential Cabinet was ever more harmonious. This was partly because of the temperaments of the ministers themselves, and the habit of cooperation they had gained as members of the opposition. Even more, probably, it was due to the President, who made a special point of harmony, and to whom they were all personally devoted. In his ability to command the loyalty of his subordinates without needing to ask it, Jefferson was an executive beyond compare.[4]

Regardless of the issue, Jefferson was always the hub of his policymaking wheel. After taking office, he convened his cabinet at least once a week to discuss the issues and reach a consensus on how to deal with them. That practice gradually diminished as he realized it was more practical to work with those secretaries who were directly concerned. Jefferson did not hesitate to seek perspectives from beyond the Executive Mansion. He was a prolific letter writer who exchanged ideas with a wide spectrum of people. But his closest advisers were James Madison and Albert Gallatin.

Madison was somewhat miscast as secretary of state. He had never been out of the country and spoke or wrote little on international relations. Exhausted from years of leading the Republican crusade in the House of Representatives against the Federalists, he had retired in 1797. But Jefferson had no trouble luring his faithful protégé, friend, and political partner back to public service.

Gallatin would ably serve as the treasury secretary for the next dozen years. Like Hamilton, he was a foreigner whose brilliance brought him swift fame and fortune in America. He was born into a wealthy Geneva family, studied at the Geneva Academy, and then in 1780 at age fifteen emigrated from Switzerland after the last of his family died. He first supported himself as a merchant on the Maine frontier, but an influential connection got him a post teaching French at Harvard. After a couple of years in Cambridge, he headed back to the frontier, this time for a homestead in western Pennsylvania. Impressed by his learning, intelligence, and eloquence, his district sent him as a delegate to Pennsylvania's constitutional convention in 1789 and then to the state assembly in 1790. He was elected as a Republican to the U.S. Senate in 1793, but the Federalists blocked his admission, claiming against all the evidence that he did not meet the nine-year residence required for citizenship. Shortly after being elected to the House of Representatives in 1795, he replaced Madison as the Speaker and head of the House Republicans. His mastery of financial affairs made him Jefferson's obvious choice for treasury secretary. He would be the calm voice of reason for Jefferson and then Madison, acting as the brakeman when idealism gripped those presidents and their administrations.

In contrast to Madison and Gallatin, the remaining members of Jefferson's cabinet were better noted for their loyalty than their intellects. Henry Dearborn had been a stolid if unimaginative and cautious officer during the War for Independence, and displayed those same characteristics as the secretary of war. Benjamin Stoddert had been an outstanding navy secretary and agreed to stay until Jefferson could find his own man. Neither of his replacements had any acumen for that post: Samuel Smith agreed temporarily to be the navy secretary if he could keep his day job as a prominent Republican senator from Maryland; on July 15, 1801, he yielded that post to his brother, Robert, an Independence War veteran but whose only link with the sea was his specialty in admiralty law. Levi Lincoln was just as undistinguished an attorney general, but as a prominent Massachusetts lawyer and politician, he helped balance the cabinet's geography.

Like his predecessors, Jefferson neglected his vice president, Aaron Burr. Unlike them, he had ample cause for doing so. Perhaps only one vice president in American history has been reviled for being more divisive and devious than Burr. Most Republicans scorned him for betraying Jefferson's trust by trying to grab the presidency for himself. His notoriety worsened in 1804 when he killed Alexander Hamilton in their infamous duel. He was indicted for treason shortly after leaving office.

Jefferson managed Congress as expertly as he did his administration. He was a brilliant lawmaker. Malone explained that "Congress not only accepted practically all of his recommendations; it passed virtually no bills of any significance without his recommendation or tacit approval. That legislative record was not to be matched in American history until the presidency of Woodrow Wilson."[5]

It certainly helped that Jefferson enjoyed overwhelming Republican majorities in both houses of Congress, and "unlike both of the Presidents before him and most of those after him, he was the undisputed head of his party."[6] Yet being the head of a party that dominates Congress is not enough. Many presidents in that enviable position have found their own party as balky as the opposition. He worked closely and continuously with congressional Republicans, inviting groups of them to the Executive Mansion for talks and dinner. But he also reached across the aisle and nurtured ties with prominent Federalists, most notably John Quincy Adams, who was a frequent guest. Relations with Congress were so good that, during his eight years as president, Jefferson never once had to wield the power of veto.

But the most important reason why Jefferson racked up such an outstanding legislative record was that he was a brilliant and ruthless politician. No one excelled him as a master of political guerrilla warfare, of anonymous attacks from unexpected directions, of secretly convincing politicians and editors to say and do what he could or would not say or do publicly, for fear it would sully his image.

It was certainly not all work and no play for Jefferson and his fellow politicians of the early republic. In that leisurely age, presidents took nearly as much time off as members of Congress. Jefferson liked to spend August and September at Monticello, his mountaintop plantation. He responded to criticism of his long sojourns there by arguing that he worked just as hard on affairs of state at Monticello as at the Executive Mansion, and could keep in touch with his administrators by couriers atop fast horses.

Although Jefferson was a private man in most ways, paradoxically he enjoyed surrounding himself with others.[7] He was alone in the Executive Mansion because his wife was deceased and his one surviving daughter of six children was married and lived elsewhere. So he viewed his secretaries and Republican leaders as an extension of his household. He loved presiding over informal dinners with good food, fine wines, and convivial conversation.

He worked hard at cultivating an image of himself as the quintessential common man of an agrarian republic. Aside from elaborate meals, Jefferson shunned ostentation. He dressed simply. His manners were always impeccably polite. He avoided displays of lavish praise or enthusiasm. At times, though, he may have carried his studied "democratic" style of dress and demeanor too far. British minister Anthony Merry was offended when once greeted by the president in his bedroom slippers, and complained loudly of the indignity he and his wife suffered when they were forced to scramble with nimble-footed Americans for empty chairs at a state banquet.[8]

2

The Battle for the Courts

Politically one obstacle marred the Republican monopoly of power.[1] While Jefferson dominated the legislature, he faced a judiciary that two Federalist presidents had filled with like-minded people over the dozen years after the system was set up. The latest expansion and reform of the federal court system came with the Judiciary Act that John Adams signed into law on February 13, 1801, about three weeks before he turned over the presidency to Jefferson. The law itself was uncontroversial. It amended the 1789 Judiciary Act, which had brought about the federal court system, by adding ten district courts, three circuit courts, sixteen circuit court judges, and forty-two justices of the peace; relieved Supreme Court justices from the time-consuming duty of having to ride the circuit; and ended the potential for deadlock on the Supreme Court by reducing the number of justices from six to five.

John Adams took full advantage of that law. During his remaining time in office, he appointed Federalists to all of the new positions. He swiftly tapped candidates for thirteen of the sixteen new judges. Finding the remaining three judges and filling a list of the forty-two justices of the peace took longer, however. He submitted those final nominees on March 2, and the Senate confirmed them as they had the earlier list of judges. Although he was legally entitled to do so, John Adams left a huge political boulder in the garden that Jefferson would inherit.

The new president naturally resented what became known as the midnight appointees. But there was nothing he could do. The Senate had confirmed all of

Adams's choices. The commissions, however, had not been delivered and were piled neatly on the secretary of state's desk.

So Jefferson defied the will of both the president and the Senate that preceded him. But he did so in a way that he believed would at once assert his own administrative power and make a strong conciliatory gesture. He withheld those commissions and instead gave recess appointments to thirty people, of whom twenty-five were Adams nominees. He explained that he had not appointed the other twelve for reasons of economy. Not on that list was William Marbury, who would make a groundbreaking federal case of his absence.

For Jefferson, beneath the struggle over political power was political philosophy. And underlying that philosophy was the most profound level of all—psychology. This, however, was a realm where Jefferson, like most people, feared to tread. Jefferson was most comfortable wrapping himself in the abstractions of philosophical speculation. And by that light, he saw Adams's appointments not as those of a political leader taking advantage of legal powers granted by the Judiciary Act. Instead, he scornfully viewed that law and the subsequent appointments as a violation of a more fundamental law of political trust, thus a "nullity." This leads to a powerful facet of Jefferson's outlook on life—the idea that the earth belongs to the living. Practically this view meant that those new to power could rightfully undo the work of their predecessors. When politics gridlocked or the powerful violated the rights of the weak, a minority had the right to break away from the majority if it saw fit to do so. That was certainly the logic behind the American Revolution. If it had been in less responsible hands and reasonable voices than those of America's founders, then the revolution would have potentially been an excuse for anarchy or tyranny.

With that outlook, Jefferson worked closely with Republican leaders to repeal the 1801 Judiciary Act. The subsequent battles between the majority and minority parties were bitter and consumed much of the congressional sessions of 1801 and early 1802. The Republicans eventually triumphed with the Judiciary Act of 1802, which abolished the 1801 Judiciary Act and reverted the system to that established by the 1789 act. But that proved to be a Pyrrhic victory.

William Marbury was among the dozen justices of the peace whose nomination the Senate had confirmed but whose commission Jefferson had set aside. He and four others appealed to a federal court to issue a writ of mandamus, or legal command for the administration to fulfill its legal duty, which in this case was to deliver the commissions. The writ was issued against Secretary of State Madison because it was on his desk that the commissions fell.

The Supreme Court ruled unanimously on February 24, 1803, that Marbury, like any citizen, had the right to issue a writ of mandamus, but his case was thrown out because the 1789 Judiciary Act violated the Constitution by expanding its judicial powers beyond those clearly stated. In writing the court's opinion, Justice Marshall succinctly explained the federal court's constitutional power and its duty of judicial review.

The Supreme Court's 1803 decision of *Marbury v. Madison* was the turning point for judicial power. In finding the 1789 act unconstitutional, the Supreme Court asserted the power of judicial review, which was alluded to in the Constitution's third article and elaborated on by Alexander Hamilton in Federalist Essay 78. Since that ruling, the judiciary has been, in theory if not always in practice, as important and powerful as the executive and legislative branches within the federal government.

That ruling infuriated Jefferson and those who have shared his philosophy of government then and thereafter. Jefferson denied the power of judicial review and instead insisted on his "tripartite" theory of the Constitution whereby each branch was free to define and act upon its own powers. That concept completely conflicts with the theory of checks and balances designed to prevent any branch from dominating, thus forcing each to work with the others. The government set up by the Constitution epitomizes cooperation, elaborated on by Alexander Hamilton, James Madison, and John Jay in their eighty-five Federalist essays. But try as he might, Jefferson could do nothing to reverse the Supreme Court's *Marbury v. Madison* ruling and its crucial precedent.

3

Thomas Jefferson and American Power

Thomas Jefferson's animus toward judicial power merely reflected the key maxim of his political philosophy: the government that governs least, governs best. Government was, at best, a necessary evil and, at worst, a tyranny. To minimize that danger, most of the duties, and thus the powers, of government should reside in that level closest to the people. Only if local communities proved incapable of handling a problem should a state government involve itself. Ideally, that left virtually nothing for the federal government to do.

Of course, there was more to Jefferson's political ideals, which he most eloquently and succinctly expressed in the Declaration of Independence. Yet, as Stanley Elkins and Eric McKintrick caution, "Jefferson was not a systematic theorist, nor indeed a system-builder of any kind. He produced no fusions of theory, experience, and necessity comparable to Madison's theory of the extended republic or Hamilton's system of public finance."[1] Jefferson's mind "habitually worked on two quite different levels. One was that of broad general statement, the other that of specific technical detail. He was both a utopian and something of a gadgeteer."[2]

And therein lies a huge problem. There was often not just a gap but a contradiction between his principles and his practices or what he felt was practical. Elkins and McKintrick captured his central intellectual dilemma, and thus his moral deficiency:

> This disjuncture in Jefferson's thinking between the general and particular, the long range and the short, and between broad conception and concrete

16

realization, might seem belied by his historical reputation for "pragmatism." He was quite aware that hard facts frequently got in the way of his ideal constructs. . . . [Yet] true "pragmatism" consists not simply in adjusting one's actions but also in adjusting one's mind; indeed, an odd thing about a man who lived as long as Jefferson is that he seldom changed his mind about anything.[3]

Jefferson was a strict constitutional constructivist whenever his political foes, especially Hamilton, cited the "supremacy clause" and "implied powers" in order to promote their programs. But he would turn a blind eye to his own ideology when it obstructed what he wanted to do, most glaringly for the Louisiana Purchase. Shortly after completing his second presidential term, he made the following argument, which would have provoked him to condemn Hamilton had the latter uttered it: "A strict observance of the written laws is doubtless one of the high duties of a good citizen, but it is not the highest. The laws of necessity, of self-preservation, of saving our country when in danger, are of higher obligation. To lose our country by a scrupulous adherence to written law, would be to lose the law itself, with life, liberty, property, and all those who are enjoying them with us; thus absurdly sacrificing the end to the means."[4] When it came to the development of the nation's economic power, Jefferson was strictly a libertarian by contemporary political yardsticks. He believed that "a wise and frugal government, which shall restrain men from injuring one another, shall leave them otherwise free to regulate their own pursuits of industry and improvement, and shall not take from the mouth of labor the bread it has earned. This is the sum of good government."[5]

Throughout his career, Jefferson would be a deficit hawk for public spending, even if he was profligate in his private expenses. "To expend the public money with the same care and economy we would practice with our own" and "impose on our citizens no unnecessary burden."[6] He most succinctly explained his outlook in a letter to Gallatin:

I consider the fortunes of our republic as depending, in an eminent degree on the extinguishment of the public debt before we engage in any war: because that done, we shall have revenue enough to improve our country in peace and defend it in war, without recurring either to new taxes or loans. But if the debt should once more be swelled to a formidable size . . . we shall be committed to the English career of debt, corruption, and rottenness, closing with revolution. The discharge of the debt, therefore, is vital to the destinies of our government.[7]

Unlike contemporary conservatives, Jefferson was serious about cutting back the size of government and reducing the national debt. His priority after taking power was to devote himself to "demolishing useless structures of expense, lightening the burthens of our constituents, and fortifying the principles of free government."[8]

Like contemporary conservatives, Jefferson wanted to get rid of all internal taxes, which had contradictory effect on his desire to diminish the national debt. Ideally, the government would fund itself solely from the revenues skimmed from trade. Gallatin explained patiently that if internal taxes were abolished, the national debt would rise. Jefferson could either lower taxes or the national debt, but he could not do both. Jefferson believed that he could eliminate all internal taxes and reduce the national debt by cutting back on government expenses.

Jefferson proved to be right. Defying Gallatin's advice, one of his first acts as president was to rally the Republican Party to pass a law that abolished all internal taxes. He signed that act into law on March 8, 1801. He then confronted the national debt. On April 19, 1801, he signed a law that required a strict frugality in federal spending.

Those policies were as popular as they would be successful. Jefferson merits high marks for his fiscal policies. During his eight years in office, he reduced the national debt by $25 million, from $82 million to $57 million, and left a $9.5 million budget surplus despite the Louisiana Purchase. Had he survived, Hamilton would have heartily congratulated the outgoing president.[9]

Much like his view of government, Jefferson saw international trade at best as a convenience. He conceded that Americans could not make all they desired while they gained wealth by selling to others. He admitted that "access to the West Indies is indispensably necessary to us."[10] But he preferred autarky. Ideally, the United States could "abandon the ocean where we are weak, leaving to neutral nations the carriage of our commodities."[11]

Jefferson bitterly lamented America's economic dependence on Britain and would have outright abolished trade with that country if he could have. In 1797, he wrote that the British

> have wished a monopoly of commerce & influence with us; and they have in fact obtained it. When we take notice that theirs is the workshop to which we go for all we want; that with them centre either immediately or ultimately all the labors of our hands and lands; that to them belongs either openly or secretly the great mass of our navigation; that even the factorage of their affairs here, is kept to themselves by factitious citizenships; that these foreign and false citizens now constitute the great body of what

are called our merchants, fill our sea ports, are planted in every little town & district in the interior, sway everything . . . by their votes . . . are advancing fast to a monopoly of our banks & public funds, and thereby placing our public finances under their control; that they have in alliance the most influential characters in and out of office.[12]

Jefferson's accusations may have a familiar ring to today's readers. If anything, those lines on the evils of the corporate class are far more descriptive of America two centuries after they were penned. Jefferson certainly and correctly diagnosed a perennial problem with America's economic and political system. Yet, for all his brilliance, he was incapable of understanding that his own ideology was the principle cause of that very dependence. It was Jefferson and his fellow Republicans who championed the ideal of an American economy and government dominated by yeoman farmers. That sentiment would ensure a trade of American foodstuffs and other raw materials for British finished goods and capital, and thus perpetuate and worsen American inferiority and dependence as Britain's economy developed and America's stagnated.

Alexander Hamilton sought to break these bonds by promoting related American financial, commercial, and industrial revolutions. Those revolutions would take generations to realize and would involve a brainy and brawny federal government working closely with the private sector to cultivate America's economy. That would in turn allow the United States eventually to surpass Britain in wealth and power. But Hamilton's vision was ideological heresy for Jefferson and his fellow Republicans, and they did everything possible to block or dismantle his policies. The result would be to delay and distort the development of American wealth and power for decades.

American exports nose-dived during Jefferson's first two years in power, from $94 million in 1801 to $54 million in 1803, and then more than doubled to $108 million in 1807.[13] The president's policies had little to do with this fall and rise. The fleeting peace allowed British and continental merchants to recapture some of trade that the United States and other neutral countries had grabbed during the war. Exports subsequently soared when Europe plunged back into the abyss of war after 1803, and neutral Americans could once again take over the carrying trade.[14]

Jefferson's beliefs and acts could be downright muddled, at times with tragic results. While the economy is a nation's ultimate foundation of power, a military is also essential to deter and, if necessary, defeat aggressors. Here Jefferson was lost at sea over the vital national security question of how to defend America from foreign and domestic armed threats. Jefferson, that most unmartial of men, opposed both a standing professional army and navy for the United States. For defense he would rely on gunboats to shield the coast and on militia to defend the land.

Indeed, he would go so far as during

> the occasions of making war, it might be better for us to abandon the ocean altogether, that being the element whereon we shall be principally exposed to jostle with other nations: to leave to others to bring what we shall want, and to carry what we can spare. This would make us invulnerable to Europe, by offering none of our property to their prize, and would turn all our citizens to the cultivation of the earth; and, I repeat it again, cultivators of the earth are the most virtuous and independent citizens.[15]

He was well aware that his sentiments provoked apoplexy in the nation's merchants and shippers. Although autarky was Jefferson's ideal, he recognized that his isolated Arcadian republic was an elusive dream since "the actual habits of our countrymen attach them to commerce." Thus "wars then must sometimes be our lot."[16]

So the question then was what would be the best strategy in a time of war. Jefferson had as little regard for regulars as army veterans had for the militia. He wrote that it "is nonsense to talk of regulars. They are not to be had among a people so easy and happy at home as ours. We might as well rely on calling down an army of angels from heaven."[17] His philosophy celebrated the ideal of virtuous yeomen farmers cultivating the land and contemptuous of making and selling things to others, who would grab their muskets and march off to battle rapacious invaders. But when he thought more about the problem, he admitted that maybe the sea should be America's first line of defense:

> Providence has placed their richest and most defenseless possessions at our door; has obliged their most precious commerce to pass as it were in review before us. To protect this, or to assail us, a small part only of their naval force will ever be risqued across the Atlantic. . . . They can attack us by detachment only. . . . A small naval force then is sufficient for us, and a small one is necessary. . . . To aim at such a navy as the greater nations of Europe possess would be a foolish and wicked waste of the energies of our countrymen. It would be to pull on our own heads that load of military expense which makes the European laborer go supperless to bed.[18]

Actually the United States tried this naval strategy during the Revolutionary War but it failed to prevent the British from sailing armadas and landing armies freely along the American coast. While the privateers and a handful of state and national warships did pick off scores of British merchant ships, they destroyed only a portion of Britain's immense trade. The Americans fought few naval battles with His Majesty's ships and won even fewer of those engagements. Given their inherent weaknesses, the Americans had no choice but to follow that strategy.

But the greatest folly would be to do so a generation later with a greatly expanded economy, population, merchant fleet, and government revenues. Yet that was exactly Jefferson's plan. The result left the United States far weaker militarily than it might otherwise have been, first in a war with Tripoli and then, after Jefferson left office, with the British empire.

Although the Federalists repeatedly issued Cassandra-like warnings, Jefferson made his ideology the foundation for the military's budget and structure. Ideally, he would have done away with a standing army and navy altogether, but he conceded that a skeleton of each was politically expedient and strategically sound. To that end he ordered Treasury Secretary Gallatin to spend no more than $2 million annually on the military, split equally between the two services.[19]

Thanks largely to Hamilton's ceaseless efforts, first as treasury secretary and then as an unofficial adviser behind the scenes, the United States had an army and navy in 1801, although far short of what he had envisioned. When Jefferson took the oath of office, the army's authorized strength was 5,438 troops in four infantry regiments, two companies each of engineers and artillery, and two troops of light dragoons. Jefferson's 1802 Military Peace Establishment Act cut that official army by approximately one-third to 3,289. That cutback was not as sharp as it seemed. The army's actual strength may have been roughly 3,600 when the new law took effect, so the administration may have only dismissed several hundred troops.[20]

Jefferson was more zealous in ridding the officer corps of Federalists and replacing them with loyal Republicans, a practice that Madison would just as enthusiastically continue. That purge was partly realized by privatizing staff positions and then appointing loyal Republicans in those now civilian jobs. The corps was also downsized by reducing the ratio of officers to enlisted men by consolidating the four existing regiments into two. All the dragoons and a company each of engineers and artillery were eliminated. Finally, the War Department was able to weed out forty-one officers who were identified as "unworthy" of their commissions. The rank of colonel was reintroduced.

All of this enabled Jefferson to place Republicans in nine of the ten top posts and many others further down the pyramid. The most notorious appointee proved to be the army's highest-ranking officer, Brig. Gen. James Wilkinson; that fervent Republican was eventually unmasked as not only a murderously incompetent field commander but also an outright traitor to the United States. After a dozen or so years of Jeffersonism, the officer class of the army that fought the 1812 War was mostly ideologically correct but militarily inept. Not surprisingly, morale was abysmal. Winfield Scott, who proved his leadership gifts during that war, dismissed his fellow officers as "imbeciles and ignoramuses . . . swaggerers, dependents, decayed gentlemen, and others—fit for nothing else."[21]

The 1802 Military Peace Establishment Act also established the military school at West Point, a long-standing goal of Alexander Hamilton's. Initially the classes were confined to engineering and natural sciences and consisted of only five teachers and ten cadets. Gradually West Point's curriculum, faculty, and cadets grew to embrace the whole spectrum of the art and science of war, although only about seventy-five cadets received their commissions before the 1812 War erupted. The United States did not have a professional officer corps until the Mexican War, whose veterans did not truly come of age until the Civil War nearly a generation beyond that.

Jefferson also forged full speed ahead with a sharp cutback of American naval power. The Naval Act of March 1, 1801, passed in the twilight of the Adams administration, empowered the president to sell off the entire navy except for thirteen frigates, of which only six would be on active service and the others anchored for an emergency. The ambitious project launched during the Quasi-War to construct six ships of the line was canceled, and whatever progress had been made was auctioned off. Those cutbacks were not deep enough for Jefferson. He slashed the navy budget in half, the number of active-duty frigates to three, and the list of fifteen captains to nine. At the end of his first term in March 1805, he had the Republican majority in Congress pass a bill that appropriated $60,000 to build twenty-five gunboats, the first batch of an eventual 276. That vast gunboat fleet would mostly prove to be utterly worthless when the United States eventually went to war with Britain.[22] In all, he largely succeeded in replacing a budding blue-water navy with a brown-water navy.

If Jefferson wanted no more than the bare bones of a military, he hoped to wipe America's diplomatic slate completely clean up to the time he took power. He declared his "wish to let every treaty we have drop off without renewal." Jefferson especially despised the Jay Treaty, which he called "a millstone round our necks." Ideally, Jefferson believed that a foreign policy founded upon the Golden Rule would make war less rather than more likely. The United States should try "to cultivate the peace and friendship of every nation." He had "but one system of ethics for men and for nations: To be grateful, to be faithful to all engagements and, under all circumstances, to be open and generous."[23]

What if that policy invited rather than dissolved aggression? Jefferson did not believe in turning the diplomatic cheek in domestic or international politics. There were times in the life of a man or nation when the show and even assertion of strength was essential. The reason was simple: "A coward is much more exposed to quarrels than a man of spirit. Weakness provokes insult and injury, while a condition to punish it often prevents it. . . . I think it to our interest to punish the first insult: because an insult unpunished is the parent of many others."[24]

When it came to diplomacy, Jefferson was as much of two minds on that vital dimension of national power as he was on every other issue. To Madison, he wrote, "An American contending by strategem [sic] against those exercised in it from their cradle would undoubtedly be outwitted by them."[25] That pessimism would prove to be misplaced. Jefferson and the envoys he dispatched overseas would be as adept at wielding the art of diplomacy as their predecessors, while arguably no administration in American history would exceed as a diplomatic coup the purchase of the Louisiana Territory.

4

The Louisiana Dilemma

lthough Napoleon Bonaparte acquired the Louisiana Territory from Spain
in 1800, the idea had not originated with him. That had been a secondary French policy goal since the alliance Second Treaty of San Ildefonso
signed between France and Spain on June 26, 1796, which required Spain to trade
Louisiana for Gibraltar and fishing rights off of Newfoundland. The Directory
refused to ratify the treaty because it would commit France to the unlikely prospect
of persuading Britain to agree to those goals in any future peace treaty. Nonetheless,
the French devoted themselves to regaining a North American empire.[1]

For Americans, that ill-concealed French ambition held alarming possibilities.
In a 1797 letter to Rufus King, America's minister in London, Secretary of State
Thomas Pickering noted that "we have often heard that the French government
contemplated the repossession of Louisiana; and . . . that . . . the cession of Louisiana
& the Floridas may have been agreed on. You will see all the mischief . . . from such
an event. The Spaniards will certainly be more safe, quiet, and useful neighbors."[2]

Pickering did more than fret about the threat. In February 1797, he dashed off
letters to America's ministers in Madrid and Paris. David Humphreys was to ask
the Spanish about the rumors and express his nation's deep regret if they were
true. Charles Pinckney was to explain bluntly to the French that should they take
Louisiana and the Floridas, the United States "could not fail to associate themselves with Great Britain, and make common cause against France."[3]

An even worse fear was that Britain would win the Floridas and Louisiana from
Spain and thus contain the United States from three sides. That indeed was a British

24

goal during the peace talks at Lille in July 1797. Prime Minister William Pitt instructed his envoy, James Harris, Lord Malmesbury, to assert Britain's "interests as the town and port of New Orleans with a sufficient territory to be annexed to it."[4]

Charles Maurice de Talleyrand-Périgord replaced Charles Delacroix as foreign minister in July 1797. Talleyrand was well aware that France's acquisition of Louisiana might transform the Quasi-War with the United States into a full-fledged war. And that might mean that France would lose Louisiana to an American army unless a French army disembarked there first. Discretion and swift action on any deal was essential. A French fleet had to disgorge troops at New Orleans not long after the ink was dry on a treaty with Madrid. That proved to be impossible from 1797 through 1800 as French armies suffered defeats on all fronts. It was only after Napoleon Bonaparte took power in a coup d'état in 1799 and defeated the Austrians the following summer that the French could assert their ambitions beyond Europe.

Talleyrand interested Bonaparte in retaking Louisiana as an essential part of restoring French power in the New World. In early July 1800, Bonaparte sent his chief of staff, Louis Alexandre Berthier, to Madrid on the mission of negotiating Louisiana's return. The Third Treaty of San Ildefonso was signed on October 1, 1800, two days before the Treaty of Mortefontaine, which resolved the Quasi-War between the United States and France. In return for granting France Louisiana and six ships of the line, Spain would receive the Grand Duchy of Tuscany for Fernando, the Duke of Parma and the queen's brother. The Louisiana Territory was seen as a financial and thus a strategic liability. Tuscany, in contrast, was a land as rich as it was prestigious. For now Bonaparte insisted that the treaty be kept a secret for fear that Britain might attack France's vulnerable new possession.

There was a catch to this deal between Paris and Madrid. Although French troops occupied Tuscany, France did not yet formally own it. To take and then transfer the title, Bonaparte had to win three more diplomatic campaigns. The first came on February 9, 1801, when as part of the peace treaty between France and Austria, France received the Grand Duchy of Tuscany. Bonaparte imposed a French-style constitution on that realm and renamed it the Kingdom of Etruria. The First Consul then sent his brother Lucien to Madrid to alter the Ildefonso treaty. The Convention of Aranjuez, signed on March 21, would grant the Kingdom of Etruria not to Fernando, whom Bonaparte despised, but to Luis, the queen's son-in-law. The final crucial step was peace with Britain. A preliminary treaty was signed on October 1, 1801, and would be confirmed by the Treaty of Amiens on March 27, 1802. Now Bonaparte could send an armada across the Atlantic without fear that the Royal Navy would destroy it.

Such important transfers of territory could not be kept secret for long. Rumors began to circulate even as the deal was being cut. In August 1800, David Humphreys, America's minister to Spain, saw an article in a French newspaper that revealed Berthier's mission. Both Berthier and Spanish foreign minister Pedro de Cevallos denied the article's truth when Humphreys asked them for an explanation. In late March 1801, Rufus King was the first to send word back to Washington that Spain had apparently ceded Louisiana to France. Upon reading his report, Jefferson wrote, "There is considerable reason to apprehend that Spain ceded Louisiana and the Floridas to France. It is a policy very unwise to both, and very ominous to us."[5]

Madison summoned the newly arrived French chargé d'affaires, Louis Andre Pichon, and queried him on that vital question. Pichon denied any knowledge of the transaction but thought it unlikely. Then, in a deft display of diplomacy, he turned the inquisitorial spotlight on Madison. If the rumor were true, what was wrong with France retaking land that it had once possessed? Regardless, for France the issue was whether the United States had any ambitions to expand west of the Mississippi. Madison could only meekly reply that he hoped that the rumor was untrue, while he denied any plans to take Louisiana.[6]

The want of a minister in Paris prevented the administration from directly confronting the French foreign minister on that question. Jefferson tapped Robert Livingston for that post. The choice was curious to say the least. Although he was a bright and prominent member of the Republican Party elite, he had serious liabilities that would hobble his diplomacy—he was nearly deaf and spoke no French. But he had plenty of time to ponder his instructions on the long voyage to France. His central mission was to determine whether that transfer of territory had taken place. If not, he was to dissuade the French from doing so. If so, he was to see if Bonaparte would be willing to cede New Orleans and the Floridas to the United States. He was to make clear that a failure to do so could force the United States into an alliance with Britain and then expose all French colonies in the New World to "the joint operation of a naval and territorial power."[7]

Within a few months that threat of an American alliance with Britain to war against France would ring hollow when word arrived of the preliminary peace treaty signed between Paris and London. For Bonaparte, peace with Britain did not eliminate the potential American danger to his ambitions. If mustered, an American army of hardened frontiersmen could reach New Orleans far sooner than any army sailing from France. Pichon wrote Talleyrand that "I am afraid they may strike at Louisiana before we can take it over."[8]

Livingston set foot in Paris on December 3, 1801. He was soon able to ask Talleyrand the key question of his mission. With a straight face, the foreign minister replied that no such deal had been consummated. Bonaparte may have had Talleyrand's statement in mind when he officially received the American minister with a sympathetic warning: "You have come to a very corrupt world."[9]

It would take nearly another year before the Jefferson administration received the evidence of that transaction. Once again it came from King, who enclosed a copy of the treaty in a letter to Madison in November 1801. The newspapers soon picked up the story, resulting in a political uproar.[10]

Sooner or later the duties and limits of power would have a sobering effect on all but the most extreme ideologues. The news that France had taken the Louisiana Territory back from Spain had just such an eye-opening effect on Thomas Jefferson. Like most Americans, he assumed that eventually the Louisiana Territory along with the Floridas would fall into America's hands like so many ripe fruits. The Spanish were seen as weak, inept, corrupt, and few in number, as opposed to the Americans, who were restless, enterprising, ever more numerous, and greedy for new lands. American settlements in those Spanish territories would eventually convert them to American domination. Then it would be a relatively easy diplomatic matter to arrange a transfer of formal ownership. Faced with overwhelming American power within their territory and on the frontier, the Spanish would have no choice but to cede those lands. Thus, for now, Spain's possession of those territories was seen as a mere annoyance.[11]

In contrast, word that France had taken Louisiana set off alarm bells across the United States. Jefferson fired off instructions to Livingston to offer to purchase New Orleans and the Mississippi valley from France. The prospect of not doing so was grim. Jefferson explained that "there is on the globe one single spot, the possessor of which is our natural and habitual enemy. . . . It is New Orleans through which the produce of three-eighths of our territory must pass to market. . . . The day that France takes possession of New Orleans . . . seals the union of two nations who in conjunction can maintain exclusive possession of the ocean. From that moment we must marry ourselves to the British fleet and nation." Jefferson penned those words more from sorrow than anger. He had once loved France as much as he hated Britain. Those days were long past. The realities of defending American interests from the depredations of both imperial powers had muddied those fine distinctions.[12]

Separately, Madison told Livingston to make clear that the French takeover of New Orleans and the Floridas would provoke "the worst events." Livingston drafted a long report on why France should cede these lands to the United States and presented it to Talleyrand in August 1802.[13]

The urgency of the New Orleans question prompted Jefferson to open a second diplomatic channel to Bonaparte. He asked Pierre Samuel du Pont de Nemours, a Frenchman who had lived for years in the United States but was about to return to Paris, to convey to the First Consul the seriousness with which Americans viewed France's possession of New Orleans and their willingness to purchase it for a fair price. Du Pont was to reassure Bonaparte that the United States needed to possess New Orleans and the Floridas for purely defensive purposes and that it had no ambitions beyond the Mississippi. Nine months later, after this gentle approach had obviously failed, Jefferson had Du Pont issue a blunt warning to Bonaparte's government: "Whatever power . . . holds power east of the Mississippi, becomes our natural enemy."[14]

Conducting diplomacy amid the perennial web of intrigue in Paris was no easy task even when relations between the United States and France were at their best. All the war threats and rumors of secret territory swaps had obviously soured feelings. Livingston complained that it was bad enough that Talleyrand was unfriendly and haughty, but worst of all was that with Bonaparte in power, "there never was a Government in which less could be done by negotiations than here. There is no people, no Legislature, no counsellors. One man is everything. He seldom asks advice, and never hears it unasked. His ministers are mere clerks." Yet he was optimistic about his mission's outcome: "I am persuaded that the whole will end in a relinquishment . . . to the United States."[15]

Faced with Talleyrand's officious stonewalling, Livingston turned to Bonaparte's older brother, Joseph, in October 1802. Like Talleyrand, Joseph Bonaparte sidestepped the question of who now owned Louisiana, but at least he was pleasant in his dissemination. He asked whether the United States would prefer Louisiana or the Floridas. Livingston stated the Executive Mansion's official position of the desire for both New Orleans and West Florida and its disinterest in expansion beyond the Mississippi.[16]

Meanwhile, the diplomacy was even more intense on the other side of the Atlantic. In their meetings with Pichon, Jefferson and Madison asserted that if France did not sell New Orleans and West Florida, it would lose them in war. To back that threat, Jefferson instructed War Secretary Henry Dearborn to reinforce Fort Adams on the Mississippi River, thirty-eight miles south of Natchez. Pichon conveyed word of those warnings and preparations to Talleyrand with the advice to heed them.[17]

A final step Bonaparte had to take before he could take possession of Louisiana was to crush the rebellion on Saint-Domingue and make it again the world's richest sugar island. He entrusted that task to his brother-in-law, Charles Victor Emmanuel Leclerc, and a twenty-thousand-man army. Leclerc's armada sailed from Brest on December 14, 1801, reached Saint-Domingue on February 1, 1802, and began the reconquest. By June 1802, Leclerc had captured Toussaint Louverture, the rebel leader, and secured Saint-Domingue's ports.

Upon hearing of these successes, Pichon asked Jefferson for help in restoring Saint-Domingue to French rule, arguing that it was in American interests to do so. Otherwise a nation of free blacks in the Caribbean would soon become a pirate state that preyed on American shipping and inspired slave revolts in the United States.

Jefferson faced a dilemma. Pichon's points were genuine fears among slave owners and many merchants within the United States, including the president himself. Yet Jefferson also saw Saint-Domingue as a possible solution to America's own intractable problems over slavery and race; that land could be a refuge for blacks expelled from the United States. The president at first thus leaned toward aiding France. Then word arrived that Leclerc had confiscated the cargoes of a score of American vessels in Saint-Domingue's ports. Jefferson demurred from providing any direct aid to France and instead insisted on compensation for the confiscations. The French eventually did pay for the provisions they had seized.[18] In all, the pressure was building for some sort of land deal, but its outline remained hazy.

5

Squaring Off with Spain

T he United States perceived France as a worsening threat with its acqui-
        sition of Louisiana and attempt to reconquer Saint-Domingue. That
        tension and fear ratcheted up on October 18, 1802, when Louisiana's
intendant, Juan Ventura Morales, issued an edict forbidding Americans from placing any goods in the warehouses of New Orleans.

That unilateral act clearly violated the 1795 Treaty of San Lorenzo, negotiated
by Thomas Pinckney, which gave Americans the right to travel the Mississippi
River through Spanish territory to the sea, and along the way deposit goods at
New Orleans or another mutually agreed-upon site. All had gone well for the first
seven years that the treaty was in force. The first American flatboat to legally
complete the journey arrived in December 1796. The process and place for
Americans to deposit goods in New Orleans was formally established in 1798.
That outlet to the sea provided an economic boom to the hardscrabble western
settlers of Kentucky, Tennessee, and elsewhere, and thus quieted once fervent separatist sentiments among most of them.[1]

The 1802 policy was not as severe as it seemed. Americans could still carry
goods down to New Orleans, but they suffered the inconvenience of tying their
flatboats to barges and transferring their goods amid the Mississippi's relentless
current. Nonetheless, that policy provoked howls of rage among westerners, which
were soon heard in Washington City.

The secretary of state fired off a letter to Charles Pinckney, America's minister
in Madrid. Pinckney was to ask Foreign Minister Pedro de Cevallos to restore the

right of deposit. Madison then summoned Spanish minister Don Carlos Martinez de Irujo y Tacón to discuss the matter. Irujo apologized for knowing nothing about it and promised to write both Morales and Cevallos about reversing the policy. He was good to his word. He and French minister Pichon wrote Morales in an attempt to convince him that his policy could provoke a disaster for Spanish and French interests if he did not soon change course: "If the proclamation of the Intendant is not revoked in three months the clamor of the Federalists, the impulse of public opinion, and party policy will force the President and the Republicans to declare war against their wish."[2]

Finally, Madison had William Claiborne, the Mississippi Territory's governor, issue Louisiana governor Don Manuel Juan de Salcedo a letter lodging a protest and requesting an explanation. Salcedo replied that Morales had acted on his own authority and his act did not represent the king's instructions or intentions. However, he made no promise that the policy would be swiftly overturned.[3]

Salcedo's reply did not necessarily mean that he was being two-faced. Spain's colonial administration, like that of France, included two chief administrators, a governor, and an intendant. Among their complementary duties was to keep an eye on the other. The governor was in charge overall and presided over official ceremonies, while the intendant, much like a prime minister, devoted himself to the daily minutiae of running a colony. The system worked well enough. But at times a governor and intendant could act at cross-purposes, especially with an unhappy mix of bloated rival egos, vague or conflicting instructions from Madrid, and genuine disputes over what could best advance Spanish interests. That essentially summed up relations between Salcedo and Morales.

That said, Morales appears to have been acting on instructions from Madrid but was required to keep them secret from everyone else, including the governor. It remains a mystery why King Charles IV and his advisers would commit such a provocative act when Spain was already at war with Britain and would be outgunned by the United States. The archives are silent. Did officials reconsider rendering the province to France, and did they thus seek to provoke a crisis that would give Bonaparte pause?[4]

While awaiting Madrid's official explanation, Jefferson defused explosive political tensions at home simply by announcing that Morales's act was unauthorized and would be overturned. That did not stop Federalist politicians and newspaper editors from arguing that Spain would not respect the Pinckney treaty as long as Jefferson persisted in cutting back the nation's military strength and refusing to confront foreign aggression. They demanded that he turn over to Congress all documents concerning Louisiana.

The political uproar spotlighted the dangers to the United States latent in the eventual transfer of Louisiana from Spain to France. Would the new proprietor feel bound by the old treaty? Would the United States have to negotiate a new treaty? If so, how could the Americans win the same benefits from a vigorous France that they had from a decrepit Spain?

6

The Louisiana Purchase

Jefferson addressed the controversy over Louisiana in three ways. First, in his address to Congress on December 15, 1802, he asked that body and the nation to patiently await an explanation from Madrid on the closure of New Orleans. Second, his Republican majorities in Congress sweetened a resolution on January 5, 1803, by lauding the president for his handling of the crisis as they requested all related documents. Finally, to undercut his critics, placate westerners, and hopefully resolve the Louisiana crisis, he nominated on January 11, 1803, James Monroe as an extraordinary minister to Paris to negotiate with the French and, if necessary, the Spanish. The Senate swiftly approved Monroe's nomination by a largely party-line vote of 15 to 12 that same day. The following day, Congress armed the envoy with a $2 million appropriation to purchase New Orleans and West Florida. The president and his supporters then settled back to wait and see what sort of explanation, if any, Madrid rendered and what sort of deal Monroe could win.[1]

These measures did not mollify most Federalists. They were especially upset over the selection of Monroe for such a vital mission. They feared that he would give too much and receive too little, a trait they attached to Jefferson's entire foreign policy. Sen. Gouverneur Morris condemned the president for believing "in payment of debts by diminution of revenue, in defense of territory by reduction of armies, and in vindication of rights by appointment of ambassadors."[2]

Alexander Hamilton, as always, backed his criticism with calls for decisive action. The nation was faced with two choices: "First to negotiate and endeavor to purchase; and if this fails, to go to war. Secondly, to seize at once the Floridas and New Orleans, and then negotiate."[3] He hoped that Jefferson would follow the second path, not merely because that would best advance American interests, but because in doing so the president "might yet retrieve his character."[4]

Sen. James Ross, who was at once a fervent Federalist and from Pennsylvania's far-western region, championed Hamilton's plan. He sponsored a resolution, mostly ghostwritten by Hamilton, that would have required the president to "take immediate possession of such place or places" that were "fit and convenient" for securing America's rights to navigate the Mississippi River and make a deposit at New Orleans. To that end, Congress would appropriate $5 million and raise fifty thousand troops.[5]

The subsequent Senate debate lasted from February 23 to 25, 1803. Hamilton had helped Ross carefully craft the resolution not only to force the president to act decisively, but also to split the Republican Party. The resolution had a wide appeal in the western states, which were Republican strongholds. That forced each western Republican senator to choose between his region or his party leader. And if the majority of Republicans supported Jefferson's purely diplomatic approach, they would appear weak to many Americans. In the end, the resolution was defeated on February 25 by a strict party vote of 15 to 11.

The Republican Party stayed united because John Breckinridge of Kentucky sponsored a face-saving resolution that authorized the president to raise eighty thousand militiamen if he thought those troops were necessary. Now the Federalists faced a dilemma. Would they hold their noses and vote for what they believed was a "milk and water" resolution? Or would they stick literally and figuratively to their guns? The Breckinridge resolution unanimously passed on March 2. So Jefferson had a saber to rattle after all, if need be.[6]

A report from William Claiborne, the Mississippi Territory governor, highlighted the importance of time in favorably settling the issue: "We have in this part of the Territory, about two thousand Militia, pretty well organized, and with a portion of this force (say six hundred men) my opinion is that New Orleans might be taken possession of provided there should be only Spanish troops to defend the place."[7] Obviously that overwhelming American advantage would disappear should battle-hardened French regiments disembark at New Orleans.

As for timing, that of Monroe's appointment certainly could not have been better for him. He had recently finished his term as Virginia's governor and was going to return to his law practice after a quick trip to Kentucky to survey his land investments. Nonetheless, it still took him two months to settle his affairs and prepare for his trip. His mission was to purchase New Orleans; the Mississippi

River to the sea; and lands eastward along the Gulf Coast at least as far as the Perdido River, which included the strategic port of Mobile; and ideally all of Florida to the Atlantic for not more than fifty million livres, or $9,375,000. If necessary, he was authorized to issue the none-too-subtle threat that "the western people believe, as to their Atlantic brethren, that they have a natural and indefensible right to trade freely through the Mississippi. They are conscious of their power to enforce this right against any nation whatsoever."[8]

After Monroe sailed from New York on March 9, the president and his government would not hear from him for another four months. But when they did, the news was electrifying.

Until then, the word from Paris was mostly dismal. Talleyrand rejected the parallel requests of Livingston and DuPont to buy Louisiana. He did, however, provide at least one vital answer that Livingston promptly passed on to Jefferson. The Floridas were not included in the trade with Spain. The United States would now be hemmed in by three great powers—France on the west, Spain on the south, and Britain on the north.[9]

This caused Jefferson to reach a reluctant conclusion. On April 8, he forged a consensus among his cabinet that he would ask Congress for a war declaration and alliance with Britain if France refused to cede New Orleans and the Gulf Coast. Madison then sent word to Monroe that if he failed in Paris he should immediately head to London and seek an alliance "on the ground that war was inevitable."[10]

There was some good news amid the gloom. America's outrage, war talk, and warnings, which erupted on news that Morales had forbidden American merchants from depositing their goods, had a powerful diplomatic effect. On February 28, 1803, Manuel de Godoy, Charles IV's closest adviser, informed Charles Pinckney that the right of deposit would be restored. The formal notice came in April with a letter from Foreign Minister Cevallos to Secretary of State Madison. Cevallos apologized for the "misunderstanding" and explained that he had sent word to Morales to reopen New Orleans to American merchants. At the foreign minister's request, Madison had his letter published in the *National Intelligencer*, the Republican Party's leading newspaper. The Morales crisis had passed peacefully.[11]

Monroe reached Paris at a time when distant events strengthened America's diplomatic hand. Napoleon Bonaparte's dream of conquering a New World empire had become a nightmare. Yellow fever was wiping out the French expedition to Saint-Domingue. On January 7, 1803, Bonaparte learned of General Leclerc's death atop seventeen thousand other soldiers' so far. The guerrillas had regrouped to besiege the survivors in a handful of coastal towns and forts. His response to that news may not have been eloquent, but it succinctly captured his rage at the disaster his policy had wrought: "Damn sugar, damn coffee, damn colonies!"[12]

Meanwhile, France and Britain once again teetered at war's brink. The First Consul realized that he had to sell Louisiana to the United States before the Americans—or worse, the British—took it. At least then he would receive some badly needed gold to fight enemies much closer to home.

Although Robert Livingston was hardly pleased to find James Monroe on his doorstep on April 12, the arrival was not unexpected. Livingston had received a dispatch from Madison in January informing him that "Mr. Monroe will be the bearer of the instructions under which you are jointly to negotiate." Livingston would deeply resent having to share the diplomatic stage. He would later write that "I had prepared everything, first by creating a personal interest, next by showing the inutility of Louisiana to France. . . . I had advanced so far as to have been upon the point of concluding when the appointment of Mr. Monroe stopped my operations."[13]

Yet for America if not Livingston, the timing of Monroe's arrival could not have been better. Word that Monroe had disembarked at the port of Le Havre on April 8 galvanized Bonaparte into action. Two days later, he summoned Foreign Minster Talleyrand, Treasury Minister François de Barbé-Marbois, and Marine Minister Denis Decrès to forge a negotiation strategy over Louisiana. The First Consul explained that they had to wrap up a deal quickly or else Britain would take Louisiana—"I have not a moment to lose in putting it out of their reach." Well aware of the animosities between Talleyrand and Livingston, he asked Barbé-Marbois to lead the negotiations with the Americans. The treasury minister had lived in the United States for six years and was generally sympathetic toward Americans. Bonaparte told him to "not even await the arrival of Mr. Monroe. Have an interview this day with Mr. Livingston. But I require a great deal of money for this war. . . . I want fifty millions [francs] and for less than that sum I will not treat."[14]

Talleyrand enjoyed being upstaged even less than Livingston. He invited the American minister over that afternoon to ask him if he would like "the whole of Louisiana." Livingston could only respond by citing his instructions limiting any purchase to New Orleans and the Floridas. The foreign minister then asked how much he thought Louisiana would be worth to the United States. Livingston reckoned 20 million francs might be about as far as his government would go. Talleyrand replied that was much too low and asked him to think about it while he awaited Monroe.[15]

Jefferson and Madison had penned their instructions before they learned that Madrid had restored the right of deposit at New Orleans. Thus, taking that city was crucial. As Jefferson put it to Livingston in a separate letter, "We must know at once whether we can acquire N. Orleans or not. We are satisfied nothing else will secure us against war at no distant period." Both Jefferson and Madison made that clear in separate meetings with French minister Pichon, on January 12 and 14, respectively. But neither the president nor secretary of state then considered taking by force any lands west of the Mississippi River.[16]

Instead Livingston first broached the idea. On February 18, 1803, he wrote Madison his suggestion that the United States acquire all land between the Arkansas River mouth and Canadian border to split the British and French empires. The secretary of state and president would not receive that letter until weeks after they dispatched Monroe with his instructions. Yet after receiving it, they would have weeks to mull over the idea of taking lands west of the Mississippi before getting word that their diplomats had signed a treaty doing just that.[17]

Livingston hosted a dinner party for Monroe on the day of his arrival. Barbé-Marbois showed up as they were dining and invited Livingston to his home later that night. With regrets he explained that Monroe could not come because he had not yet officially presented his diplomatic credentials. After Livingston arrived, the treasury minister quickly got to the point. He asked him how much the United States could pay for Louisiana. When Livingston repeated the 20-million-franc figure he had made to Talleyrand, Barbé-Marbois claimed that the First Consul wanted 100 million francs for the territory, doubling his actual demand. When Livingston expressed shock at the price, Barbé-Marbois lowered it to 60 million francs plus the American assumption of all reparation claims against France. Livingston explained that he would have to consult Monroe. The haggling began in earnest the day after Monroe was presented to Talleyrand on April 14. It would take two weeks before they worked out all details. The Americans' opening offer was 40 million francs. When Barbé-Marbois dismissed the amount, they countered with 50 million and not a franc more. Even though that was the sum that Bonaparte had wanted, the treasury minister said he would have to speak with the First Consul. Monroe and Livingston then shifted the discussion to Louisiana's borders. They were especially eager to learn whether it included West Florida. They pointed out that when Britain owned the Floridas, the Apalachicola River formed the border between the two. Barbé-Marbois claimed that the exact borders were unknown, thus open to interpretation, but that Louisiana did not include West Florida, which the Spanish still owned. The Americans insisted that the treaty's wording should be vague enough to allow the United States to claim West Florida. Here the treasury minister was happy to indulge the Americans. He also agreed to their request that France use its good offices to encourage Spain to transfer West Florida to the United States.

Barbé-Marbois then presented his conditions. For twelve years French and Spanish ships would pay the same duties as American ships in Louisiana's harbors. Louisiana's inhabitants would enjoy the same constitutional rights as American citizens. Ratifications would be exchanged within six months of the official signing. The Americans found those requests reasonable enough.

It took them longer to agree to Barbé-Marbois's next position. The United States could take title to Louisiana for 60 million francs ($11,250,000) plus the 20 million francs ($3,750,000) worth of American claims against France, totaling 80 million francs or $15 million. Since the federal government's treasury was nearly empty, the sum would have to be borrowed in bonds at a 6 percent annual rate not to be redeemed for fifteen years. On April 27, they drew up all the particulars in a treaty and two conventions.

With each undoubtedly taking a deep breath, François de Barbé-Marbois, James Monroe, and Robert Livingston signed the treaty and conventions of Louisiana on April 30, 1803. After they stepped back with mingled relief and trepidation, Talleyrand made a remark to the Americans that was at once gracious and prescient: "You have made a noble bargain for yourselves and I suppose you will make the best of it."[18]

On May 1, Napoleon Bonaparte ratified the treaty and then celebrated their achievement with a grand reception for the diplomatic community at the Louvre Palace, followed by a private dinner with the Americans, Barbé-Marbois, and Talleyrand at the Tuileries Palace. Livingston was exultant: "We have lived long, but this is the noblest work of our whole lives. The treaty which we have just signed has not been obtained by art or dictated by force; equally advantageous to both parties, it will change vast solitudes into flourishing districts. From this day the United States takes their place among the powers of first rank." Bonaparte typically saw the deal in strategic terms: "This accession of territory strengthens for ever the power of the United States; and I have just given to England a maritime rival that will sooner or later humble her pride."[19]

Bonaparte soon needed all the help he could find. Britain declared war on France on May 18, 1803. Meanwhile, the first steps in fulfilling the deal were implemented in the days following the signature. The documents were translated into English. Barbé-Marbois struck a deal with two firms, Baring Brothers & Co. of London and Hope & Co. of Amsterdam, to convert the American bonds into cash.

Monroe and Livingston were nervous about having so dramatically exceeded their instructions. On May 13, they jointly penned a letter that gave their reasoning.

Money and West Florida were their two biggest worries. They had spent far beyond their allowance and had failed to gain clear title to West Florida. While they assumed that the president and Senate would eventually approve their purchase, they feared being criticized for only partially accomplishing their mission.[20]

Jefferson first received news of the Louisiana Treaty not from them but, on July 3, from Rufus King who had just returned from London. The official documents and the accompanying explanation from his envoys in Paris reached Washington City on July 14. If Jefferson was disappointed over the treaty's ambiguities and seeming exclusion of West Florida, he did not publicly say so.

Jefferson presented the documents to his cabinet for discussion on July 16. The president and his men soon forged a consensus in support of the purchase, but they also recognized that it might be a tough sale to the Senate, House, and public. The deadline for the exchange of ratifications was October 30. Convincing two of every three senators to endorse the treaty before then would take a well-crafted political offensive. Fortunately, Bonaparte had agreed to conduct the exchange in Washington in order to expedite it. Jefferson called for a special session of Congress on October 17 and released to the press a summary of the agreement, but not the text. It was essential to assert firm control over New Orleans as soon as the transfer was finalized. He sent orders to Governor Claiborne of the Mississippi Territory, to prepare for occupying New Orleans and other key Louisiana Territory towns and posts.

The primary concern of Jefferson and other strict constructionists was that the treaty was illegal; the Constitution said nothing about acquiring territory. In their battles against the Federalists over issues like Hamilton's Bank of the United States and other programs, Jefferson and his fellow believers had wielded a literal interpretation of the Constitution. If that text did not specifically mention a power or practice, then it was unconstitutional. Now the Jeffersonians were entangled in their own ideological web. For a while, Jefferson seriously thought he would need to amend the Constitution before the United States could take title to Louisiana.

Treasury Secretary Albert Gallatin saw a way around that objection. In a letter to Jefferson, he conveniently ignored ideological correctness and presented three arguments for acquiring Louisiana that were straight out of Hamilton's "implied powers" playbook. As a sovereign nation, the United States had the right to acquire territory. The Constitution states that treaties are part of the law of the land; thus, if ratified, the Louisiana Treaty would justify itself. Congress has the choice of admitting new land in the United States as a separate state, as part of an existing state or states, or as a territory.[21] Jefferson jubilantly accepted those arguments from Gallatin that he would have scorned had Hamilton made them:

"You are right . . . there is no constitutional difficulty as to the acquisition of territory." He did, however, suggest that perhaps it might be helpful to pass a constitutional amendment to make that explicit.[22]

He would soon discard this notion. On August 17, he read a letter from Livingston that lent urgency to the ratification process: "Be persuaded, that France is sick of the bargain, that Spain is much dissatisfied, and that the slightest pretense will lose you the treaty." That turned the tug-of-war in Jefferson's mind completely from lofty ideals to practical political needs. He wrote Gallatin his decision "that we execute it without delay." Jefferson justified his ideological waffling by citing a higher principle, the betterment of mankind: "The world will see here such an extent of country under a free and moderate government as it has never yet seen."[23]

The Louisiana Purchase faced a potentially far more serious obstacle. In April 1803, Spanish minister Irujo conveyed a disturbing message to Madison. Madrid condemned the treaty as illegal because France had promised not to sell Louisiana. That vow was not in the Ildefonso Treaty, but came later. After ratifications of the Ildefonso Treaty were exchanged, Charles IV had second thoughts. He refused to transfer Louisiana until the First Consul promised not to resell it. Laurent de Gouvion St. Cyr, the French minister in Madrid, wrote a letter to that effect to Foreign Minister Cevallos on July 12, 1802. Three months later, on October 12, 1802, Charles IV signed a document officially ceding Louisiana to France. Yet Louisiana remained in Spanish hands. Bonaparte did not want to take the territory until he had enough troops there to keep it. What would the United States do if the Spanish refused to yield that vast land?[24]

Foreign Minister Cevallos echoed Irujo's protest in May and, after receiving no official reply from the United States, again in September. Jefferson initially treated the protests as he did most problems—he delayed any action in the hope that the problem would resolve itself. But receipt of the second protest on the eve of Congress's return to debate the treaty prompted Jefferson to take action.

The president convened his cabinet on October 4 and called for discussion on a vital question—had France illegally sold Louisiana to the United States? A consensus was quickly reached on the validity of the treaty signed by Monroe and Livingston. Jefferson then shifted the debate to whether Louisiana was worth fighting for. The answer was a swift and resounding yes.[25]

But Jefferson and his men naturally hoped that eventually the Spanish would gracefully yield what they could not possibly defend. The best way to encourage that was to stroke rather than provoke Spanish pride. To that end, the same message would be conveyed by Jefferson and Madison to Irujo in Washington City and by Pinckney to Cevallos in Madrid. As Jefferson put it, any broken promises by Bonaparte to Charles IV "were private questions between France and Spain which they must solve together. . . . We derived our title from the First Consul, and did not doubt the question of it."[26] Lest the Spanish mistake his determination, Jefferson summoned Irujo and issued a blunt warning—war would result if the Spanish refused to yield Louisiana, and the United States would take not just that land but also the Floridas. The president backed up those words with action. He sent instructions to Governor Claiborne and General Wilkinson to prepare the region's regular troops and the pick of the militia to conquer Louisiana if necessary.[27]

The treaty's actual ratification was easy enough. Congress reconvened on October 17. The Senate debated the treaty over the next two days before ratifying it by 24 to 7 on October 19, 1803. Madison and Pichon exchanged ratifications of the treaty and two conventions on October 20.

The following day, Jefferson sent a message to both houses of Congress that they now had to pay for the purchase. Recalling the Republican demand that President Washington submit all documents concerning the Jay Treaty, the Federalists issued a similar resolution for the Louisiana Treaty. That resolution was defeated in a close vote of 57 to 59. The enabling appropriations bill passed the Senate by 26 to 6 on October 22, by acclamation in the House that same day, and was signed into law by Jefferson on October 31, 1803. The president was empowered to appoint a governor, spend up to $1.5 million, and mobilize as many as eighty thousand militiamen to assert control over Louisiana.

The Jefferson administration's insistence that the treaty was valid and that the United States would take possession by whatever necessary means prompted the Spanish to reinforce their garrisons in Louisiana and the Floridas, and bar any foreigners from entering. But, in the end, while their protests may have been heartfelt, the Spanish were incapable of backing them with force. Madrid fatalistically released the territory. Irujo summed up the feelings of most: "That colony cost us heavily and produced very little for us."[28]

A beautiful plaza lies in the heart of old New Orleans, today known as the French Quarter. The St. Louis Cathedral stands on the north side; elegant buildings with tall doors and windows and wrought-iron balconies line the east and west sides; the south lies open to the levee and the Mississippi River beyond.

A huge crowd gathered there on December 20, 1803. Three men stood before the cathedral: Pierre Clément de Laussat, the French prefect for Louisiana, flanked by Gov. William Claiborne and Gen. James Wilkinson, representing the United States. Detachments of French and American troops faced each other across the square. Hundreds of onlookers were of French and Spanish descent, along with many free and enslaved of mixed or pure African descent; also included were a scattering of Americans. Most of those of French, Spanish, and free people of African descent probably witnessed the ceremony with mingled fear and sadness, and some with ill-disguised loathing; their varying degrees of economic, social, cultural, and political power would soon be challenged by Louisiana's transfer and the influx of Americans who would follow. Those who were slaves had the most to fear—it was well known that America's slave laws were far harsher than those of Spain. As for that handful of Americans, most of them probably could not contain their pride at what was about to take place.

The sight of the French tricolor being hauled down and the American stars and stripes being raised in its place was too much for Laussat. He burst into tears and fled the ceremony. Later he composed himself and presided unhappily over a banquet celebrating the transfer.

Nearly four months later, Capt. Amos Stoddard took possession of St. Louis and Upper Louisiana for the United States on March 10, 1804. After the Spanish flag was lowered, Stoddard graciously allowed the French flag to fly for twenty-four hours before replacing it with the American flag.

Charles IV formally acknowledged Louisiana's transfer from France to the United States on January 10, but it was not until February 10 that Cevallos informed Pinckney. In his generosity and benevolence, Charles IV was withdrawing his "opposition to the alienation of Louisiana made by France, notwithstanding the solid reasons on which it is founded." Irujo conveyed the same message to Madison on May 15, 1804.[29]

There was one final battle over the Louisiana Territory—one that would not be decisively resolved until 1865—and that was over how to govern it. The Jefferson administration and Congress initially debated two questions: under American rule what would be the status of the Creoles and of slavery?

Most Americans, including Jefferson, did not believe that the Creoles were ready for democracy and thus should be denied its rights. As the president put it, "the principles of popular Government are utterly beyond their comprehension."[30] The Creoles would beg to differ. The struggle of the Creoles for their rights, which were guaranteed both by the Louisiana Purchase Treaty and the U.S. Constitution, would persist for years thereafter.

The slavery question was at first finessed rather easily, but it reemerged as the most fiery issue in American politics over the next six decades. Since slavery was already established there, the Louisiana Territory would be administered under the Southwest rather than the Northwest Ordinance. The territory would be carved up into states as settlers poured into its different regions. Madison captured this sentiment: "It may fairly be expected that every blessing of liberty will be extended to them as fast as they shall be prepared and disposed to receive it."[31]

These complications aside, the Louisiana Purchase was unquestionably Jefferson's greatest achievement. But he scored this diplomatic coup only by setting aside ideological correctness and acting on concrete American interests. John Quincy Adams was among many who noted the irony that Jefferson's Louisiana Purchase was "an assumption of implied power greater in itself and more comprehensive in its consequences than all the assumptions of implied powers in the years of the Washington and Adams administrations put together."[32] In his eagerness to seize a chance to double America's size, Jefferson trampled his ideal of the United States as a small, agrarian republic based on states' rights and a weak national government. Ultimately no one in the early republic aggrandized America's physical power more than Jefferson with the Louisiana Purchase.

7

Where to Draw the Line?

While most Americans celebrated the doubling of their nation's territory, for many others that acquisition was merely a consolation prize. Interest groups exerted enormous and persistent pressure on Jefferson to insist that Madrid render at the very least West Florida along with Louisiana. Indeed the president welcomed public expressions of that pressure because he felt it strengthened his position against Spain. First, he persuaded Congress to approve in January 1804 a bill whereby the United States would pay for West Florida by assuming the American claims against Spain for seizing American ships during the Quasi-War, an amount that came to about $5 million. Then, on February 24, 1804, he approved the Mobile Act, which claimed those lands between the Mississippi and Perdido rivers that were designated West Florida.

All along, the Spanish steadfastly denied that West Florida was ever part of Louisiana. The president cautioned his followers to be patient. The last thing he wanted was to go to war over territory he assumed would sooner or later fall to the United States. He was right, although it would take much longer than he had hoped. The Adams-Onís Treaty, which officially transferred both Floridas from Spain to the United States, would not be signed until 1819, although the United States marched into the Baton Rouge district in 1810, and the rest of West Florida to the Perdido River in 1813.

Connected with the dispute over Louisiana's eastern frontier was its western frontier. Here again, the United States and Spain were at loggerheads over where to draw the line. Jefferson initially seized on French claims that Louisiana's western frontier rested on the Rio Bravo, or Rio Grande River, which cuts from north to south through New Mexico's heart and then runs southeast to form the present boundary between the United States and Mexico. The Spanish asserted a watershed theory for Louisiana's territory that included all those waters running east into the Mississippi River; that not only precluded New Mexico and Texas but most of the current state of Louisiana from the United States.

Jefferson and his cabinet reached a consensus in February 1804. They would split the difference with Spain over Louisiana's western boundary as a compromise to assert the Perdido River as its eastern boundary. The Sabine River, which today forms the boundary between the states of Louisiana and Texas, would be the Louisiana Territory's western frontier. When Madison shared that latest position with Irujo, he rejected it as vehemently as he had all other claims.

With that local diplomatic channel stalemated, Jefferson assigned James Monroe the task of going to Madrid and winning West Florida for the United States. He would do his preliminary work in Paris by presenting to the French government and Spain's minister three arguments that West Florida was part of Louisiana. First, the Spanish had administered West Florida and Louisiana together. Second, the French had extended Louisiana to the Perdido River when they owned it, as cited by the 1762 treaty whereby France ceded that land to Britain. Finally, the 1803 treaty guaranteed America's interpretation of boundaries.

The Spanish countered each of these arguments. First, they pointed out that West Florida was always separate from Louisiana even if at times the latter's governor had directed its affairs. They dismissed the map that the Americans had cited and revealed others where boundaries appeared to shift from one to the next. Finally, they argued that the 1803 treaty did not delineate Louisiana and thus was irrelevant regarding the border question. The Treaty of Ildefonso clearly stated that Louisiana consisted of what the Spanish had designated and governed as such.

Monroe asked that the French government support America's claim to West Florida. Bonaparte had no intention of doing so. It was in French interests to minimize Madrid's outrage at the transfer and maximize the tensions between the United States and Spain along their frontier. Indeed, the First Consul discouraged Monroe from immediately opening talks with the Spanish over West Florida.[1]

That prompted Monroe to postpone his planned trip to Madrid. Instead, he journeyed to London in July 1804 to replace Rufus King, who had left for the United States, as minister temporarily. Having deadlocked on issues with Whitehall, Monroe returned to Paris in October and conferred with Livingston and his recently arrived replacement, John Armstrong.

The Americans assumed that their best diplomatic card in a poor hand was strategic rather than legal. They assumed that Bonaparte would prefer American to British possession of West Florida. Thus they played up the fear that if Spain did not quickly cede that stretch of the Gulf Coast with its strategic port of Mobile, the British would sooner or later conquer it, thus shifting the region's power balance in its favor. More subtly they hinted that the United States might unilaterally assert its claim to that territory, especially to preempt a British takeover.

Bonaparte viewed each scenario as a disaster for French interests. He opposed possession by the United States only slightly less adamantly than possession by Britain. It was in France's strategic interests that the Spanish Empire control as much of the surrounding lands and islands within the Gulf of Mexico and Caribbean Sea as possible. If neither the French nor Spanish forces in the region were powerful enough to capture Jamaica, the jewel in the crown of Britain's West Indian colonies, they could at least do what they could to confine the British there and on a handful of tiny other islands. That in turn would complicate Britain's strategy of trying to conquer France's Caribbean colonies. And however militarily inept Spain might be as an ally, the alternative was worse. Madrid would certainly rethink its relationship with Paris if the First Consul pressured the Spanish into ceding West Florida to the United States.

The chance of Spain handing over West Florida was rendered even more unlikely by differences between Monroe and Livingston, who more often than not clashed in fulfilling their overlapping duties. In November 1804, Livingston attempted to entice the French and Spanish into ceding West Florida by hinting that the United States would be willing to make a huge loan to Madrid. That angered Monroe, who rejected any notion of gaining the territory for what he believed amounted to a bribe.

An opportunity arose for the United States on December 12, 1804, when Spain declared war on Britain. Monroe fired off a letter to Madison in which he explained that Whitehall might well welcome an ally against Spain and France.[2] Britain's command of the seas would make America's conquest of the Floridas a relatively easy matter. Thus the United States could take by force what Spain refused to yield by sale. With the assumption that the president would follow his advice, Monroe finally traveled to Madrid. That mission's result would not be apparent until after Jefferson began his second term.

8

Rising Tensions with Britain

Jefferson's belief that America should be an autarkic, agrarian republic might be dismissed as quaint or crankish if he were just penning such thoughts at Monticello. But his ignorance about such fundamentals of international diplomacy as the relationship between national wealth, interests, power, and policy was a dead weight on American diplomacy. The United States desperately needed to find overseas markets and investors that would swell profits for American entrepreneurs and finance infrastructure, industries, and depleted government coffers. Understanding and acting on that reality was a vital presidential duty.

But Jefferson also harbored an Anglophobia that was as deep as it was soft-spoken. His policy toward Britain was shaped by the fervent belief that "England is still our enemy. Her hatred is deep-rooted . . . and nothing is wanting with her but the power to wipe us and the land we live on out of existence."[1] While that may have been largely true, if exaggerated, Jefferson was definitely projecting his own feelings on the former mother country.

The result of his hatred of England and ignorance of power would undercut American national security in his second term. Despite all contrary evidence, he clung to the notion that somehow cutting off American trade with Britain would bring that empire to its knees. Instead he provoked the opposite. His policy enfeebled America by depriving it of wealth while forcing the British to diversify their trade and thus their sources of wealth and power.

Fortunately, Jefferson's animosity was not powerful enough to provoke him into leading the United States into war against that country. Indeed, for now he was careful not to do anything to provoke Whitehall. He turned down an appeal by French minister Pichon in March 1801 that the United States join the League of Armed Neutrality.

The British were highly concerned that the United States would do so. Foreign Secretary William Grenville called in Rufus King and pointedly asked him if that would happen. King assured him that the United States, in order to preserve its neutrality, preferred to remain aloof from any association of states, even one dedicated to neutrality.

It was probably good that the United States did avoid that entangling alliance. Britain viewed the League of Armed Neutrality as a declaration of war and reacted accordingly. On April 2, 1801, a British fleet under Adm. Hyde Parker destroyed Denmark's fleet at Copenhagen. Denmark swiftly withdrew from the league, followed by Sweden. Word arrived that on March 20 Czar Paul had died; rumor accurately had him murdered in a coup that brought to power his son Alexander. The new czar promptly denounced the league. Had the United States been a member, it would have had to beat a hasty retreat or probably suffer a disaster from British naval power similar to that inflicted on the Danes.

When Jefferson took power, negotiations were ongoing over who would pay what for the debts to British creditors who had lingered from before American independence. John Marshall had initiated the talks, and Rufus King had concluded them in January 1802, when he persuaded Whitehall to agree to limit the pre-revolution debts of Americans to 600,000 pounds sterling, which the British government would in turn distribute to the claimants. The debt convention was signed in November 1801 and ratified by the Senate on January 8, 1802. The joint-commission handling claims finished its work on February 23, 1804. Then something extraordinary happened. In sorting out the conflicting claims of Britons and Americans, it was found that Americans had already received $5,849,082 and Britons $2,807,428 for damages.[2]

King scored a second diplomatic coup while in London. On May 12, 1803, he settled the boundary dispute between the United States and Canada with a line between the Lake of the Woods and the Mississippi River in the northwest, and the Passamaquoddy Bay islands in the northeast. Jefferson submitted that treaty to the Senate in October 1803. The Senate rejected the northwest boundary line, fearing that it might yield land that had been won with the Louisiana Purchase.

When James Monroe journeyed to London in July 1804 to serve as an interim minister, his top priority was to argue that there was no "right" of impressment and that the British should stop forcing Americans into the British navy. The legal arguments against the practice were airtight. No treaties codify impressment, and any British laws allowing it are valid only within that kingdom. Indeed, doing so on the high seas is a form of piracy and thus violates the law of nations. On legal grounds alone, it had to end.

But the policy was rooted in British power and interests rather than law. The practice, however, was not without limits. Of 1,949 acts of impressment from 1797 to 1801, only 102 men were proven to be British subjects, 805 men were detained for lack of contrary proof, while 1,042 men were released upon proof of being American or another nationality.[3]

Monroe failed in his attempts to negotiate a treaty that settled impressment along with other maritime issues. As if British stonewalling was not frustrating enough, Foreign Secretary Robert Banks Jenkinson, Lord Hawkesbury, deliberately tried "to wound and to irritate. Not a friendly sentiment toward the United States or their Government escaped him. . . . Every thing that he said was uttered in an unfriendly tone, and much more was apparently meant than was said."[4] After enduring nearly four months of such treatment, Monroe finally gave up and hurried back to Paris in October 1804. The festering wounds between America and Britain would steadily worsen.

9

To the Shores of Tripoli

The United States first warred against an Arab state more than two centuries ago. Chronic threats to American people, profits, and pride provoked that war. And it was Thomas Jefferson, among the most gun-shy of the presidents, who launched it.[1]

For the previous two decades, an array of more pressing issues and a want of revenue had forced America's leaders to put relations with the Barbary states on the diplomatic back burner. Congress had ransomed the crew of an American ship captured by Morocco in 1783 but rejected any notion of doing the same for twenty-two Americans from two vessels captured by Algeria in 1786. That policy shift reflected an excess of pride, a paucity of money, and the sensible fear that ransoming captives would simply encourage more kidnappings. So those American prisoners continued to rot in prison and die one by one. Their fate preyed on the consciousness of sensitive Americans. A potential breakthrough emerged in 1792 when Hassan Bashaw, the new dey or ruler, came to power.

George Washington asked Congress to appropriate $40,000 to ransom the prisoners and negotiate a treaty of commerce and friendship with Algiers. The Senate upped the ante to $50,000 and appointed Capt. John Paul Jones as the envoy. But Hassan was insulted by the bribe's miserliness. He ordered his corsairs to sail forth and rake in more American ships. By late 1792, the Algerians had captured eleven ships and 119 sailors. The ransom demanded for those captives ranged from $800,000 to nearly $2.5 million, depending on Hassan's feelings at any one moment. And that payment would free only those survivors. The dey swore that his fleet would take more vessels and their crews unless the United States paid annual fees like the other states and provided him naval stores and two 36-gun frigates.

This demand was the last straw for Washington and a majority in Congress. The national interests of profit, pride, and pity left them no choice now but to go to war. The only problem was that the United States lacked the means of doing so. In March 1794, with the battle cry of "millions for defense, but not one cent for tribute," the president and Congress worked together to enact a bill that would construct and man six frigates, three of 44-guns and three of 36-guns, which would initially cost $2.4 million.[2] Constructing that flotilla would take years to complete.

Nonetheless, word that the United States might actually build a navy and send it against Hassan prompted him to slash his price. A deal was struck for the United States to pay $642,500 for the release of the captives and thereafter two 36-gun warships and an annual fee of $21,600 in naval stores.[3] The Senate approved the treaty on March 2, 1796. With the promise of peace, a majority in Congress no longer saw the reason for a navy so it halved the number of vessels and drastically cut appropriations. Although Hassan released the prisoners, the United States did not promptly pay. As a result, the dey threatened war. The envoy Joel Barlow was able to make an immediate payment of $18,000 and promise the swift delivery of the two 36-gun frigates. Hassan would later rage and threaten vengeance when other payments and the warships did not appear.

But now, at least, the United States had some means to retaliate. In 1797 the government launched three frigates—including the *Constitution* and *United States*, with 44-guns each, and the 36-gun *Constellation*—and purchased and converted into warships a score of smaller merchant vessels. But that flotilla was scattered across the Atlantic and Caribbean in search of French vessels rather than concentrated to retaliate against the Barbary states. The United States could fight only one "quasi-war" at a time. So to keep the peace, the United States paid $992,463 to Algiers that year and renewed its promise of the two frigates. Forking over any bribe, let alone one that stiff, enraged most Americans. Yet that payoff along with the launch of the navy was good for America's economy, as marine insurance rates dropped.[4]

The downside was that Tunis and Tripoli felt empowered to more loudly demand their own bribes. Given America's weakness, President John Adams had no choice but to ask his envoys to strike the best possible deals. Tripoli was made a "one-time payment" of $56,496 in 1797, but it would soon demand more. That same year the dey of Tunis received a $20,000 gift and the promise of an annual payment of $107,000 and fifty barrels of gunpowder.

The latest insult to the United States occurred in September 1800, when USS *George Washington*, captained by William Bainbridge, was anchored in Algiers harbor beneath the citadel's guns. The dey, Bobba Mustapha, demanded that Bainbridge convey a diplomatic mission to Constantinople. The humiliation came when the American flag was hauled down and Algiers' banner was hoisted in its place. After returning from that mission, Bainbridge sensibly anchored beyond the reach of Algiers' cannon and refused a demand for a second errand.

A far worse insult occurred on September 25, 1800, when Tripoli's bashaw, Yusuf Karamanli, ordered his corsairs to capture USS *Catherine*, a brig, and hold it as a bargaining chip in shaking down the United States for tribute. The American minister in Tripoli, James Cathcart, secured the *Catherine*'s release only by pledging that the United States would give Yusuf $225,000, an annual tribute of $25,000, and a 20-gun warship. But the dey scuttled that deal and demanded even more rapacious bribes. Cathcart replied that he was not authorized to give more, but he did pledge to ask his government for instructions. Yusuf warned him that war would soon result without a deal.

Jefferson received word of Yusuf's threat on March 13, 1801, roughly one week after taking the oath of office. He was not intimidated. With the 1800 Treaty of Mortefontaine, the Quasi-War with France ended, freeing up twenty-nine American warships for service elsewhere. The president wrote each Barbary state leader, informing him that a naval flotilla would soon be cruising in those waters and would undoubtedly ask for fresh provisions. Undercutting Jefferson's show of strength was his 1801 Naval Reduction Act, which dry-docked seven of the navy's thirteen frigates and dismissed their crews. The flotilla that eventually sailed to the Mediterranean numbered three frigates and a schooner under the command of Cdre. Richard Dale.

Jefferson's letter did not cow Yusuf. On May 14, 1801, he declared war by having troops march to the United States consulate, chop down the flagpole, and drag away the American flag. Cathcart left the city for safety in Livorno, Italy. On July 24, Dale anchored his flotilla just beyond cannon shot of Tripoli and began a blockade. After seizing several vessels, he traded those crews for six captive Americans. The first battle took place on August 1, when the American schooner, the 12-gun *Enterprise* commanded by Lt. Andrew Sterett, captured a Tripolitan 14-gun corsair after a three-hour battle. Despite those successes, Dale ended the blockade and sailed away to Gibraltar after provisions dwindled and sickness broke out among the crews.

Dale received much-needed reinforcements when Cdre. Richard Morris appeared with a flotilla at Gibraltar on May 25, 1802. For the next year, either together or separately, they would hover off Tripoli for a few weeks of blockade followed by months sailing between or anchored in various other Mediterranean ports. It was hardly a decisive way to wage war, but there was no alternative.

The understrength American navy was supposed to not only win the war against Tripoli but also prevent wars from breaking out with the other Barbary states. That policy was severely tested after June 19, 1803, when Morocco's emperor, Muley Soliman, declared war on the United States. Fortunately, he was bluffing. Capt. Edward Preble sailed with a flotilla to Tangiers and pacified Soliman by delivering that year's tribute.

Preble's successful mission, however, weakened the blockade at Tripoli, where only two American warships, the *Vixen* and the 44-gun *Philadelphia*, captained by William Bainbridge, rode at anchor. On October 31, after the *Vixen* sailed off for provisions, Bainbridge moved the *Philadelphia* closer to the port in order to boost the blockade's effectiveness. Suddenly there was a harsh grinding sound and abrupt halt as the *Philadelphia* ran aground and listed badly. A swarm of nine gunboats sailed out, surrounded the *Philadelphia*, and demanded surrender. For Bainbridge the only wise course was to lower the flag. The *Philadelphia*'s cannons pointed either toward the sea or sky, and the 307 men were outnumbered and would be slaughtered in a fight. While Bainbridge and his officers were housed in the former American consulate, the crew was crammed into the castle dungeon. When the tide came in, the Tripolitans refloated the *Philadelphia*; they anchored it in the harbor and under the name the *Gift of Allah*.

Upon hearing of the *Philadelphia*'s capture, Captain Preble sent word to the scattered American warships and flotillas to concentrate at Tripoli. Yusuf demanded $3 million for the crew; he would keep the ship. For now the Americans could only dismiss that demand and ask for a lower price.

News of the *Philadelphia*'s capture emboldened Hamuda Pasha, the dey of Tunis. He threatened war if he did not receive more tribute and a 36-gun frigate. William Eaton, the American consul, backed by a flotilla led by Commodore Morris, managed to defuse that crisis with a timely payment.

The Americans hoped that they had boosted their bargaining position at Tripoli when the flotilla captured the *Mastico* on December 23, 1804. But Yusuf rejected an offer to exchange the *Mastico*'s 60 crew members and passengers for 60 of the *Philadelphia*'s 307 crew members. The *Mastico* was repaired and pressed into American service as the *Intrepid*.

The Americans retrieved some of their honor on February 16, 1804. With Lt. Stephen Decatur and eighty marines and sailors hiding below deck, a skeleton crew dressed in Arab garb sailed the *Intrepid* into Tripoli harbor under a

British flag and anchored beside the *Philadelphia*. Suddenly Decatur and his men burst onto the deck, swarmed aboard the *Philadelphia*, cut down its defenders, and set a fire in the powder magazine. As an inferno consumed the ship, Decatur and his men reboarded the *Intrepid* and sailed to the open sea under a hail of cannon fire from the citadel and other shore batteries. Although a deafening explosion blew apart the *Philadelphia* behind them, the daring raid did not break the stalemate.

It was not until July 25, 1804, that Preble massed most of the navy at Tripoli. On August 3, the Americans captured three gunboats and bombarded the city. That prompted Yusuf to drop his price to $1 million. Richard O'Brien, the American consul, offered $60,000. For now the haggling ended with that gap. Preble ordered another bombardment on August 28 and three more in September, but still Yusuf stood firm on his last demand. The Americans packed the *Intrepid* with gunpowder and tried sailing it as a floating bomb into Tripoli's harbor on September 4. The vessel exploded prematurely into a million flaming splinters and killed the dozen men aboard; fortunately, Decatur was on another vessel. Cdre. Samuel Barron arrived with the frigates *Constellation* and *President* on September 9 and relieved Preble of command.

Jefferson, meanwhile, reluctantly agreed to a strategy submitted by William Eaton, who had been the American consul at Tunis since 1797. The Americans would support Hamet Karamanli, Yusuf's exiled brother, in his claim for the Tripoli throne. In authorizing Eaton to do what he could to instigate that coup, Madison expressed his and the president's qualms: "Although it does not accord with the general sentiments or views of the United States to intermeddle in the domestic contests of other countries, it cannot be unfair . . . to turn to [our] advantage the enmity and pretensions of others against a common foe."[5] Actually, Americans had been playing that game with the Indians for more than a century and a half, and would do so in ever more foreign countries as American power and interests spread around the world in the centuries to come.

William Eaton must rank among America's greatest special operations officers. Few have ever matched and perhaps none have exceeded him in brain and brawn. Before becoming the consul at Tunis, he had earned a Dartmouth degree between stints in the Independence War and Gen. Anthony Wayne's campaign against the northwest Indians. As a linguist alone he was brilliant—he spoke four Indian tongues along with French, Greek, Latin, and Arabic. He was a crack shot and deadly with a sword. He had that rare mix of courage and charisma that inspired men to follow him to death's door and beyond if need be. For his mission, he would require all of those skills.[6]

For his expedition, Eaton was allocated three officers, six marines, and $20,000. On February 23, 1805, Eaton and Hamet signed at Alexandria a contract whereby Hamet agreed that Eaton would command all the forces in return for placing him on the throne and arriving there by land rather than sea. By March 8, 1805, Eaton had recruited 80 Greek and 300 Arab mercenaries, and set off at their head west across 520 miles of desert leading to Derne, Hamet's former residence. From there it would be nearly another thousand miles to Tripoli itself.

That odyssey severely tested Eaton's indomitable will and array of skills. Provisions dwindled, water was rarely found, the various factions among his men repeatedly threatened to mutiny against him or fight each other, and Hamet got fainthearted and demanded that he be allowed to go back to Alexandria. Yet Eaton overcame each of those challenges and kept his expedition moving. Along the way he recruited several hundred more armed men.

The expedition reached Derne on April 26. To the governor's refusal to surrender, Eaton replied, "My head or yours, Mustifa."[7] The governor had reason to believe he would soon be parading Eaton's head on a pike. His troops manning Derne's citadel were ten times more numerous than his enemy. As a flotilla of three American warships bombarded the town, Eaton led an assault whose ranks were bolstered by sixty marines. Eaton was wounded and fell behind. Led by Lt. Presley O'Bannon, the marines fought their way into the citadel, hauled down the enemy flag, and raised the stars and stripes in its place. Mustifa fled with most of his men. Derne was the first foreign city beyond North America that the United States ever took by storm.

News of Derne's fate atop the blockade of fourteen warships, including six frigates, convinced Yusuf to negotiate. Tobias Lear, the latest envoy, held out for the $60,000 deal, the exchange of prisoners, and a most-favored-nation trade treaty. Yusuf dropped his demand to $200,000 and the exile of Hamet back to Alexandria. When Lear refused to budge, Yusuf gave in on the money as long as Hamet was sent packing from Derne. Lear agreed. The two signed a treaty on June 3, 1805. The $60,000 ransom amounted to $277 for each of the surviving 297 captives from the *Philadelphia*. There would be no annual tribute.

Although it was a relatively good deal, it was controversial. Congressmen and newspaper editors questioned why Lear had agreed to any ransom when he could have swapped Derne for the captives. Had Yusuf refused, the massed fleet could have pounded Tripoli to rubble. But Lear had spurned either option. The Senate committee that investigated the war and Lear's treaty found plenty to criticize. Nonetheless, the Senate ratified the treaty on April 12, 1806. In all, the Tripoli war had cost the United States $3.6 million and about thirty dead.[8]

America's conflicts with the Barbary states did not end there. The ink was no sooner dry on the treaty with Tripoli than Cdre. John Rodgers, the latest commander, had to sail much of his fleet to Tunis and deter the dey from declaring war. That intimidation worked. American naval power in the Mediterranean peaked in 1806 with thirty-one ships, including a half-dozen frigates. But following HMS *Leopard*'s attack on USS *Chesapeake* in June 1807, virtually all of those warships would be withdrawn to American ports and waters. Fortunately, although the rulers of the Barbary states periodically tried to shake down more money from the United States, another war did not erupt. Like the European powers, American leaders recognized that it was cheaper to pay than fight the Barbary states.

During the early republic, the United States chalked up few genuine feats of arms or diplomacy in its policy toward the Barbary states. Appeasement prevailed for all but three of those four decades, although occasionally a president would rattle his saber. From 1784 to 1815, the Barbary states seized thirty-five American ships and enslaved seven hundred sailors, and all the surviving captives were ransomed. The "war" with Tripoli involved only a few skirmishes and at best a sporadic blockade. Tripoli scored the only significant victory when it captured the *Philadelphia*. Certainly Decatur's raid that burned the *Philadelphia* was daring, but he destroyed an American vessel and did not free any prisoners. Likewise, Eaton's expedition that crossed five hundred miles of desert and culminated with the capture of Derne was an extraordinary feat of leadership and endurance, but it was not fully exploited by Lear at the diplomatic table. The United States eventually sent Hamet back into exile, not the last time that the Americans would be fickle with an initial favorite. And, in the end, the United States paid for the "peace" with a huge sum.

Americans can be forgiven if they believe that the United States won that war. The actual dismal record was deliberately obscured by celebrating the exploits of Decatur and Eaton. Since then that conflict has been kept alive in the popular imagination with a line in the "Marines' Hymn" about "the shores of Tripoli," although few Americans actually know what happened there and would be astonished if they did. Yet, even if the war was at best a draw, many Americans might take some comfort that President Jefferson stood up to Tripoli and the other Barbary states when the European powers merely appeased them. They might, however, ask themselves whether that war was worth the cost in treasure and blood.

IO

To the Ends of the Earth

The west had fascinated Thomas Jefferson for as long as he could recall. When a small boy, he had gazed at sunsets over the Blue Ridge Mountains and imagined what lay beyond, all the way to the Pacific pounding the continent's western edge. He loved listening to or reading about the wondrous or fearful tales of those who had explored that seemingly endless wilderness, whether they had gone to survey, hunt, trap, settle, trade, or speculate, or to join or fight the Indians on the receding frontier. Indeed his own father, Peter, had with three neighbors received a colonial commission to tramp across much of Virginia and map its dimensions.

Yet Jefferson never dared to head west himself. He would always be an armchair explorer living vicariously through the adventures of rugged, daredevil frontiersmen. Had he known what lay ahead, he could take enormous pride in being responsible for sponsoring America's greatest expedition before the moon walk. In the American imagination, Jefferson's launching of the Lewis and Clark expedition ranks with authoring the Declaration of Independence and the Louisiana Purchase as his crowning achievement. Indeed, no mission in all of American history demanded more courage, skill, and sheer endurance.[1]

That trek to the Pacific and back was a long time coming. Jefferson's first effort dates to 1783, when he tried to convince George Rogers Clark to lead an expedition across the continent; Clark declined. In 1785, while he was in Paris, Jefferson met John Ledyard, who had sailed with James Cook's third voyage to the Pacific and was the first American to set foot in the northwest. Jefferson inspired Ledyard and John Paul Jones with the scheme of sailing to the west coast, whereupon Ledyard would lead an expedition east across the continent; that venture never passed the talking stage. In 1792 he learned that American sea captain John Grey had discovered the Columbia River's mouth and had claimed that entire watershed for the United States. In an effort to solidify that claim, Jefferson interested the American Philosophical Society into backing an expedition led by the botanist André Michaux; that plan died in 1793 when Michaux was implicated in French minister Edmund Genet's schemes to conquer Louisiana. And with that, Jefferson's dream would lay dormant for nearly a decade.[2]

The turning point came in 1802 when Jefferson read with mingled awe and jealousy Scotsman Alexander Mackenzie's account of being the first known white man to traverse the continent in 1793. The British had beaten the Americans in realizing his vision. Jefferson was determined that an American expedition would be the second to reach and return from the Pacific, but surpass the first in the wealth of knowledge of nature, native peoples, and geography it collected along the way.

The press of other issues prevented him from asking Congress to sponsor such an expedition until January 18, 1803. He justified the expedition "for the purpose of extending the foreign commerce of the United States."[3] A majority in Congress agreed and appropriated $2,500 for what became known as the Corps of Discovery. Jefferson proudly signed the act into law on February 28, 1803.

That bill was a roll of the dice on two crucial matters. The first was how so few men could survive a two- or three-year trek across thousands of miles of wilderness beset with dangerous natives, beasts, and weather. The second was whether the Corps of Discovery would even be allowed to traverse lands that were legally owned by the French and administered by the Spanish. At that time, the United States was committed to trying to buy from France not the Louisiana Territory but just New Orleans, and even that transaction was hardly certain. No one then could anticipate that Americans would soon own the entire Louisiana Territory, and thus could do what they wanted with it. Given the well-justified fears among the Spanish and French alike of American expansion, the expedition would most likely be turned back at the Mississippi. Jefferson had prepared a legalistic argument for "innocent passage," but that would not have swayed the foreign officials. With the door barred, the Corps of Discovery would have had to make a humiliating withdrawal.

To surmount that gauntlet of daunting challenges, the expedition would have to be led by a truly extraordinary individual. Jefferson could think of no one better than his secretary, Capt. Meriwether Lewis, who was then only twenty-nine years old and had served for nine years in the army.[4] Jefferson knew Lewis from his childhood, which was spent on a neighboring plantation. Lewis had served with the militia for a year before, in 1795, he wrangled an ensign's commission with the regulars. He joined the army for adventure, but the war against the northwest Indians was over by the time he was posted there. For the next half-dozen years his duties would be solely administrative. His diligence in performing these mostly thankless and dreary tasks earned him promotions to the rank of captain. The only solace was the opportunity to travel across much of the Northwest Territory when he carried dispatches from one post to another. On February 23, 1801, little more than a week before taking the oath of office, Jefferson tapped Lewis to be his secretary. He chose Lewis because he wanted someone who was trustworthy, capable, and familiar with the people, politics, and places of the "western country."

Jefferson described Lewis as possessing "courage undaunted" and "a firmness & perseverance of character which not but impossibilities could divert from its direction."[5] Lewis would certainly live up to those accolades during his expedition. Yet he masked a tormented soul. He was torn between wild swings from the most intoxicating elation to the deepest melancholy. He was hot-tempered, solitary by nature, and often drowned his sorrows in alcoholic binges. He was court-martialed in 1796 for his drunken challenge of a lieutenant to a duel; his acquittal and reassignment reflected political rather than legal considerations. He briefly courted a series of women, but they seem to have found his Byronic temperament disturbing rather than beguiling. Left fatherless at the age of five, he would truly love only one woman—his adoring mother. His life's only sustained happiness was during the two-and-a-half-year journey to the Pacific and back, when he would often range alone across the plains and forests far from his companions.

Jefferson explained to Lewis that his mission was to ascend the Missouri River to its source, find a way over the Rocky Mountains, descend to the Pacific, and then return. In doing so, the Corps of Discovery would bolster America's claim to the Pacific Northwest initiated by Captain Grey. Along the way, he was to map the territory; conduct diplomacy with the Indians; note tribal customs, dispositions, and numbers; discern any commercial opportunities; and collect or sketch samples of all the plants, animals, and minerals. Essentially Lewis was to do across a swath of the continent what Jefferson had done in his only book. In "Notes on Virginia," Jefferson systematically explored the historic, cultural, social, economic, and psychological relations between man and nature in his beloved home state.

Exploration and diplomacy were the expedition's most important goals. The Indians were to be treated "in the most friendly & conciliatory manner which their own conduct will admit; allay all jealousies as to the object of your journey, satisfy them of its innocence, make them acquainted with the position, extent, character, peaceable & commercial dispositions of the U.S., of our wish to be neighborly, friendly, & useful to them."[6]

Lewis asked his army friend, William Clark, to be his partner in heading the expedition.[7] Clark was the youngest brother of George Rogers Clark and had acted as an older brother to Lewis, who was four years his junior. Clark may not have been as bright as Lewis, but he provided an emotional stability lacking in his volatile companion. While their men knew them as captains, Clark was actually only a first lieutenant during the journey.

Although the Louisiana Purchase would be ratified by the time the Corps of Discovery set forth, Lewis, Clark, and their men would travel through American territory only until they reached the continental divide. Thereafter they would pass through lands claimed by Spain, Britain, and Russia, as well as the United States. The strongest claim to that territory would come from who best mapped, exploited, settled, and defended it, or, in other words, who was the most powerful.

The Corps of Discovery that headed up the Missouri River on May 21, 1804, from St. Charles, twenty miles upstream from the Mississippi River, numbered forty-five men, including the leaders, thirty-one soldiers, eleven hunters, and Clark's slave, York. Of the soldiers, twenty-five would journey all the way to the Pacific, while the rest would winter with the expedition and then return to St. Louis in the spring. The men and supplies were split among a huge keelboat and two dugout canoes. As they poled upriver on that sultry spring day, none could be confident that any of them would survive the journey, let alone imagine that their exploits would be forever celebrated as a dazzling triumph of American power.

PART 2

Jefferson, 1805–1809

*What an awful spectacle does the world exhibit at this time, one man bestriding the
continent of Europe like a Colossus, and another roaming unbridled the sea.*

THOMAS JEFFERSON

*An American contending by strategem against those exercised in it
from their cradle would undoubtedly be outwitted by them.*

THOMAS JEFFERSON

The efficacy of an embargo cannot be doubted.

JAMES MADISON

*War will be a most calamitous event. Our immense commerce will be destroyed,
our progress and improvement retarded, and a thousand fortunes will be ruined.*

ALBERT GALLATIN

We have only to shut our hand to crush them.

THOMAS JEFFERSON

11

Faltering Steps

Although a lawyer and politician, Thomas Jefferson was not a powerful speaker. His voice was soft and easily lost in the rustling of a crowd, the far corners of a large hall, or the sighing of the wind. But delivery was not the most disappointing facet of his second inaugural address.

What was missing was the reconciliation and vision of his first. He hinted at rather than asserted a foreign policy. He spoke mostly of philosophical rather than practical matters. He alluded to problems over trade, the American Indians, and defense without offering any concrete proposals to resolve them. To those who were still concerned about how the United States could settle and govern the Louisiana Purchase, he tried to reassure them by asking, "Who can limit the extent to which the federative principle may operate effectively?"[1]

What explains that studied vagueness? Jefferson was a complex, often contradictory man. He was at once a visionary and an opportunist, a lofty philosopher and a crafty politician. His leadership was more consensual than decisive. He rarely favored quickly sizing up a situation, making a plan, and then swiftly acting on it. He took his time, a characteristic that his supporters called prudence and his critics called procrastination.

Then there was a side of Jefferson that is little considered today but was well known then. Jefferson could be loose with the truth. As John Quincy Adams diplomatically put it, he had "an itch for telling prodigies."[2] While Jefferson may have been the first, he was hardly the last popular president to confuse fantasy with reality. That tendency could be dangerous if it hampered a president's ability to understand and defend American national interests and security.

The political and policy successes of his first term seem to have bolstered Jefferson's natural complacency.[3] The nation was at peace, his party was in power, and no immediate crisis threatened that happy state. And, after all, the heart of his political philosophy was the notion that the government that governs least governs best.

Yet the United States faced a chronic if distant threat. So far Jefferson and his two predecessors had managed to avoid dragging the young nation into Europe's latest conflagration. But an America at war was only as far away as the mishandling of the next crisis.

Jefferson clearly recognized this problem but did not want to alarm the public by spotlighting the danger in his speeches. He would only privately confess his growing fear: "What an awful spectacle does the world exhibit at this time, one man bestriding the continent of Europe like a Colossus, and another roaming unbridled on the ocean." Yet he saw opportunity in that peril. Having defined the threat, Jefferson explained how to handle it: "But this is better than that one should rule both elements. Our wish ought to be that he who has armies may not have the Dominion of the sea, and that he who has Dominion of the sea may be one who has no armies. In this way we may be quiet; at home at least."[4] Logically that meant the best way to defend American interests amid those giants was to play one against the other. That would be easier said than done.

The domestic political situation reinforced the leisure with which Jefferson inaugurated his second term, which could not have been more compatible. He had won a landslide reelection with 162 electoral votes over the Federalist candidate Charles Pinckney's 14, and had won every state except Connecticut and Delaware. This time he was spared the tension of having a political foe as his vice president. The Twelfth Amendment, which allowed the vice president to be the president's running mate, was ratified on September 25, 1804. George Clinton, New York's governor and a longtime Republican stalwart, seconded him. Congress remained a Republican bastion, with solid majorities in both houses. Jefferson continued his highly successful practice of schmoozing with congressional leaders over dinner at the Executive Mansion. Then there was his cabinet, whose core was largely unchanged in composition and temperament. His two closest advisers remained Secretary of State James Madison and Treasury Secretary Albert Gallatin, while Henry Dearborn plodded on as the war secretary.

It was in his second tier of advisers where there would be turnover before the year was out. When Levi Lincoln resigned as attorney general, several prominent

Republicans turned down the post before Jefferson was able to persuade Robert Smith, his navy secretary, into switching portfolios. Smith was eager to do so, having felt overwhelmed by the duties and details of running the navy. But that left the navy post open. Jefferson's first choice, Jacob Crowninshield, resigned for personal reasons shortly after the Senate approved him. John Breckinridge took the post but died before the year was out. So Smith ended up returning to the Navy Department and heading it until he was finally able to resign on the day of Madison's inauguration.

As for policies, Jefferson maintained his minimalist approach to government. He continued to cut taxes and spending. Despite the reality that the war with Tripoli was being fought with frigates and marines, he clung to the notion that gunboats and the militia best defended the United States. Neither the president nor the Republican Party favored doing more. On March 25, 1805, a proposed House resolution that called for building six ships of the line failed to pass. Thus did Jefferson at once shape and reflect the era's parsimony and parochialism.[5]

1 2

The Fate of West Florida

West Florida's fate was the most notable unfinished business of Jefferson's first term. He had charged James Monroe with convincing the Spanish to agree that the Louisiana Purchase included the Gulf Coast east to the Perdido River. That mission proved to be doomed from the very start.

Having failed to elicit any serious talks with the Spanish minister in Paris, Monroe journeyed to Madrid for direct negotiations. Soon after arriving on New Year's Day, 1805, he learned to his dismay that he faced the same stonewalling by officials that he had endured in Paris.

Napoleon, who had been crowned France's first emperor the previous December, was disappointed that Monroe had left Paris for Madrid. Although Napoleon had recently ratified a treaty guaranteeing Spain's territorial integrity on January 5, 1805, he was having second thoughts. Any agreement for Napoleon was only as good as the immediate interests that prompted it. When those interests changed, then old deals were crumpled and new ones drafted and imposed. He passed on word to Monroe that he was willing to pressure Charles IV to yield West Florida if the United States first loaned Madrid 70 million livres, which would pass through French to Spanish hands. No French official was willing to explain just how much the handling fee would be. And even after the loan reached Madrid, there was no certainty that Charles IV would be any more amenable to rendering West Florida.[1]

Monroe angrily rejected any notion of a loan. He wrote Madison, explaining that Spain "would never cede one foot of territory otherwise than by compulsion."

Thus, only one card was left to play, but it was the trump—the United States should "take possession of both the Floridas and the whole country west of the Mississippi to the Rio Bravo."[2] Faced with a deadlock in Madrid, Monroe headed back to the United States.

The initiative for winning West Florida then passed back to the American minister in Paris, John Armstrong, who replaced Robert Livingston in 1805. Armstrong was a curious choice as a diplomat. John Quincy Adams described him as "morose, captious, and petulant."[3] Armstrong was unprepared for the frustrations of diplomatic life in Paris. In his reports back to Madison, he painted ever bleaker portraits of not just French stubbornness but also venality. Officials from Talleyrand on down appeared to be always fishing for bribes for even the most inconsequential of meetings. That provoked an angry reaction from Madison, who called on Armstrong to stand firm against such pressure: "The United States owed it to the world as well as to themselves to let the example of one government at least, protest against the corruption which prevails."[4] As for West Florida, Armstrong soon came to the same conclusion as Monroe, that diplomacy was futile and that the United States could assert its interests only through force. He advised Madison to impose a trade embargo against Spain, arguing that this action might provoke Napoleon to pressure Charles IV to render the territory. If that failed, then only the military option remained.[5]

Jefferson was sojourning at Monticello in August 1805 when he received copies of the letters from Monroe and Armstrong. The Spanish and French intransigence and arrogance, which his diplomats described, angered the president. But even if he had wanted to act, he had to sit tight. The entire federal government had shut down for a prolonged summer vacation. Only Dearborn was at hand for a prolonged visit. As for the rest of his cabinet, Madison was in Philadelphia, Gallatin New York, and Smith Baltimore. Congress had adjourned. Such was that era's casual approach to governance.

All Jefferson could do was write Madison wondering whether "we ought not immediately to propose to England an eventual treaty of alliance, to come into force whenever . . . a war shall take place with Spain or France."[6] That message most likely surprised Madison. After all, Jefferson had for years counseled patience over West Florida, arguing that the Spanish would sooner or later agree to relinquish it.

But Jefferson now argued that brinksmanship was justified. America's strategic position was sharply altered by Adm. Horatio Nelson's crushing victory over the combined French and Spanish fleets during the battle of Trafalgar on October 21, 1805. That victory would prove to be a double-edged sword for American national security. The destruction of much of France and Spain's naval power gave the

United States the freedom to do as it pleased with the Floridas and west of the Mississippi River. But it also led to uncontested British naval supremacy.

Meanwhile, when it was clear that the United States would not loan Spain 70 million livres via Paris, Napoleon made a new offer in September 1805. He told Armstrong that he could convince Spain to yield West Florida and a western boundary for Louisiana at the Colorado River, which runs from northwest to southeast through central Texas, for $10 million. When Armstrong rejected the offer, Napoleon dropped the price to $7 million. At this point, the emperor's need for quick cash exceeded his need to prop up Spain's sagging pride by clinging to money-losing colonies.[7]

Upon hearing the offer, Jefferson convened his cabinet to debate what to do. They concluded that $5 million plus the assumption of the $3 million in American claims for Spanish depredations was a reasonable counteroffer for both Floridas.[8] Jefferson wanted to back that offer with the threat of force. In a secret address to Congress on December 6, 1805, his statement that "formal war is not necessary for now" was a relief to some and a disappointment to others. But then he went on to argue that "the spirit and honor of our country requires that force should be interposed to a certain degree." As commander in chief, he reserved the right to determine just what form that would take. But he hoped to win both Floridas through diplomacy and asked Congress to scrape up $2 million to that end.[9]

It took nearly two months of debate before Congress finally passed a bill appropriating $2 million for the acquisition of the Floridas, with the House agreeing on January 16 and the Senate on February 7. Jefferson signed the bill into law on February 13, 1806.[10]

The biggest resistance to Jefferson's policy came when he submitted the names of John Armstrong and James Bowdoin as the official commissioners to the negotiations. Both men were already serving respectively as the ministers to France and Spain. Senate confirmation, especially with a Republican majority, should have been automatic. Yet Armstrong was widely reviled for his bullying personality and less-than-scrupulous business practices. After an impassioned debate, he passed muster in the Senate by only one vote. But that was only the beginning of the problems with the commission. Armstrong and Bowdoin despised each other.

In Paris, the haggling continued over the Floridas. Talleyrand suggested that Napoleon might be willing to drop the price to $6 million. Armstrong hinted that Jefferson might be willing to go as high as $4 million. The next logical step in the diplomacy would have been to split the difference at $5 million. But neither side budged.

Spain's image in the United States did not improve when a scandal erupted over its minister to the United States. In January 1806, Carlos Martinez de Irujo y Tacón was revealed to have tried to enlist William Jackson, a Federalist newspaper editor, to support Madrid's position. Republicans condemned Irujo by evoking images of French minister Edmond Charles Genet's machinations of siding with the Republicans against George Washington and the Federalists more than a decade earlier, even though there was no comparison between the two. Embarrassed by the scandal, Irujo received permission to return home. Yet he lingered, both so that his American wife would not have to leave her family and because he genuinely enjoyed living in the United States. Jefferson finally had Madison declare Irujo persona non grata and required him to set sail from the United States at the first opportunity. Irujo was replaced by a minister who lacked his understanding and appreciation for the country in which he served.[11]

In early 1806, Jefferson faced a diplomatic problem over the machinations of another Spanish subject. Francisco de Miranda was dedicated to liberating his homeland of Venezuela from Spanish rule. He had spent more than a decade traveling from one European capital to another to drum up support for his cause. In November 1805, he had arrived in New York with a letter of introduction from Rufus King, America's minister in London. During his three-month stay, he tried to find both private and public backers, bought a merchant ship called the *Leander*, equipped it for war and recruited a crew, and eventually sailed for Venezuela. Irujo, who was still in Washington, and the latest French minister, Louis Marie Turreau, protested Miranda's activities.

These intrigues put Jefferson on the spot. He sympathized with Miranda yet was duty-bound to uphold American law. He ordered an investigation. Federal officers arrested two men—Samuel Ogden, the *Leander*'s owner, and William Smith, New York's port surveyor and John Adams's son-in-law—on charges of rendering military aid against a country with which the United States was at peace. Ogden and Smith submitted memorials to both houses of Congress arguing that they were unjustly accused and calling for the dismissal of charges. Both houses overwhelmingly rejected those memorials. The men went on trial in the summer of 1806 and were acquitted of all charges.

The United States and Spain appeared to be marching steadily toward war against each other. Jefferson sought to back up his diplomacy with military strength. In March 1806, he had all troops in St. Louis except for one company journey down the Mississippi River to Fort Adams and had nine warships sail from the East Coast to New Orleans. On April 14, 1806, Congress passed a bill that appropriated $2 million if the president deemed it necessary to call up and provision 100,000 militia into service. In June, the War Department ordered Gen. James Wilkinson to prepare to transfer his headquarters from St. Louis to New Orleans.

The Americans were not alone in rattling the saber. Spain did so through Lt. Col. Simón de Herrera y Leyva, the military commander of the vast Spanish province of Nuevo León, which encompassed what is today northeastern Mexico and Texas eastward to its vague border with Louisiana. In July 1806, Herrera acted on orders from Governor Antonio Cordero y Bustamante to lead his men across the Sabine River and occupy Bayou Pierre, just thirty miles west of Natchitoches. The United States and Spain had previously agreed that that territory was American. After tarrying a couple of weeks, he withdrew his force to Los Adaes, on the stream Arroyo Hondo between the Red and Sabine rivers. The Spanish claimed the Arroyo Hondo as the boundary, while the Americans insisted that the Sabine River was Louisiana's proper western frontier. Jefferson would respond belatedly to that invasion of American soil. He was preoccupied with accusations of a plot by one of the nation's most prominent political leaders. Eventually he learned to his dismay that the internal and international crises fed on each other.

13

The Burr Conspiracy

The number of known traitors in American history is mercifully few. Two of the highest-ranking figures in that notorious lineup betrayed America during Jefferson's presidency—Aaron Burr, who had just finished his term as vice president, and James Wilkinson, the army's senior general. To this day, just what they intended to do remains impossible to unravel with precision. However, it is clear that they were paid agents of foreign powers and were conspiring, among other things, to detach the trans-Appalachian west from the United States.[1]

Wilkinson had been a Spanish spy and subversive for nineteen years. During that time, whispered rumors of his treason eventually came to President Adams's attention. To his later deep regret, Adams dismissed the notion and reassured Wilkinson that "I esteem your talents, I respect your services, and feel an attachment to your person, as I do to every man whose name and character I have so long known in the service of our country, whose behavior has been consistent."[2] Like most true patriots, Adams could not imagine how anyone could stab his fellow countrymen in the back, especially when he served in uniform.

Wilkinson was then the American army's highest-ranking officer. Even without the suspicion of his being a foreign agent, he owed his rise to that position of power to politics and luck rather than to military prowess. His service during the revolution was controversial. He was a competent enough aide successively to Benedict Arnold, Horatio Gates, and George Washington. But in 1778 he was involved in the Conway Cabal, which tried to replace Washington with Gates as commanding general. Rather than cashier him, Congress made him the clothing commissary; he was forced to resign in 1781 on corruption charges. After the war, he journeyed to Kentucky, where he boosted the fortune he made as a merchant and land speculator by his salary as a Spanish secret agent. In March 1791, he led the Kentucky militia against the Indians north of the Ohio River. With the army starved of experienced high-ranking officers, Washington granted Wilkinson a lieutenant colonel's commission in the regular army when he asked to be reinstated. Wilkinson was soon promoted to brigadier general under Gen. Anthony Wayne and became the army's senior general after Wayne died in December 1796.

Washington granted Wilkinson his commission and promotions with mixed feelings. He had not forgotten Wilkinson's disloyalty and corruption during the revolution. He was well aware of the more recent rumors of his Spanish ties, including warnings from General Wayne that Wilkinson was not fit for command as a soldier or patriot. But Washington hoped that the duties of office would lash down a loose cannon. He explained to Hamilton that the post would "feed his ambition, soothe his vanity, and by arresting discontent produce a good effect."[3]

It would not quite turn out as the president wished. Wilkinson may have been a lousy soldier, but he was a natural intriguer and politician. All along he shamelessly exploited his official posts to cut backroom financial deals, take payments under the table, and plot with a cabal of prominent, disgruntled western leaders for secession from the United States.

Those intrigues reached a new height in 1804 when he received orders to journey to New Orleans and join Governor William Claiborne in accepting the transfer of the Louisiana Territory on behalf of the United States. He stayed on to command American forces in that region as well as to secretly resume pocketing Spanish bribes that had been suspended for several years. Then, on March 11, 1805, Jefferson named Wilkinson the governor of the Upper Louisiana Territory, eight days after Congress had passed an act officially setting up that territory with its capital at St. Louis. Jefferson made that recess appointment on the recommendation of Samuel Smith, a prominent Republican senator and old friend of Wilkinson's. The appointment allowed Wilkinson to double-dip his income with a $2,000 salary as governor and $2,700 as a brigadier general.

Aaron Burr and James Wilkinson first met during the revolution when they served together as aides to Arnold and later to Washington. Like Wilkinson, Burr earned a reputation for his political rather than battlefield skills. He rose to lieutenant colonel before receiving permission to resign for reasons of bad health in 1779. That let him return to his study of law, and he passed the bar later that year. After the war, he embarked on a political career, serving as a New York assemblyman from 1784 to 1785 and from 1798 to 1799, as New York's attorney general from 1789 to 1791, and as New York senator to Congress from 1791 to 1797. His reputation for shady business deals, avarice, and corruption deepened with his political influence, causing George Washington, whom President Adams had enticed from retirement to head the army during the Quasi-War with France, to reject Burr's request for a commission. "Burr is a brave and able officer," Washington remarked, "but the question is whether he has not equal talents at intrigue."[4]

Burr blatantly displayed that latter talent during the 1800 election when he brokered a deal with Jefferson not to compete with him for the presidency. The electoral college tied at 73 votes each, and the subsequent election in the House of Representatives went through 36 tallies before a crucial vote shifted in Jefferson's favor. For the next four years, Jefferson was saddled with Burr as his vice president. Jefferson pointedly did not include Burr in his cabinet's deliberations.

Burr and Wilkinson most likely first discussed plans for carving out a western empire during a meeting in New York on May 23, 1804. The urgency to act on that dream was magnified after July 11, 1804, when Burr killed Alexander Hamilton in a duel in which Hamilton, who was a crack shot, appeared to have fired deliberately into the air. The outpouring of hatred against Burr, and demands for his resignation and even trial for murder, forced him into hiding for several weeks.

With his political career in the United States ruined, Burr now had nothing to lose by trying to conquer his own country. On August 6, he secretly met with Anthony Merry, the British minister, and requested a half million dollars and a British fleet at New Orleans to detach the trans-Appalachian western states and territories from the United States. Although Merry encouraged Burr's machinations, Whitehall nixed the plot. Around the same time, Burr most likely floated the same scheme to Spanish minister Irujo.[5]

In the face of constant pressure and a grand jury indictment for murder on August 14, 1804, Burr clung to the vice presidency until his term expired on March 3, 1805. On April 10, he embarked on a half-year tour of the western states to knit together a web of conspirators behind what he claimed was a plan to conquer Mexico. In New Orleans, Burr closeted himself with Juan Ventura Morales, the former Spanish intendant, a rather curious tête-à-tête for someone who was supposedly dedicated to stealing part of the Spanish Empire. Burr then journeyed back up the Mississippi and joined Wilkinson at Fort Massac on the lower Ohio River in June and again in September for a week together at Wilkinson's St. Louis headquarters. Burr spent the autumn in Washington, New York, and Philadelphia seeking additional backers. In November, during his latest meeting with Merry, he asked again for massive British financial and military aid. Merry handed him $1,500 and said that that was all he could give. Burr also dined with Jefferson at the Executive Mansion. He met again with Irujo and explained that his goal was not merely to detach the western states but to actually take over Washington City; Irujo donated several thousand dollars to the cause.

Burr felt he needed another year of organizing before he could trigger his plot. In April 1806, Burr and Wilkinson spent several days together on that wedge of land where the Ohio River flows into the Mississippi River. In an encoded letter dated July 29, 1806, Burr informed Wilkinson that they should join forces in their "enterprise" at Natchez in early December.[6] He spent much of August through October gathering men, supplies, and boats at his base of operations on Blennerhassett Island in the upper Ohio River.

Jefferson received ample warning of Burr's conspiracy. In February 1806, he read an anonymous letter revealing that Burr was a British agent. That same month, Joseph Daviess, the U.S. attorney for Kentucky, sent the first of eight letters to the president alerting him of a plot to "cause a revolt of the Spanish provinces, and a severance of all the western states from the Union—to coalesce and form one government."[7]

Yet Jefferson rejected those warnings. After all, Daviess was a Federalist and Jefferson suspected the same of the anonymous writer. He did not want such a prominent fellow Republican as Burr exposed in a public scandal. His restraint toward Burr is especially questionable given that Burr was a longtime political foe and had a well-deserved reputation for intrigue and corruption. So rather than order an investigation, Jefferson turned a blind eye to the charges in the hope that they were untrue. Indeed, he even invited Burr to dinner at the Executive Mansion on February 22, 1806.

A barrage of revelations in the spring of 1806 finally began to pry Jefferson's mind open to the plot's reality and danger. He received a letter in March from Col. George Morgan, a staunch Republican, reporting that Burr had spent several days at his farm near Pittsburgh and attempted to entice Morgan's sons into his secession scheme. Within a few days, he received a similar letter from yet another Republican, John Nicolas, who reported that a Burr agent was trying to recruit in his region of upper New York State. Secretary of State Madison opened his own warning letters from Gen. Presley Neville, Judge Samuel Roberts, and Chief Justice William Tilghman of Pennsylvania, all from the Pittsburgh region. Gen. William Eaton, who was among the heroes of the Tripoli War, met with the president to explain Burr's attempts to recruit him as second in command after Wilkinson.

Even then it took another half year before the president finally convened his cabinet for a series of meetings in October to figure out what to do. The United States faced twin and quite likely related crises. Burr was conspiring for the western lands to secede while a Spanish force had penetrated and set up camp on territory claimed by the United States. The Spanish flag had flown from Los Adaes on the stream Arroyo Hondo since July, well east of the Sabine River border between the two countries. A different Spanish force had turned back the scientific expedition of Thomas Freeman up the Red River on lands that should have been part of the Louisiana Purchase.

Jefferson and his cabinet agreed that some show of American force was essential to asserting American territorial claims in the region. War Secretary Dearborn sent orders for a detachment of regulars to march to Natchitoches, for Wilkinson to hurry from St. Louis down the Mississippi to take command, and for Capts. Edward Preble and Stephen Decatur to sail with their frigates to New Orleans. While the regulars and Wilkinson did promptly act as ordered, the naval captains could not do so because the president's budget cuts left them with only skeleton crews and provisions. John Graham, the secretary of the Orleans Territory who was in Washington for consultations, was authorized to follow Burr's trail, amass evidence, and muster local forces to arrest the traitor.

The frontier crisis was defused through restraint and wisdom by both sides. Lieutenant Colonel Herrera withdrew his force west of the Sabine River. Wilkinson and Governor Cordero corresponded and eventually cut a deal. On November 5, 1806, Wilkinson and Herrera signed a document by which Spanish forces would stay west of the Sabine River and American forces east of Arroyo Hondo until their respective governments could agree on the frontier. Jefferson endorsed the Neutral Ground Agreement as soon as he received it.

Marching to the brink of war sobered Wilkinson from his dreams of conquering and heading a western empire. Nearly two weeks before he reached the understanding with Herrera, he had made a crucial decision, as the border crisis had put him in a precarious position. Here he was on the far southwestern frontier entrusted with the nation's security at a time when Burr was planning to descend the Ohio and Mississippi rivers with an army and capture New Orleans, whereupon Wilkinson was to join him. But what if his own troops refused to join the rebellion and instead turned their guns against him? Or what if fighting broke out with the Spanish?

Wilkinson reasoned that he had no choice but to save his own skin by betraying Burr. So he wrote but did not sign two letters to Jefferson detailing Burr's plans and had an aide hurry them to the Executive Mansion. His "confession" whitewashed the conspiracy's true gravity. He claimed that Burr had tried to enlist him in a scheme to mass an army in New Orleans and then sail to Vera Cruz to begin the conquest of Mexico. He said nothing about provoking the revolt of the trans-

Appalachian West against the United States. And he claimed to have spurned Burr's offer. His only fault, he claimed, was not to have revealed the plot sooner.

A few weeks later, Wilkinson forwarded to Jefferson a doctored version of the ciphered letter dated July 29 that he had received from Burr on October 8. In it Burr explained the preparations he had made, including troops, supplies, and even the support of a British squadron based in Jamaica, and confirmed Wilkinson as his second in command. To give the impression that the letter was the first he had heard of the conspiracy, Wilkinson omitted incriminating details, including a reference to a previous letter Burr sent on May 13.[8]

Upon reading Wilkinson's first two letters, Jefferson took another step toward dealing with the crisis. On November 27, 1806, he issued a proclamation that exposed the conspiracy and called for all public officials—federal, state, and territorial—to thwart it. He did not, however, name Burr as the ringleader. Nor did he then authorize the U.S. Army to search out and destroy the rebels. It was not until December 11, 1806, that a grand jury indicted Burr and his coconspirators.[9]

Jefferson's reliance on state militia to deal with such a potentially dangerous crisis reflected his principle that as president he could do only what was explicitly worded in the Constitution. If the Constitution does not state that a president can use regulars to arrest armed men suspected of conspiring against the United States, then he cannot do so. It was for that reason that Jefferson had privately condemned Washington's federalization of state militia to suppress the Whiskey Rebellion in 1794. A subsequent 1795 law had authorized the president to use militia only to confront domestic rebellions. But so far there was no rebellion, only rumors of a vague plot. Jefferson asked Congress to pass a bill that granted him the authority to use federal forces in a domestic crisis. He did not sign that bill into law until March 3, 1807, after the crisis had passed.

As if Jefferson's preceding actions against the Burr plot were not open enough to criticism, his next move would be even more controversial. He swayed the Republican majority in the Senate to pass with a voice vote in secret session on January 23, 1807, a bill that would have suspended habeas corpus for three months. That bill's text provoked an outcry that it was not only unconstitutional but hypocritical since it resembled the Sedition Act that Jefferson and his Republican Party had fiercely contested just a half-dozen years earlier. Cooler heads prevailed in the House, where the bill was soundly defeated by 113 to 19.[10]

Meanwhile, for several months, Burr wielded his powerful mind and luck to elude both militia patrols and court indictments. On December 5, 1806, he persuaded a Kentucky grand jury to dismiss charges against him. Ohio militia invaded Blennerhassett Island, arrested many of his followers, and confiscated his supplies, but Burr was far away. He was near Vicksburg on January 10, 1807, when he learned of Wilkinson's betrayal and the federal government's arrest warrant. A week later, he surrendered with 120 men to a court in Mississippi. He then skipped bail, abandoned his men, and dashed for a safe refuge at Mobile, in Spanish West Florida. He almost made it but was run to ground near Fort Stoddert, Alabama, on February 19, and eventually delivered under armed guard to the court at Richmond, Virginia, on March 26.

How the trial ended up in Richmond reflects the inadequacy of America's federal legal system in that era. Jefferson had no Justice Department to handle the case, only an overworked attorney general, Levi Lincoln, and his few secretaries. Lincoln advised that Burr be put on trial at the Fifth Circuit Court in Richmond, Virginia, with jurisdiction over Blennerhassett Island in the upper Ohio River, which was the conspiracy's headquarters.

Supreme Court Justice John Marshall opened a preliminary investigation on the charges against Burr of treason, a capital offense, and conspiracy on April 1. Marshall dismissed the treason charge for lack of two required witnesses, but he did find probable cause for conspiring to invade another country. He then convened a jury. Meanwhile, he ordered two of Burr's confederates, Erick Bollman and Samuel Swartwout, released for the same reason.

Jefferson unwittingly contaminated his own case against Burr in several ways. On January 22, he told Congress that Burr's guilt was beyond doubt. He then secretly promised Bollman that he would not use Bollman's confession against him if he testified against Burr, but later broke that promise. His worst failure, however, was not to have Wilkinson indicted even though numerous witnesses and documents incriminated him.

In his desire for Wilkinson to be the star witness against Burr, the president blindly accepted his claims of innocence. He reassured Wilkinson that "I am thoroughly sensible of the painful difficulties of your situation, expecting an attack with overwhelming force, unversed in law, surrounded by suspected persons, and in a nation tender as to everything infringing liberty, and especially from the military."[11] In loyalty to his belief, Jefferson would derail a later effort by John Randolph to lead a congressional investigation of Wilkinson. A court-martial of Wilkinson found him not guilty. So Wilkinson would not only escape indictment but remain firmly in command of the American army.

Finally, Jefferson himself refused to testify in the case by claiming what later became known as executive privilege. That provoked the latest debate over the Constitution. Could a president, unlike all other Americans, ignore a subpoena? Was a president above the law?

Marshall finessed the potential constitutional crisis by ruling that while a president was just as beholden to the law as anyone else, Jefferson did not have to show up because of his busy schedule. He did require the president to submit to the court all relevant documents. The crisis ended when Jefferson accepted Marshall's compromise.

Jefferson advanced some powerful precedents for executive privilege. As for obeying a subpoena, "to comply with such calls would leave the nation without an executive branch whose agency . . . is understood to be so constantly necessary to be always in function." As for documents requested by another branch of government, just what, if any, the president would send would be for him alone to decide. Here his reasoning was rooted in politics rather than the Constitution: "All nations have found it necessary that for the advantageous conduct of their affairs, some of these proceedings, at least should remain known to their executive functionary only."[12]

After the trial opened on May 22, over 140 witnesses were eventually called. Although John Hay, the prosecuting attorney, was armed with blanket pardons, he could not find a witness with an unassailable testimony. Burr mounted a vigorous defense by systematically picking apart the words and written evidence against him and issued a series of motions to have the case thrown out on various grounds. The trial ended on September 1, 1807, when the jury found Burr not guilty. Whether that decision represented genuine "reasonable doubt" or political bias has been debated ever since. One thing is for certain: Aaron Burr got away with treason.

14

The *Chesapeake* Atrocity

The worst crisis of Jefferson's second term overlapped with the next worst. Two days before Aaron Burr's indictment, the captain of the British frigate *Leopard* ordered three broadsides fired into the American frigate *Chesapeake*, leaving three men dead and eighteen wounded on June 22, 1807.

Such an atrocity was all but inevitable.[1] That unprovoked British assault was the culmination of years of worsening tensions and confrontations. Since war in Europe had broken out in 1792, the United States had struggled to benefit from the peace and prosperity of remaining neutral. Since joining that struggle in 1793, Whitehall had bitterly resented the profits the Americans enjoyed from trading with both sides. Even worse, that trade seemed to dilute Britain's naval supremacy when British blockades might otherwise have brought its enemies to their knees. Fear as well as rage rose in Britain as it became more and more difficult to find trained sailors to man the nation's war and merchant ships. Desertion from the harsh conditions aboard a royal warship was a key reason for that shortage. Countless of the thousands of those who were lucky enough to escape found refuge aboard American vessels.

In order to deal with these and other problems of fighting a world war against a powerful enemy, Whitehall issued a tougher series of Orders in Council that authorized the Royal Navy to stop and search neutral ships, confiscate war contraband heading to Britain's enemies, and apprehend suspected deserters.

The British could cite international law to justify at least part of that policy. It was an accepted practice that warships of a nation at war could indeed stop and search neutral vessels for "contraband" heading to an enemy port. The Americans did not dispute that concept. Just what constituted contraband, however, was in the mind of the beholder. The British list included food shipped by a neutral vessel from one enemy port to another. The Americans countered that with the principle of "free ships, free goods," which meant that any nonmilitary cargo on a neutral ship was legitimate regardless of its origin. They also insisted that food was a humanitarian, rather than war, good.

Britain's Rule of 1756 had no moorings in international law but was merely a policy that dated from the Seven Years' War. The policy asserted that trade forbidden in peace should not be allowed in war. Whitehall wielded that axiom as an excuse to sweep the seas of neutral merchant vessels to which its enemies had opened their ports. The policy actually violated international law, which recognized a sovereign state's right to determine when, how, and with whom it traded. To that the British retorted that if sovereignty meant anything, it meant that a state could do what it could get away with. And with their naval hegemony and determination to crush their enemies, the British got away with a great deal.

Impressment was Whitehall's worst practice, at least from the standpoint of the victims and national honor. To add deliberate insult to injury, many of His Majesty's captains took a perverse pleasure in deliberately violating America's three-mile territorial sea to stop vessels and snatch sailors. Perhaps as many as one of two among the eighteen thousand seamen manning American vessels were indeed of British origin, and many were, in fact, deserters from British warships. Royal Navy captains and press gangs may have hauled away as many as six thousand seamen from American vessels between 1803 and 1812. While a victim could sue for his release, the catch was that the process took years, was expensive, and rarely resulted in liberty. Courts not only dismissed any case without proof of citizenship, but they also often condemned even those with documents back to a berth in the Royal Navy.[2]

While impressment continued to rankle, for the five years that overlapped Jefferson's first term, American shippers enjoyed a loophole from the Rule of 1756. In 1800, the American merchant vessel *Polly* was brought into a British prize court. The captain explained that he should be allowed to sell his French cargo as he pleased because he had first taken it to an American port and paid a duty before shipping it across the Atlantic. With its 1800 *Polly* decision, the court ruled that a so-called broken voyage did not violate the rule.

Then came the *Essex* decision of June 22, 1805, which reversed the *Polly* decision. The *Essex* was an American merchant ship caught in the web of Britain's Orders in Council. When brought before the Admiralty Court, the captain pleaded for release, arguing that his cargo was "broken" during the voyage. The court dismissed his documents and instead ruled that his ship and cargo be confiscated. Henceforth, with that precedent, any cargo was "fair" game for British warships and courts.

Word of the *Essex* decision galvanized Jefferson into diplomatic action. On March 16, he wrote James Monroe, America's minister in London, that he would soon dispatch William Pinkney with instructions for them to negotiate a treaty with Britain that ended impressment and accepted the principle of "free ships, free goods." It would be another two months before Secretary of State Madison sent the actual instructions.[3]

Despite that initiative's turtle-like pace, there was a good chance that the Americans and British could reach a diplomatic breakthrough in 1806. Charles James Fox became foreign minister in the new "All Talents" cabinet formed after William Pitt's death in January 1806. The cabinet's nickname came from its composition as a coalition of leaders from across the political spectrum. Fox led the liberal opposition Whig Party in Parliament and advocated friendly, mutually beneficial relations with the United States.[4] He would indeed try to alleviate tensions with several substantive measures, but the relationship would worsen before word of his efforts reached Washington.

Joseph Nicholson, a Maryland representative, authored the Non-Importation Act, which barred any British goods that could be obtained from other countries or at home. The bill passed the House by 93 to 32 on March 26, 1806, and the Senate by 19 to 9 on April 19. Jefferson signed that bill into law on April 18, 1806. The bill had two tenets that made it a subtle rather than blunt diplomatic instrument. First, it would not take effect until seven months later on November 15, and then only if Whitehall refused to rescind its Orders in Council. Second, the bill could be suspended if the president and a majority in Congress believed that it was in American interests to do so. Thus the bill was crafted in a way that gave American diplomats enough bargaining power and time to cut a deal with the British. The Non-Importation Act was not the only legal display of resolve. Jefferson and the Republican majority deluded themselves with the belief that the bill authorizing fifty new gunboats, which the president signed into law on April 21, 1806, would somehow cow the British or defend American waters.[5]

As coincidence would have it, a tragedy that gunboat supporters would use to justify their policy occurred four days later. On April 25, 1806, the captain of HMS *Leander*, hovering off Sandy Hook near the entrance to New York Bay, ordered a warning shot fired when an American merchant vessel failed to halt at his command. The shot struck another ship and killed a man.

After consulting with his cabinet, Jefferson issued on May 3, 1806, a proclamation charging the British captain with murder and called for his arrest and trial.
He also ordered the *Leander* and two other accompanying war sloops, the *Cambrian*
and the *Driver*, out of American waters and forbade their return. The president did
not explain just how he hoped to reconcile those two policies.[6]

Amid these escalating tensions, word of Fox's conciliatory measures reached
Washington. Fox's first step was to recall Anthony Merry, who had been a
provocative figure ever since he set foot in Washington to serve as Britain's minister in November 1803. Merry sneered at what he considered American vulgar-
ity and all along downplayed the seriousness of American protests against Britain's
rapacious policies. He tended to place too much faith in those politicians and merchants who dismissed the notion of going to war with Britain because the nation
would lose more than it could possibly gain. Likewise, he ignored the powerful
interest groups that urged the United States to prepare itself for an inevitable war.
Fox recognized Merry as a liability to British interests, and thus he had to go. Fox
hoped that Jefferson and his cabinet would appreciate his gesture, along with the
time it would take to find someone appropriate to replace Merry.

Jefferson certainly seized on that gesture and its author as a golden opportunity.
He wrote Monroe of his confidence that skillful diplomacy would soon resolve all
the conflicts between the United States and Britain. That once-fierce Anglophobe
asserted that "no two countries on earth have so many points of common interest
and friendship, and their rulers must be great bunglers indeed if with such dispositions, they break them asunder."[7] The worsening crisis with Spain and Burr's
conspiracy had forced Jefferson to set aside his prejudices.

Word would soon arrive of an even more substantive shift in British policy. Fox
was the driving force behind the Order in Council of May 16, 1806, that imposed
a strict blockade on Napoleon's empire in Europe, but beyond those waters neutral ships would be allowed to carry products from an enemy if the voyage was
"broken" by paying duties in a neutral port.

Unfortunately, Fox fell gravely ill shortly after Pinkney arrived and formal
talks began on August 28; he died on September 13. Fox had designated William
Eden, Baron Auckland, and his nephew Henry Richard Fox, Baron Holland, to
negotiate with Monroe and Pinkney, and ensured that they would treat the
Americans with respect and warmth. That was an abrupt and welcome change
from the condescension and arrogance that previous American envoys had
endured. Auckland actually invited the Americans to his country estate with the
remark, "I trust we shall be able to do some good to mankind, if your powers are
sufficient enough."[8]

Although the talks were friendly, the British firmly refused to put the impressment issue on the table. Instead they insisted that by requiring all sailors manning American vessels to carry proper documents, the U.S. government could greatly reduce any inconvenience. They also expressed their hope that American law would prohibit captains from enlisting sailors without proper documents or for officials to grant citizenship papers to British nationals. Monroe and Pinkney replied that those suggestions might make a solid foundation for a treaty only if Whitehall pledged to renounce impressment. Auckland and Holland agreed to seek the cabinet's approval.

Meanwhile, the November 15 deadline passed and the Non-Importation Act took effect on December 14, 1806. The bill listed British manufactured goods that would be barred from the United States. Federal officials prosecuted several people who were caught violating that law. Then Jefferson received word from Monroe and Pinkney of progress in London, so he asked Congress on December 3, 1806, to suspend the act for another six months. Congress dutifully complied. When the next deadline loomed, the president would ask for yet another half-year suspension.[9]

Jefferson's optimism was further boosted when David Erskine replaced Merry in the fall of 1806. With an American wife and longtime residence in the United States, Erskine understood American interests, sentiments, values, and, most important, just how much Americans would endure before they struck back. Unlike his predecessor, he did not mince his words in reporting to his superiors the swelling anti-British feelings among Americans: "I think it in my duty to observe to your lordship that all the parties in this country take a warm interest on the point of the non-impressment of sailors (claimed as British) out of American ships on the high seas, and . . . I am persuaded that no cordiality can be expected from this country whilst it is deemed necessary by His Majesty to enforce that right." He later expressed his sympathy for the United States by noting how "highly grating to the feelings of an independent nation" to be "watched as closely as if it was blockaded, and every ship coming in or going out of their harbors examined in sight of the shore by British squadrons within their waters."[10]

Whitehall eventually authorized Auckland and Holland to grant an array of concessions. With the treaty signed on New Year's Eve, 1806, Monroe and Pinkney sent to Jefferson a diplomatic glass that was nine-tenths full. The only missing piece was impressment, which the British adamantly refused to yield, although they conceded all the other American demands. Most important, the British codified in treaty what had been practiced since Fox issued his Order in Council in May 1806. Henceforth, Whitehall would respect the "broken voyage" of neutral vessels as long as the duty paid in an intermediate port was documented. American vessels would be allowed to sail on to Britain's West Indian colonies after dropping anchor in Britain. Duties would be reduced from 3 percent to 2 percent for goods bound to Britain and 1 percent for those heading to the West Indies. An order would be issued to the Royal Navy not to intercept vessels within five miles of the American coast. Finally, the British offered insurance so that any American vessel that was unjustly taken would be promptly compensated for any losses.

Whitehall's concessions did not end there. Privately Holland and Auckland offered a deal on impressment. If the United States issued a declaration that it would not give refuge to any British deserters and would return those who were apprehended, Whitehall would pass on by word of mouth to the Royal Navy's captains that impressment was suspended for now.

Monroe and Pinkney had secured a formal treaty and secret understanding that resolved the major problems between America and Britain. In reality, the diplomats conceded little of substance. The United States would have to officially forfeit the principle of "free ships, free goods," forbid privateers from using its ports or Americans from serving in the armies and navies of Britain's enemies, and return deserters to British authorities.[11] That treaty and the subsequent policies would have all but eliminated the two major excuses by which Madison led the United States into war in 1812.

Monroe and Pinkney were well aware that without a formal impressment ban, Jefferson would likely scuttle the deal, so they included a twenty-one-page explanation with the treaty when they sent it to the president on January 3, 1807.[12] Letters and conflicting intentions would cross in the mail. The hearts of Monroe and Pinkney must have scraped bottom when they read a letter sent by Madison in February. He warned the envoys that "if no . . . formal stipulation on the subject of impressment be attainable, the negotiation should be made to terminate without any formal compact whatever."[13]

That hard-line stance was inspired by the latest bitter lesson about power recently inflicted on Jefferson. Issuing a proclamation against the British navy was much easier than enforcing it, especially with little more than a gunboat flotilla. Indeed it would have been suicidal for the gunboats rotting in the harbors of New York or other ports to square off with any of the British warships cruising American waters. Those puny pop-gun vessels only provoked British scorn and emboldened them to more outrages.

HMS *Cambrian*, which was among the three ships that Jefferson had banned from American waters, tested the president's resolve by sailing into the Chesapeake Bay in December 1805. Jefferson was enraged when he learned of it, but with no other available power than his pen, he could only dash off another proclamation. He had no sooner condemned the *Cambrian* and forbade Americans from any communication with the warship, when he learned that it had sailed back to sea. Then would come word that HMS *Driver* had violated his orders by sailing into Charleston Harbor. These tests were a clear indication of the shift in British policy since Fox's death.[14]

That humiliation merely provoked Jefferson to ask Congress to fulfill his vision of a 200-gunboat fleet, with 40 on the Mississippi River and the rest scattered along the Eastern Seaboard. Since the navy already had 73 of his cherished vessels, only 127 more needed to be built at a cost of no more than $600,000. He cited economy as well as strategy to justify that expansion—the cost of those new vessels was less than that for two frigates. Each gunboat was about fifty feet long, could be rowed and sailed, mounted an 18- or 24-pounder cannon, and would cost an estimated $5,000 to build.[15]

Critics revealed that the existing gunboats had cost twice the estimated amount. That fact was enough to raise some powerful congressional eyebrows. The worst doubt was sown by the prediction that the gunboat fleet would not just prove to be militarily worthless, but would also weaken the United States by diverting scare money, men, and materials from warships that might otherwise have hurt America's enemies.

Although Jefferson irritably deafened himself to those arguments, congressional majorities listened. The result was a deadlock. The House appropriated only one-quarter of the president's gunboat request, or $150,000, and authorized another $150,000 for coastal forts. The Senate was willing to spend another $300,000 for defense, but only for fortifications. A tragedy would soon occur that would not only convince Congress to allocate more money for defense but also bring America and Britain to war's brink.[16]

Meanwhile, a copy of the treaty reached Washington in March 1807. It was not, unfortunately, the one sent by the American envoys along with their carefully reasoned arguments for the treaty. Erskine obtained his copy from Whitehall and immediately hurried to Madison with what he thought was wonderful news.[17]

Jefferson was stunned when he received it. He considered the treaty worthless without a formal British renunciation of impressment and never sent it to the Senate, which was to soon adjourn. "I do not wish any treaty with Great Britain," he angrily declared, and added that "a concession on our part would violate a moral and political duty of the Government to our citizens."[18]

And so Jefferson tossed away a golden diplomatic opportunity, one that Hamilton and any other pragmatist would have happily seized. He clung to his belief that his non-importation policy would bring Britain to its knees. If so, then why should he agree to any concessions at all? Soon Whitehall would yield to his demands on impressment, or so his logic went.[19]

The latest Order in Council appeared to reflect parts of the treaty. On January 7, 1807, Whitehall decreed that the Royal Navy would intercept any neutral vessels sailing between any two ports of France and its allies. That was an explicit rejection of the American assertion of "free ships, free goods," which said that neutral ships could sail anywhere and carry anything, but which Monroe and Pinkney had conceded in their treaty. A tacit approval could be read into Whitehall's silence on the "broken voyage" concept, whereby neutral vessels could trade with belligerents if they broke their voyage in a neutral port and paid duties on those goods. The treaty had formally accepted that concept.

The president, along with most Americans, assumed that Whitehall's latest tightening of the screws on international trade was primarily directed against them. Prime Minister Spencer Perceval succinctly captured the essence of Britain's policy: "The object of the Orders in Council was not to destroy the trade of the Continent, but to force the Continent to trade with us."[20] It was an attempt to retaliate against Napoleon, who, flush from his conquest of Prussia, issued his Berlin Decree of November 21, 1806, which implemented a Continental System of blockade against the British Isles. But Napoleon had done so partly in retaliation for a British Order in Council of May 16, 1806, which declared a blockade from Brest to the Elbe River. Thus was American trade increasingly trampled in the tit-for-tat broadsides of those two behemoths. While Britain's policy was understandable, it did have a potential downside. With most of Europe cowed or conquered by Napoleon, Whitehall could ill afford to further alienate the United States. But that was exactly the effect of each Order in Council. The British enforced their latest policy immediately and vigorously, in contrast to the French, who did not begin to implement their policy against American ships until September 1807.

Those dueling blockades would devastate America's merchant fleet and trade. With their command of the sea, the Royal Navy and British privateers would capture several times more American vessels than the French navy, which was mostly blockaded in port. With only a handful of warships in the American navy, the United States could do nothing to deter or retaliate against those depredations.

Among America's tiny fleet was USS *Chesapeake*, a 38-gun frigate moored in Norfolk, Virginia. James Barron, its captain, spent most of spring 1807 preparing the *Chesapeake* for a long voyage to the Mediterranean to show the flag before the Barbary states. In February, a group of sailors escaped from HMS *Melampus*, which was anchored in Hampton Roads. Three of those deserters would lash their hammocks aboard the *Chesapeake*.

That was hardly the first time that British sailors had deserted to an American warship. The month before the *Melampus* incident, Erskine had asked Madison to apprehend and return some other deserters. Madison rejected the request, arguing that no treaty bound the United States to do so. After learning of the *Melampus* deserters, Erskine again asked for Madison's aid. Madison would have repeated his position in any event but was especially forthright in doing so because he believed those sailors were impressed Americans. American law forbade citizens from serving with foreign nations that were at war when the United States was neutral, and this reinforced the illegality of their impressment by the British. Undaunted by the logic of Madison's position, Whitehall would later cite his refusal as an excuse for taking the matter into its own hands.[21]

If the *Melampus* deserters were impressed Americans who had escaped, then genuine British deserters were also aboard the *Chesapeake*, including five from HMS *Halifax* who enjoyed taunting their former officers in Norfolk's teeming streets and smoky grogshops. Word of that enraged Vice Adm. George Berkeley, who commanded the North American station at his headquarters at Halifax, Nova Scotia. To the flotilla in the Chesapeake Bay, he had Capt. Salusbury Pryce Humphreys set sail with his HMS *Leopard* with word that all means were justified to apprehend and try deserters. The 52-gun *Leopard* dropped anchor off Hampton Roads on June 21, 1807.

The following day the *Chesapeake* set sail for the Mediterranean. It would never reach its destination. Barron had ordered a hasty departure. Supplies still cluttered the deck, and his crew was poorly trained in most ship operations, including gunnery.

The *Leopard* intercepted the *Chesapeake* off Cape Henry. Humphreys ordered Barron to permit a party to board his vessel to search for British deserters. Barron refused to do so, explaining that he knew of no such men in his service. Humphreys ordered his gunners to open fire. Three broadsides killed three Americans and wounded eight, including Barron, who ordered the colors struck. British marines boarded the *Chesapeake* and eventually arrested four suspects. Three feet of water filled the *Chesapeake*'s hold before the survivors began to pump out more than seeped in.

The *Chesapeake* atrocity was a turning point in British policy. It was the first time a British warship had impressed sailors from an American naval vessel. Much worse, it was the first time that a British warship had fired on an American warship in peacetime.

The battered *Chesapeake* sailed back to Norfolk, while Humphreys had the *Leopard* defiantly drop anchor in nearby Lynnhaven Bay. On June 24, the citizens of Norfolk and Portsmouth issued resolutions condemning the attack and forbidding any British sailors to step ashore or else suffer arrest. As the news spread across the nation, the reaction among nearly all Americans was ire. In a letter to Jefferson, Sen. Samuel Smith captured the prevailing national view: "There appeared but one opinion—War."[22]

Although the attack shocked Jefferson when he learned of it on June 25, war was the last option he wanted to consider. He called for his cabinet to convene, but it would take a while for them to gather; War Secretary Dearborn was in Philadelphia on his way to summer in Maine, while Treasury Secretary Gallatin was in New York. Meanwhile, Madison and Erskine met several times. The British minister conveyed his regret, assured Madison that the attack was unauthorized, and urged patience until Whitehall could offer a suitable response.

The cabinet was finally able to open discussion on a course of action on July 1, a week after the attack. Its members unanimously agreed that the president should issue a proclamation condemning the attack, order all British warships from American waters, and demand an "honorable reparation." But before then, Jefferson wished to explain to the public what had happened and prohibit anyone from offering aid, comfort, or communication of any kind to the British. He issued those two proclamations on July 2 and July 7, respectively.[23]

Then there was the question of how America's diplomats should support the policy. The president dispatched the *Revenge*, a small sloop of war, to carry dispatches to America's ministers. Those to James Monroe and William Pinkney in London ordered them to lodge a strong protest with Whitehall, demand reparations and release of the four abducted sailors, and call for a British emissary to journey to Washington for negotiations to resolve all outstanding differences. Those to John Armstrong and James Bowdoin in Paris would have them halt any negotiations over purchasing West Florida for the practical reason that the United States needed as much money as possible if it were to go to war. They were also to ensure that good relations prevail with France and Spain. Should a war break out, the United States would be fighting a parallel war with those nations against Britain. Jefferson explained to Bowdoin that "in this state of things, cordial friendship with France, and peace at least with Spain, become more interesting."[24]

The British, meanwhile, heaped aggression upon aggression. Commodore George Douglas, the ranking commander in the Chesapeake, led the squadron at Lynnhaven Bay to Norfolk, blockaded that port, and demanded that the citizens resume supplying his warships. Jefferson had a copy of his proclamation sent to the British flotilla.

It took several days for news to travel between Norfolk and Washington. The crisis reached a potentially new dangerous stage when militia captured a party of midshipmen and three sailors who had come ashore to secure supplies. Virginia governor William Cabell reacted to that event with alarm. He hardly wanted to provoke an attack on his state. He wrote Jefferson that while he was trying to uphold the supply embargo on the British fleet, he did not believe that that extended to incarcerating stray sailors.[25]

In his reply, Jefferson cited a congressional act of March 3, 1805, that empowered the president to maintain order in America's harbors. The British attack and block-ade were acts of a "qualified war." As such the governor was to consider and treat those captives prisoners of war. Nonetheless, the governor was to do all possible to prevent escalation to a general war. Indeed, after praising the militia, he told Cabell to let them disperse to their homes. As for Norfolk's defense, he reckoned that the twelve gunboats, the *Chesapeake*, and the French frigate *Cybele* at anchor in the harbor, along with the small detachment of regulars manning Fort Nelson, would be sufficient.[26]

Fortunately, the British did not test Jefferson's faith in the strength of those local forces. After receiving the proclamation, Douglas lingered for another week simply to show the Americans they were impotent to back up their demands. Finally, he ordered his flotilla to return to Lynnhaven Bay.

Jefferson was indeed powerless to do anything about that blatant defiance of his order to leave American waters. Yet he did not allow his frustration to effect his policy. All along, his response to the crisis was measured, calm, and moderate. While trying to sidestep war at virtually all costs, he made it clear that the United States expected full compensation for the attack. But the British could ignore his diplomacy since it lacked any military backup.

Even had he wanted to, he could not bolster the strength of the army or navy without congressional approval. Congress was then in recess and was not scheduled to reconvene until November. For Jefferson, that absence was fortuitous. He was well aware that if he called its members back now their rage would pressure him into an unwanted war. And if that were going to happen, he would "procrastinate 3 or 4 months only to give time to our merchants to get in their vessels, property, and seamen, which are the identical materials with which the war is to be carried."[27] That was a prudent policy given the estimate that at sea there were 2,500 American vessels packed with over a hundred million dollars worth of goods, most of which was uninsured.[28] So he rejected the advice of Treasury Secretary Gallatin and Navy

Secretary Robert Smith that he immediately recall Congress. Instead he put off issuing any recall until July 31, and then asked it to reconvene on October 26, just a couple of weeks before its members' scheduled return.

He hoped to settle the crisis through diplomacy before Congress next met. But diplomacy took time. A ship took around six weeks to sail between Washington and London. With favorable winds and currents, and a prompt Whitehall response, he would get word within four months. By that time, if the British did not offer a face-saving way of backing off, he would face overwhelming pressure from Congress and the newspapers to go to war.

During those four months, Jefferson did nothing of substance to ready the nation for a war that he believed was inevitable. His personality and philosophy conspired to keep him from doing anything more. He was naturally contemplative and patient and hated confrontations of any kind. He believed that most problems would either go away or diminish in importance with time, regardless of one's actions. Those traits and outlooks reflected and reinforced his political outlook that the government that governs least, governs best. All that combined to produce in Jefferson an almost languorous fatalism that Dumas Malone likened to that of Russian general Mikhail Kutuzov as depicted by Leo Tolstoy in his novel *War and Peace*.[29]

That fatalism could have been disastrous. Thanks to Jefferson's belief that the nation's defense should rest largely on militia and gunboats, the United States was completely unprepared for a war. The army's actual number of soldiers was about a third less than its authorized strength of 3,495. The undermanned regiments were mostly scattered in small detachments on the frontier. Then there was the navy, which Jefferson considered "a ruinous folly." Only seven of the thirteen warships were seaworthy, and most of them were sailing in distant waters and would take months to recall. Of course, there were plenty of gunboats—176 of Jefferson's cherished vessels would be built between 1805 and 1807—but they would be useless if shooting broke out. And then there was the militia, which historically had been of mostly dubious military value except at Concord, Bunker Hill, and Bennington. All of this mattered not to Jefferson, who had Dearborn call on the governors to prepare their militia for possible mobilization. He also anticipated a fleet of 250 privateers if a war broke out. He hoped that Britain would not add the United States to the list of countries it was warring against. But if worse came to worst, he was confident that the United States could quickly win a war with Britain by conquering Canada and holding it for ransom.[30]

Yet another critical issue had to be resolved when the president and his men finally figured out what to do. Wars must somehow be paid for. Gallatin explained to Jefferson that a war would be difficult to finance even if it lasted only a year, a very unlikely scenario. A war budget for 1808 would be $18 million while revenues would plummet to only $11 million, leaving a $7 million deficit.[31] Given the Republican hatred of taxes, that gap could be filled only by borrowing. Finding creditors might be tough. As the treasury secretary put it, "People will fight, but they will never give up their money for nothing." He, for one, had no illusions about America's fate if a war broke out. To his wife, he confided, "War will be a most calamitous event. Our immense commerce will be destroyed, our progress and improvement retarded, and a thousand fortunes will be ruined."[32]

Fortunately, Jefferson's gamble paid off. As he had hoped, America's diplomatic hand was indeed bolstered by a series of critical faraway events. Napoleon finally decisively defeated Russia and Prussia with which he had been warring since the previous autumn. In July 1807, on a raft on the Niemen River at the Russian frontier, Emperor Napoleon had imposed the peace of Tilsit on Czar Alexander and King Frederick William. Although Russia lost no territory, Prussia was stripped of half of its land and population, while its army was limited to forty-five thousand troops. Britain was left to fight alone against Napoleon, who now dominated the continent with allies, friends, or outright conquests from Spain to Russia. Whitehall did not need yet another enemy, even one as weak as the United States.

Jefferson understood that America's fate depended to a great extent on the shifting power balance and wars in Europe. Months before he would learn of Tilsit, he confessed that "I never expected to be under the necessity of wishing success on Buonaparte. But the English being equally tyrannical at sea as he is on land, & that tyranny bearing on us in every point of either honor or interest, I say 'down with England' and as for what Buonaparte is then to do to us, let us trust to the chapter of accidents. I cannot, with the Anglomen, prefer a certain present evil to a future hypothetical evil."[33]

Although Monroe did not receive his instructions until August 31, he had learned of the attack on the *Chesapeake* from a July 25 letter by Foreign Secretary George Canning, who expressed his "deep regret" for what happened. In their subsequent meetings, they spoke at length about ways the crisis might be resolved, but neither could go further until Monroe received his instructions and Canning learned the nationality of the impressed men. Monroe hastened to tell Canning that impressing sailors from American naval and merchants ships was the key issue, while the victims' nationality was irrelevant. Knowing his words would eventually be picked up by American newspapers, Canning expressed his wish in the House of Commons that peace would prevail between Britain and the United States. Once he received his instructions, Monroe issued a formal demand for reparations for the deaths, wounds, and damage, and the repatriation of the impressed sailors. Canning followed his script and refused any discussion of impressment, even informally as Monroe suggested. He would treat the *Chesapeake* only as an isolated tragedy untied to any British policy. Monroe grew so exasperated at Whitehall's stonewalling that he sailed back to the United States, leaving Pinkney in charge.[34]

Among Monroe's instructions was to ask the Russian czar to act as an intermediary between the United States and Britain. As he had when Tripoli had captured the *Philadelphia* three years earlier, Alexander agreed to do what he could, only to be once again politely rebuffed by Whitehall. Jefferson attempted to upgrade America's relationship with Russia from a consul general to a minister, but the Senate refused to approve his nomination of William Short for that post, citing financial constraints and a lack of need.[35]

When Jefferson addressed Congress on October 27, 1807, the day after it reconvened, he explained the diplomatic steps he had taken and asked for patience until they learned Whitehall's official response. He made no reference to the possibility of war.[36]

Patience surely was needed. It would be more than another month, and five months after the *Leopard* attacked the *Chesapeake*, before Jefferson received that official British response on November 31. The day before, John Quincy Adams had complained that the "President's policy is procrastination, and if Great Britain does not wage complete war against us, we shall end with doing nothing this session."[37]

As Adams penned those words, Jefferson was angrily mulling a sneak preview of Canning's response that he had received from Erskine a couple of days earlier. He had found the tone of Canning's message "unfriendly, proud, and harsh" rather than conciliatory as he had hoped. As for substance, Canning did explain that the attack was unauthorized and thus the United States was entitled to compensation. But there was a catch. He accused the United States of hostility and thus Britain would determine a just amount of reparation. A special envoy, George Rose, would investigate the matter and determine damages. As for the impressed sailors, the three Americans would be released. But Britain would never render its right of impressment.[38]

15

Within the Turtle Shell

Canning's haughty message outraged Americans. The British had murderously violated the nation's sovereignty and honor. It was America's prerogative to determine what compensation was just.

The president responded by crafting with his Senate cohorts a bill that forbade British warships from American waters until Whitehall offered compensation the president deemed appropriate. The bill was introduced on November 23, passed by 26 to 3 on December 2, 1807, and sent to the House. At the same time, Jefferson approved Navy Secretary Smith's plan to build more gunboats at a cost of $853,000, bringing the existing total to 261. That bill passed the Senate by 26 to 3 on December 2, and the House by 111 to 19 on December 11, 1807.[1]

Yet that buildup was mostly for diplomatic and political show. Jefferson's wish was that all those gunboats might somehow convince the British of the seriousness of his demand for justice and placate those at home who demanded he do more. Certainly most Republicans and nearly all Federalists did not want to go to war; no one was more gun-shy than Jefferson.

But war seemed inevitable. Word arrived of Britain's latest acts of aggression. King George III had proclaimed on October 16 that no British subject would be permitted to serve on any foreign ship. The latest Order in Council of November 11, 1807, decreed that to better enforce Britain's right of impressment henceforth British nationality would be considered permanent and thus naturalization papers from another country would be invalid. Jefferson and leading Republicans and

Federalists condemned that policy as an insult to the United States and an infringement of American sovereignty.

Americans would learn in March that Napoleon, not to be outdone, had responded in kind with his Milan Decree of December 17, 1807. Thus, the French navy would confiscate any neutral vessel that traded with Britain or whose captain allowed it to be searched by a British warship. With most of the French navy bottled up in port or sunk by the Royal Navy, Napoleon had little power to enforce that decree. Nonetheless, on paper at least, it was even more predatory than Britain's policies.

The Milan Decree posed a cruel dilemma for American policymakers and merchants alike. To trade with one country meant opening oneself to capture by the other. Since Britain's navy had swept the seas or blockaded in port most French warships, it could turn its guns on American trade with France. And to that, all the president's militia and all the president's gunboats could do nothing. It made sense to swallow one's pride, cut one's losses, and trade exclusively with Britain.

Canning's message and the latest Order in Council bitterly disappointed Jefferson. What more could he do short of asking for a war declaration? Gallatin lifted his spirits by reminding him that the Non-Importation Bill, which had passed six months earlier on April 18, 1806, and which the president had twice persuaded Congress to suspend to allow time for his diplomacy to work, was finally to go into effect on December 14, 1807. This time Jefferson would not ask for another suspension.

But the president was not content with merely halting imports. On December 18, 1807, he asked Congress for a total embargo of American exports, unless the president deemed otherwise for particular vessels and cargoes. Four days later, the Embargo Bill passed the Senate by a party-line vote of 22 to 6 and the House by 82 to 44; Jefferson signed the bill into law that day. It would soon be amended. The original act allowed a coastal trade within the United States. The hard-liners feared that shippers would use that as a loophole to weigh anchor and sail to wherever they pleased. A supplementary act on January 9, 1808, forbade any ships to sail, including fishing and whaling as well as merchant vessels. The Senate passed the bill 22 to 7, but the House even more overwhelmingly approved the measure by 73 to 22. Henceforth only foreign ships would carry American trade. Yet more nails were pounded into the coffin of America's shipping industry and foreign commerce with a bill that became law on March 12, 1808. As for sea trade, bonds would be required for foreign vessels in the coastal trade, which would be forfeited if that vessel either imported foreign goods or exported American goods.

Overland trade was forbidden with the neighboring British and Spanish empires. Finally, the Enforcement Act of April 25, 1808, gave the federal government the power to use the militia and marshals to apprehend, and the courts to harshly prosecute, anyone who violated the preceding laws.[2]

Just what did Jefferson and his followers hope the embargo would achieve? The day after the original act passed, the *National Intelligencer*, the Republican Party's unofficial newspaper, published both the act's text and an anonymous essay most likely written by James Madison. The writer expressed the Republican belief that the embargo would sooner or later force Britain to yield: "We shall be deprived of markets for our superfluities. They will feel the want of necessities."[3] That view mirrored what Madison was telling the president: "The efficacy of an embargo cannot be doubted. If indeed a commercial weapon can be properly shaped for the executive hand, it is more and more apparent to me that it can force all nations having colonies in this quarter of the globe to respect our rights."[4]

Jefferson justified his policy as the lesser of two evils: "The embargo, keeping at home our vessels, cargoes & seamen, saves us the necessity of making their capture the cause of immediate war. . . . Till [England and France] return to some sense of moral duty therefore we keep within ourselves. This gives time, time may produce peace in Europe: peace in Europe removes all causes of difference, till another European war, and by that time our debt may be paid, our revenues clear, & our strength increased."[5]

While the "logic" was impeccable, that well-intentioned strategy would not only fail, it would backfire. Indeed the Embargo Act was among the more self-destructive policies in the nation's foreign policy history, the economic equivalent of cutting off one's nose to spite his face. Exports plunged from $107 million in 1807 to $22 million in 1808, while customs revenue, the most important source of money for the federal government, plummeted from a record height of $16 million in 1807 to $6.5 million in 1809. Unsold products piled up in barns and warehouses, while ships rotted alongside empty wharfs. The only clear winners were foreign producers and shippers who were allowed to sell in the United States.[6]

Americans in scores of mostly New England towns fired off to Jefferson petitions explaining that the embargo was destroying their livelihoods and humbly requesting that he rescind it. Years later the president would admit that "I felt the foundations of the government shaken under my feet by the New England townships." Yet he remained willfully blind and deaf to anything that appeared to refute his policy's wisdom. He clung to the belief that he had only two choices and had taken the better for now: "For a certain length of time I think the embargo is a less evil than war. But after a time it will not be so." He never seriously mulled the notion that either course was disastrous for American interests.[7]

Instead the mounting evidence that his embargo was wrecking America's economy made him even more dead set to stay the course. He insisted that "I place immense value in the experiment being fully made, how far an embargo may be an effectual weapon in future as well as on this occasion." Jefferson's "experiment" was destroying the fortunes not just of wealthy merchants and shipowners, but of the tens of thousands of people in all walks of life related to that entire industrial complex. Jefferson was not oblivious to the suffering his embargo was causing, he was simply indifferent to it: "I do not wish a single citizen in any of the States to be deprived of a meal of bread, but I set down the exercise of commerce, merely for profit, as nothing when it carries with it the danger of defeating the objects of the embargo."[8]

It was up to Albert Gallatin as treasury secretary to implement the embargo. While he supported the embargo in principle, he was increasingly cognizant of just how much damage it was inflicting on America's economy and how difficult it was to enforce. Six months after the embargo was decreed, Gallatin complained that increasing numbers of merchants were violating the law and pleaded with Jefferson for more power to impose the government's will, including allowing customs officials to seize the property of violators and sell it at public auction. Jefferson replied by encouraging Gallatin to do what was necessary and expressed his outrage that "so sudden & rank growth of fraud & open opposition . . . could have grown up in the U.S." So Gallatin employed regular soldiers to enforce the embargo.[9]

The president did, however, grudgingly agree to one compromise. As officials confiscated more and more shipments, the protests of merchants were too loud to ignore. Congress amended the act on February 27, 1808, to allow any ship that had sailed before December 14, 1807, to bring a cargo back to the United States by May 14, 1808. How that message would reach those ships' captains was unclear.[10]

And, to heap irony upon irony, the embargo barely hurt Britain. The timing of Jefferson's attempts to sever trade with Britain could not have been worse. The Portuguese and Spanish monarchies would soon open their empires to British trade. On November 29, 1807, the Portuguese Court set sail to Rio de Janeiro the day before a French army led by Gen. Jean-Andoche Junot marched into Lisbon. But the French would not occupy Portugal for long. Gen. Arthur Wellesley, the future Duke of Wellington, landed his army in July 1808, defeated Junot in several battles, and forced him to surrender with the Convention of Cintra on August 31. A grateful Queen Maria and her son and regent John opened Brazil to British trade. Meanwhile, on May 2, 1808, Spain rose in revolt against Napoleon, who had deposed Charles IV and put his brother Joseph on the throne. The result was a horrendous international and civil war that would not end until 1814 when the last French troops had been driven from the peninsula. Britain allied with Spain's provisional government at Cadiz, and sent an army under Wellesley and millions of pounds sterling in military and economic aid. In return, the Spanish Cortes, or national assembly, would eventually grant Britain permission to trade with its colonies.

So Britain was able to divert many of the exports barred from America and Europe under Napoleon's rule to Latin America. The value of Britain's exports to the United States dropped from 11,850,000 to 5,240,000 pounds sterling from 1807 to 1808, while its exports to Latin America increased from 10,440,000 to 16,590,000 pounds sterling. Although Britain would experience spikes of recession and joblessness in the years leading up to 1815, the impact of the combined American and French embargoes could have been much harsher and even fatal without those new markets for British goods. Thomas Barclay, Britain's consul general, actually expressed the hope in September 1808 that the Americans would continue their embargo indefinitely because the benefits to Britain were so great. Without pesky American competitors, British merchants captured foreign markets and their profits soared.[11]

For now, Jefferson's diplomatic focus was on resolving the *Chesapeake* crisis with Britain. Special envoy George Rose reached Washington on January 14, 1808, and was soon negotiating with Madison. His terms were tough. First, the impressment issue was nonnegotiable. Second, he insisted that in response to Britain's generosity in recalling Admiral Berkeley and agreeing to pay reparations, Jefferson should rescind his order that the Royal Navy stay away from American waters. Third, the reparation's amount would be at the discretion of His Majesty. But those were not Rose's most insulting demands. Finally, the United States must admit that Captain Barron was at fault for sheltering deserters on his ship and refusing to surrender them.[12]

Madison declared that the ban on British warships from American waters would continue unless Rose cited the reparation's exact amount. A purely monetary settlement, however, was not enough. Any compensation must be accompanied by a pledge to give up impressment.[13]

Jefferson and his cabinet hoped that their position would be bolstered by a bill proposed on February 26, 1808, that would nearly triple the army's size to nine thousand troops. But when Rose stuck to his position, Jefferson suggested a compromise. Compensation would be unconditional for both sides; there would be no American disavowal of Barron or British renunciation of their position on impressment. After Rose bluntly rejected any compromise, Madison ended all talks on

March 22, 1808. That same day, Jefferson passed all documents related to negotiations with both the British and French to Congress. Although Berkeley stayed away, British warships would return to skulk just beyond America's ports like so many sea wolves.[14]

William Pinkney had no more luck in his talks with Canning. He explained that the United States would rescind its embargo if Britain gave up its Orders in Council. Canning repeated the rationale for the policy. Pinkney replied that while he could not fault the logic, it damaged American interests and thus had to stop. They would periodically echo those stances in meetings throughout 1808.[15]

Jefferson once again tried to enlist Czar Alexander I into mediating a settlement between the United States and Britain. In July 1808, he sent William Short on that mission before asking the Senate to confirm his appointment. The Senate voted against the mission. Short was already on his way, however. It would take months before he learned of the rejection. Without official credentials, he could present himself only as a notable American citizen and confidant of the president with a personal appeal on behalf of the United States. Jefferson wrote directly to Alexander on August 29, 1808. The czar eventually sent a cordial but noncommittal reply.[16]

Meanwhile, relations worsened between the United States and France. Napoleon applauded Jefferson's embargo for so nicely complementing his own so-called Continental System, which attempted to shut off Europe's trade with Britain. Unfortunately, his foreign minister, Jean-Baptiste de Nompère de Champagny, could not leave it at that. On January 25, 1808, he wrote to John Armstrong threatening that the United States choose either war against Britain or suffer the loss of American vessels trapped in French ports. That blunt demand backfired. It diverted the Jefferson administration and eventually the American public from anger against Britain to anger against France. But then Napoleon decided to delay implementing that policy for now.[17]

16

Abolishing the Slave Trade

During Jefferson's second term, the president and Congress found the time and energy to deal with other festering problems. Jefferson made an extraordinary request of Congress on December 2, 1806, during his annual message. He expressed his wish "to withdraw the citizens of the United States from all further participation in those violations of human rights which have been so long continued on the unoffending inhabitants of Africa, and which the morality, the reputation, and the best interests of our country have long been eager to proscribe."[1]

Jefferson asked no less of Congress than to criminalize America's participation in the international slave trade. Yet, having initiated that policy, he turned his back on it. What led the owner of more than a hundred human beings to call for outlawing the international trafficking of slaves?

Conscience undoubtedly played an important role. In late 1807, he partly expressed his perspectives to a group of Quakers who urged him to abolish slavery: "Whatever may have been the circumstances which influenced our forefathers to permit the introduction of personal bondage into any part of these States, and to participate in the wrongs committed on an unoffending quarter of the globe, we may rejoice that such circumstances . . . exist no longer. It is honorable to the nation at large that their legislature avail themselves of the first practical moment for arresting the progress of this great moral and political error."[2]

There was also the economic interest in abolishing that trade. With a surplus of slaves in the mid-Atlantic states, their value would decline as new slaves disembarked from the ships. Cutting off the importation of new slaves arrested and eventually reversed the value of that property. The demand for slaves increased as new lands were opened in the Old Southwest. Owners with too many slaves on their hands found ready buyers in the Deep South.

The international slave trade officially ended for the United States on New Year's Day, 1808. That event passed almost without notice in southern and northern newspapers alike.[3] Yet it would be the first step in a long, violent struggle for the liberation and integration of African descendants within American society that persists through today and beyond.

17

Across the Wide Missouri

Members of the Corps of Discovery ground their dugout canoes ashore in St. Louis on September 23, 1806, two and a half years after Lewis, Clark, and their men set off up the Missouri River. During that time, each member had experienced a lifetime's worth of adventures, wonders, and miseries. Astonishingly, only one man had died along the way, and the cause was appendicitis. And only once did they shed the blood of fellow men; Lewis and his men killed two of eight Blackfeet who had tried to steal their rifles. Their diplomacy with a score of different tribes was successful, although a few times they had to back it with the threat of violence. Of crucial diplomatic aid to the expedition was Sacagawea, a Shoshone captured by the Hidatsa and married to Toussaint Charbonneau, whom Lewis and Clark hired as an interpreter at the Mandan villages. She completed the trek to the Pacific and back to the Mandans with her baby strapped on her back.

Lewis and Clark diligently mapped the swath of territory through which they passed, and described its peoples, animals, plants, minerals, and topography. In doing so they shared information and inspired confidence for countless other Americans to set forth to explore, exploit, and settle the west. Perhaps most important, the journals and stories that came from the expedition have depicted an epic American odyssey that has ever since been a source of inspiration and national pride. In all, the Lewis and Clark expedition was a brilliant assertion of American power.

The Corps of Discovery was not the only American expedition to explore west of the Mississippi River while Jefferson was in the Executive Mansion. Jefferson launched two others. William Dunbar, George Hunter, and a dozen other men traced the Ouachita River to its headwaters in 1805. Peter Custis and Thomas Freeman led fifty men 615 miles up the Red River before being turned back by Spanish troops in 1806.

Brig. Gen. James Wilkinson dispatched his own expedition in 1806. Lt. Zebulon Pike and his score of men had four missions: to escort Osages captured by the Potawatomis back to their village; to proceed to the Pawnees in the central plains and make peace with them; to head south and make peace with the Comanches; and finally to explore the Arkansas River to its headwaters, cross over to the Red River, and then return. Those were the official duties. Most likely Pike was also tasked with determining the strength and disposition of Spanish troops, and the nature of the relations between the Spanish and Indians. And he was to be back by autumn.

Pike partly accomplished this seemingly impossible mission. After leaving St. Louis in July 1806, he first got the Osages safely home. He then visited one of the Pawnee villages, although they remained loyal to Spain. He reached the Arkansas River, which he followed to its headwaters, and struggled southwest over a mountain range into what he hoped was the upper Red River. It was actually the Rio Grande. By now it was early winter, and supplies were dwindling. He had his men erect a small post and winter there as best they could. A Spanish patrol discovered them in February 1807 and escorted them to Santa Fe. They were eventually taken all the way down to Chihuahua, interrogated, and then finally escorted to the frontier between Nacogdoches and Natchitoches, where they were released. To this day, many historians assume that the Pike expedition had some connection with the conspiracy of Burr and Wilkinson.

The Louisiana Purchase exacerbated the economic rivalry between the United States and the Spanish and British empires. Despite the Louisiana Purchase, the Spanish were determined to thwart any assertions of American power across that vast region. They launched an expedition to intercept and turn back the Corps of Discovery; the Spaniards got no farther than the Arkansas River where an Indian attack forced its men to turn back. They did succeed in capturing Pike and his men. The Spanish Empire with its hazy frontier would be firmly closed to Americans until the Mexicans overthrew Madrid's rule and asserted independence in 1821. Thereafter Americans could trade across the trail linking St. Louis and Santa Fe, and trap their way across the entire southwest.

Meanwhile, the Louisiana Purchase extended America's economic rivalry with the British into yet another region. The North West Company and Hudson's Bay Company were the largest British enterprises operating in the West. Each company had a string of trading posts across the Great Lakes and Canadian Great Plains and beyond into the Rocky Mountains. Since St. Louis's founding in 1764, intrepid traders had ascended ever higher up the Missouri River in search of furs and buffalo robes. Those rivals mingled where the Missouri River nears the present American-Canadian border.

During the winter of 1804–1805, when the Lewis and Clark expedition sheltered at the Mandan village high on the Missouri River's northern arc, the explorers encountered North West and Hudson's Bay Company traders. Those meetings were at once cordial and strained. The American officers did not order the trespassers to leave, although they had the right and power to do so. But in August 1805, long before the Corps of Discovery returned, Governor James Wilkinson issued a proclamation declaring the Missouri River closed to all non-American traders unless they bought a license from the government at St. Louis, a rather inconvenient transaction for Canadians.

Until 1807, that assertion was more principled than practical. Only a trickle of enterprising Americans had dared to head upriver and join traders of French and Spanish heritage already well familiar with the Indians, opportunities, and dangers. That year, Manuel Lisa led the first of five annual expeditions as far as the Missouri River headwaters to garner beaver pelts and buffalo robes. The War of 1812 would temporarily halt those trapping, trading, and exploring ventures.

Each expansion of American territory during the early republic involved two steps: taking title to that land first from a European power and then from the native peoples. Greeting Indian delegations at the Executive Mansion was undoubtedly among Jefferson's most pleasant duties. His attitudes and policies toward the Indians, as with nearly everything else, shifted with time, but they were always a mélange of sentimentalism, paternalism, and Machiavellianism, whose center of gravity changed over the decades. He explained to William Henry Harrison, the governor of Indiana Territory, that the policy "is to live in perpetual peace with the Indians, to cultivate an affectionate attachment from them, by everything just & liberal which we can do for them within the bounds of reason, and by giving them effectual protection against wrongs from our own people."[1]

Unlike most frontier folks, he viewed the Indians as "noble savages" rather than merely "savages." Nurture rather than nature explained any lapses of their manners or mind alongside white people. He insisted that "before we condemn the Indians of this continent as wanting genius, we must consider that letters have not yet been introduced among them." He viewed them akin to northern Europeans before their exposure to Roman civilization. He extolled the eloquence of their orators and the beauty of their arts. As an ethnologist, he lamented that "we have suffered so many of the Indian tribes already to extinguish, without our having previously collected and deposited the records of literature [and] . . . the languages they spoke."[2]

Yet as president, he shed much of that "noble savage" outlook and did what he could to hurry along the process of "civilizing" the natives. In 1802, he told a group of visiting Osage chiefs that "we shall, with great pleasure, see your people become disposed to cultivate the earth, to raise herds of the useful animals, and to spin and weave, for your food and clothing."[3]

Behind those kind words, Jefferson offered the Indians a brutal choice—either assimilate or suffer expulsion. His method for dispossessing the Indians was purely Machiavellian:

> We shall push our trading houses and be glad to see the good and influential individuals among them run into debt, because . . . when these debts get beyond what the individuals can pay, they become willing to lop them off by a cession of lands. . . . In this way our settlements will gradually circumscribe . . . the Indians, and they will in time either incorporate with us as citizens of the United States or remove beyond the Mississippi. . . . But in the whole course of this, it is essential to cultivate their love. As to their fear, we presume that our strength and their weakness is so visible that they must see we have only to shut our hand to crush them.[4]

18

Passing the Torch

Eight years as president was enough. Although he could take pride at a succession of achievements, Thomas Jefferson was eager to turn his back on the nearly incessant political struggles and periodic crises in Washington, and return to his beloved Monticello. He had another good reason to retire: "The danger is that the indulgence & attachments of the people will keep a man in the chair after he becomes a dotard, that reelection through life shall become habitual, & election for life follow that. Gen. Washington set the example of voluntary retirement after 8 years. I shall follow it and a few more precedents will oppose the obstacle of habit to anyone after a while who shall endeavor to extend his term."[1] Aside from his own laurels, Jefferson could retire in confidence that the man whom he had tapped as his heir in the Executive Mansion shared his philosophy and policies.

PART 3
Madison, 1809–1813

The aim of every political constitution is or ought to be first to obtain for rulers, men who possess most wisdom to discern, and most virtue to pursue, the common good of society.

JAMES MADISON

No two countries on earth have so many points of common interests and friendship, and their rulers must be great bunglers indeed if with such dispositions they break them asunder.

THOMAS JEFFERSON

Being prepared to repel danger is the most likely way to avoid it.

JAMES MADISON

What if we get taxes and do not go to war?

FELIX GRUNDY

For what are we going to fight? We are going to fight for the reestablishment of our national character.

ANDREW JACKSON

The conquest of Canada is in your power. . . . I verily believe that the militia of Kentucky are alone competent to place Montreal and Upper Canada at your feet.

HENRY CLAY

*Go to war without money, without men, without a navy!
Go to war when we have not the courage, while your lips utter war, to lay war taxes!
When your whole courage is exhibited in passing Resolutions!*

JOHN RANDOLPH

19

James Madison and American Power

While Thomas Jefferson may have anointed James Madison as his heir to the Executive Mansion, support for his choice among Republicans was hardly unanimous. The most prominent of those who fancied keys to the Executive Mansion were Vice President George Clinton and Ambassador James Monroe. But Madison was nearly as skilled a political operative as Jefferson and had no trouble mobilizing the Republican rank and file. During the party's caucus in January 1808, he won 83 votes to 3 each for Clinton and Monroe. Madison assuaged some of Clinton's disappointment by asking him to stay on as vice president; Clinton accepted. He tried to reconcile Monroe by offering him the governorship of Louisiana; Monroe refused, saying that he would accept nothing less than a cabinet position or generalship. Having overcome these rivals within his party, Madison went on to trounce the Federalist candidate, Charles Pinckney, by a landslide of 122 electors to 47; Clinton received six, though he claimed he was not running.[1]

Who was this man that would serve eight years as president and take the nation into war against the British Empire?[2] Like many shy men with sharp minds, James Madison tended to be a bookworm. The author of twenty-nine Federalist essays and scores of other works had a gift for abstract reasoning and logic. Of America's early presidents, he was the least worldly. During his entire life, he never once set foot outside the United States and traveled little within it. The center of his world was the manor house of his Virginian plantation, Montpelier. There he immersed himself in his library and pondered the classics of political philosophy.

Physically he was among the least impressive of men, with a large, balding head atop a short, puny body. His high-pitched voice tended to disappear in large, noisy rooms or before crowds outside. Without a carefully prepared speech, he tended toward silence or short, dry statements. He was especially awkward when he was forced to socialize among the manly wits of drawing rooms and boisterous habitués of taverns. He was at his social best among the ladies, who found "his manners . . . unassuming; and his conversation lively, often playful . . . chaste, well suited to occasion, and the simple expression of a passing thought . . . in harmony with the taste of his hearers."[3]

Although he lived to be seventy-five, illnesses frequently assailed him, especially beneath the presidency's burdens. Even during the war, he would not hesitate to flee Washington for Montpelier to shut off the infinitely complex, shifting, contradictory, and paradoxical world of men, and to immerse himself in his books and thoughts.

Madison had his share of character flaws. When faced with a dilemma, he could fall into indecision and procrastination. He would not begin to ready the United States for war until after Congress approved his declaration, and then he did too little, too late. Even worse, he could be petty, petulant, and vengeful. Perhaps worst of all, Madison clung to his ideals even when reality made a mockery of them. His most prolific biographer explained that Madison had a "lifelong unwillingness to make a public display of political inconsistency."[4] In other words, his character was nearly a dead ringer for that of Jefferson, who acted as Madison's big brother, career mentor, philosophical muse, and political boss.

Yet, despite his personality and character flaws, Madison was an astonishingly successful politician. His two terms as president capped a career that included serving in Virginia's House of Delegates in 1776, from 1784 to 1787, and from 1800 to 1801; in Virginia's Privy Council from 1777 to 1779; in the Continental Congress from 1779 to 1783 and 1786 to 1788; in the House of Representatives from 1789 to 1797; and as secretary of state from 1801 to 1809. One biographer explained that he "lost only one election during his political career from 1776 to 1817, and that loss was caused by his decision to take the high ground of principle. In 1777, he refused to provide a barrel of hard cider for thirsty voters and lost to a more liberal candidate who understood such matters. He never lost again."[5]

Whatever his critics might say about his performance as president, he certainly had a clear theoretical understanding of what was essential. In Federalist Essay 57 he wrote, "The aim of every political constitution is or ought to be first to obtain for rulers, men who possess most wisdom to discern, and most virtue to pursue the common good of society; and in the next place to take the most effectual precautions for keeping them virtuous, whilst they continue to hold the public trust."[6] Unfortunately, those who know what is right either do not always do it or else lack the power to. Most observers of Madison's presidency then and since would say that he failed to know and do what was right when he was entrusted with power.

Like Jefferson, Madison believed that the golden rule should guide personal and national behavior. Yet when that failed, sterner measures were essential. Peace was at its most secure when rooted in strength. Deterrence made war less likely: "being prepared to repel danger is the most likely way to avoid it."[7] Here again, Madison's critics would pillory him for failing to heed his own principle and ready the United States for war with the world's greatest power.

While James Madison is solely responsible for the choices he made as president, in many ways they were channeled by his predecessor. During the Madison years and beyond, Thomas Jefferson tended his plantation at Monticello; high on a hill his magnificent home overlooked Virginia's flatlands stretching toward the sea and the Blue Ridge Mountains across the western horizon. There he hosted distinguished guests, read and wrote voraciously, and oversaw the labor of more than a hundred slaves planting and reaping, building and tearing down.

Yet Jefferson remained the ghost at Madison's policy table, whispering in the ears of the president and his secretaries. They listened intently, not merely out of respect but from conviction. Madison and his men not only inherited Jefferson's ideological legacy, but they also championed it. That legacy, however, would prove to be an excruciatingly painful burden for the Madison administration and the nation.[8]

The principles of Jefferson's political philosophy were and remain attractive to many, but they proved to be disastrous when put into practice. Trying to live up to the notion that the government that governs least governs best would hamstring Jefferson's and Madison's abilities to defend, let alone enhance, most crucial American interests.

Philosophically they vehemently rejected Hamilton's conception of a muscular, problem-solving government that nurtured the expansion of American wealth and power. They scorned the notion that America desperately needed more, rather than fewer, industrialists, bankers, and merchants, along with professional soldiers and sailors. Yet reality continually trumped that philosophy. So politically, time after time as presidents, Jefferson and Madison would temporarily shelve their own creed and do something Hamilton-esque. The trouble was that, more often than not, they did so belatedly and incompletely, with less-than-stellar results.

The Jeffersonians never quite admitted the contradictions in their policies. They at once lamented the weakness of American power and refused until the last minute and often beyond the means of enhancing it. The result for both the Jefferson and Madison presidencies was a fatalism, passivity, and blind adherence to a narrow set of ideological options in reacting to critical events and forces.

Madison, like Jefferson, packed his administration with loyalists who mirrored his views. Even then, he had trouble riding herd, which is surprising considering how effective a leader he had been in the House of Representatives. But he would not be the only president who led better in Congress than in the Executive Mansion.

James Madison will never be ranked among the best of chief executives. Indeed most historians place him near the bottom.[9] He was not a hands-on president who immersed himself in the details of policy or administration. Instead, he delegated not just the policy details but often the essence to his cabinet heads. He hesitated to intervene when they bungled or even when they favored their own agenda over his own or abused their office for private gain. He preferred the familiar to the unknown to the point where he retained inept, corrupt, and even hostile people in power rather than replaced them. Madison was well aware of his shortcomings. He would regret that his administration "laboured under a want of harmony & unity, which were equally essential to its energy and its success."[10]

Albert Gallatin would be the rock of Madison's administration, often displaying more courage, wisdom, and resolution than the president himself. He had at first declined Madison's plea to stay on as treasury secretary. He was thoroughly sick of being "a mere financier, a contriver of taxes, a dealer of loans, a seeker of resources for the purposes of supporting useless baubles, of increasing the number of idle and dissipated members of the community, of fattening contractors, pursers and agents, and of introducing in all its ramifications that system of patronage, corruption, and rottenness."[11] It was for those very reasons that Gallatin was ideal for the job. He was outstanding at providing both the strategic financial vision and daily leadership, while sidestepping most of the unsavory political and moral pitfalls of power.

No department had a more diverse range of duties and employed more people than the Treasury Department, which not only collected and dispersed revenues but also regulated trade, sold public lands, and guarded the coasts. In Washington City alone, the department accounted for about half of the roughly 120 federal officials. Across the nation there were more than 700 officials, with most deployed in ports, collecting duties or chasing smugglers. The branches of the department's General Land Office were largely on the frontier where settlers and speculators could most easily file claims.

Madison persuaded Robert Smith to move from the Navy to the State Department. The choice made more political than practical sense. He was the brother of maverick Maryland senator Samuel Smith. That sibling tie would not render the senator any less independent. Otherwise, Smith had no diplomatic experience other than in politics, nor had he any particular interest in or knowledge of foreign affairs. To worsen matters, Smith and Gallatin could not stand to be in the same room together, which made for uncomfortable cabinet meetings and constant intrigues of each against the other outside the Executive Mansion. In April 1811, Madison would replace an ever more cantankerous and backbiting Smith with James Monroe, who had excellent credentials to prepare him for that position. Smith would not go quietly.

Politics also guided Madison's choice of William Eustis as war secretary. Eustis had been an able enough Republican representative from Massachusetts and lent regional balance to the cabinet. His sole military experience, however, was to serve as a surgeon during the revolution. Once war was declared, the duties of his office would overwhelm him. In 1809, he had only a deputy, a paymaster, thirteen clerks, and two messengers.[12]

Madison's navy secretary had no knowledge of the sea, let alone sea power. Paul Hamilton of South Carolina was purely a political choice. The president hoped that Hamilton would get along better with the treasury secretary than his predecessor. Hamilton was not only an amiable man but also a steady advocate for more money and a reordering of priorities from gunboats to warships. But he was an alcoholic and often in his cups well before noon, which blurred his ability to deal with essential administrative details. Nonetheless, Madison would retain Hamilton for the war's duration.

Despite enjoying overwhelming Republican majorities in both houses throughout his eight years as president, Madison had more and more trouble leading his party. He began his first term with Republicans dominating the Senate by 27 to 7 and the House by 92 to 50. The Republican Party's power swelled to 30 to 6 senators and 107 to 36 representatives in the Congress that led the nation into the 1812 War. During the war, the Republicans lost a couple of Senate seats, which whittled their lead to 28 to 8, but they picked up seven more House seats for a total of 114 to 68. As for the state houses, the Republicans controlled every one except Connecticut, Rhode Island, and Delaware, although after the 1812 election, Massachusetts, New Jersey, and Maryland would join the Federalist ranks.[13]

Yet the Republican Party was anything but a monolith. A generational and ideological gap split "Old" and more recent Republicans.[14] The party's name itself became a source of contention. Its elder members, including Jefferson and Madison, continued to call themselves Republicans, while the younger ranks increasingly called themselves Democrat-Republicans or just plain Democrats.

The party's biggest rift was over foreign policy. The younger crowd spurned the cautious Jeffersonism of their elders for a more confrontational and even aggressive stance. These "War Hawks" would eventually stampede Congress and the public into the disastrous war against Britain.[15] Then there were several moderate Republican senators known as the Invincibles who frequently crossed the aisle to join Federalists on issues like the war, the Bank of the United States, internal improvements, and trade. The leading Invincibles were Virginia's William Branch Giles and Wilson Cary Nicholas, Maryland's Samuel Smith, and Pennsylvania's Michael Leib and William Duane.

Inevitably the personal became thoroughly entangled in the political. Of the Invincibles, none was more obstructive than Giles, who hated Jefferson and, by extension, Madison, and had openly supported George Clinton for president. John Randolph, perhaps the House's most important Republican, had long disliked Madison, and that animosity would worsen after Madison entered the Executive Mansion. Randolph was the source of many rumors depicting the president as corrupt, cowardly, and incompetent.

Numerous newspapers amplified that cacophony of Republican voices. By serving as the president's voice, the *National Intelligencer* was the most influential during the Madison years. The *Philadelphia Aurora* was still a powerful Republican newspaper but would side with the War Hawks when Madison hoped to keep the nation at peace. The *Boston Independent* was a solitary but clarion Republican voice in a predominantly Federalist region. Madison's home-state newspaper, the *Richmond Enquirer*, supported him more often than not.

In all, three forces would hamstring James Madison as president: his character, his ideology, and his party.

20

From Embargo to Non-Intercourse

B ritain remained the foremost foreign policy problem. Madison would continue Jefferson's policy of economic coercion toward Britain with the forlorn hope that Whitehall would soon submit. Even more than that of his predecessor, Madison's version would be warped by two powerful and ultimately self-defeating forces—delusion and hatred.

Despite all contrary evidence, Madison clung to the delusion that the United States had the economic upper hand over Britain: "Her dependence on us being greater than ours on her, the supplies of the United States are necessary to [Britain's] existence," while those imported by America "are either superfluities or poisons."[1] He insisted that if the United States pressed that advantage, it could bring Britain to its knees. Madison repeatedly tried to wield the trade card, and each time the nation suffered the same devastating results.

As if delusion was not debilitating enough, Madison's feelings toward Britain worsened matters. He still hated the British even a generation after winning independence. The war had been savage everywhere, but especially in the south; there loyalties were equally divided, and tit-for-tat vengeance of looting and burning, and often rape and murder, prevailed, all literally enflamed by Britain's scorched earth policy against the rebels. In 1781, Madison wrote Jefferson that "no description can give you an adequate idea of the barbarity with which the enemy have conducted the war in the Southern States. Every outrage which humanity could suffer has been committed by them. Desolation rather than conquest seems to have been their object." Madison went so far as to call for executing

British prisoners of war in retaliation for their nation's war crimes.[2] In leading the United States into a war with Britain, Madison would expose America to the same horrors that so enraged and terrified him. True to form, the British would once again loot, burn, rape, and murder nearly every place they rampaged for two and a half years.

Yet Congress handed the newly inaugurated president a gift that partly freed him from the worst consequences of his obsessions. On February 8, 1809, bills were introduced that would repeal the Embargo Act, which outlawed all American trade, and replace it with the Non-Intercourse Act, which only forbade Americans from trading with Britain and France. That bill passed the Senate by 22 to 9 on February 22, and the House by 81 to 40 on February 27. Jefferson reluctantly signed it into law on March 1, days before he left office. Originally the repeal would have taken place on March 4, the day Madison took the inaugural oath, but an amendment extended the date to March 15.[3]

To his credit, Madison followed up that measure. Within a month and a half of taking office, he accepted a deal with David Erskine, Britain's minister to the United States, that, had Whitehall accepted it, might have prevented the War of 1812. Rigidity at the Court of Saint James's rather than the Executive Mansion killed that chance for peace.

Foreign Secretary George Canning issued Erskine his latest set of negotiating instructions in March 1809. The Orders in Council would end only if the United States opened its markets and sold its goods freely with Britain, imposed a strict embargo with France, and accepted Britain's "right" to seize American ships trading with its enemies and to impress deserters and naturalized American citizens from American ships.[4]

Knowing that the Americans would adamantly reject those terms, Erskine did not fully reveal them in an exchange of letters with Secretary of State Smith in April 1809. Instead, the two agreed on a swap—both the Orders in Council and the Non-Intercourse Act must go. Erskine sent that deal to Canning. On April 19, Madison announced that the non-intercourse with Britain would take effect on June 10, 1809, unless Whitehall revoked its Orders in Council.[5]

Meanwhile, Whitehall issued its latest Order in Council on April 26, 1809. Henceforth the blockade on Europe under Napoleon's control and France's colonies would be total. Previously, Americans could trade in those markets if they first paid a duty in Britain. Canning cited two reasons for the new policy: the military situation in Europe that, with Austria's resumption of war with France, appeared to be tilting in Britain's favor, and Washington's replacement of the Embargo Act with the Non-Intercourse Act.

Throughout history, the quirks of those with power has often determined the fate of nations. After debating the deal between Smith and Erskine, the cabinet reluctantly agreed to accept it. Canning took it to King George III for ratification. As the document was read, the unstable monarch flew into a rage at one sentence he interpreted as personally insulting, and he refused to ratify the treaty. He demanded that Erskine be recalled for exceeding his instructions. His replacement would be Francis Jackson, who was notorious as the envoy sent to demand Copenhagen's surrender before the British bombarded the city into rubble in 1807.

Hoping that the king would ratify Erskine's pledge, Madison let pass the June 10 date for initiating the Non-Intercourse Act. Canning's rejection of Erskine's agreement reached Washington in July. Even then the president hesitated to order the trade cutoff until finally doing so on August 9.

A month later, on September 8, Jackson set foot in Washington. His reputation for being arrogant, ruthless, and vehemently anti-American had preceded him. He would do everything possible to live up to that image during his stay in the United States.

Madison would first insist that Jackson communicate with him on paper rather than in person. When Jackson's written words were as vitriolic as his spoken words, Madison took his cabinet's advice to demand his recall. Richard Wellesley, the new foreign minister and the older brother of Arthur, the soon to be Duke of Wellington, did so in April 1810, although Jackson lingered until August. Whitehall chose to leave his post deliberately empty to show its anger toward the Americans. The duties for British diplomacy in America fell on the shoulders of John Philip Morris, the chargé d'affaires.[6]

Britain's ever tighter blockade of Napoleonic Europe and Napoleon's trade embargo on Britain reduced most of Europe's trade to a trickle. Only the most intrepid of smugglers dared to sail that gauntlet in either direction. Scores of American vessels packed with goods bound for foreign markets were anchored in French-controlled ports. That collapse of trade hurt France far more than Britain. The British compensated for their loss of European markets by trading more with Spanish America, the Mediterranean, and Asia. Meanwhile, France's trade and accompanying revenues plummeted.

Napoleon faced a dilemma. He needed more money to run his empire and fight his wars. His revenue officers informed him that the stranded American vessels were filled with over $10 million worth of goods. Confiscating them would help fill his empty coffers but might force the United States into the alliance against France. Given America's puny military, a war with the United States posed no military threat to France. The damage would be political. Ideally, Napoleon could enlist the United States into a war against Britain; an American invasion of Canada would divert vital British troops and warships from the war with France. But that possibility would evaporate if he seized those ships.

With his Rambouillet Decree of March 23, 1810, Napoleon sacrificed his diplomatic to his financial needs. He ordered the confiscation of all American ships in French-controlled ports. His gamble paid off—the emperor got the wealth without a war.

Madison turned a deaf ear to word of the confiscations. The president was single-mindedly focused on somehow forcing Whitehall to yield to his demands. Whatever Napoleon did was merely a distraction from the diplomatic center ring. Those merchants who lost their investments thought otherwise. Madison ignored their protests as well. After all, most of them were Federalists and would oppose him in any event.

But non-intercourse was only slightly less destructive to American wealth and power than the embargo. As John Taylor put it, "The commercial war we have waged against both has been extremely inconvenient to ourselves, without attaining the ultimate end with either of the belligerents. We have made an experiment of this plan of fighting both nations—it won't do. . . . Why shall we from vain pride and from unyielding obstinacy, continue our fruitless exertions."[7] Why indeed?

The answer to that essential question was Macon's Bill No. Two, which the president signed into law on May 1, 1810. The bill repealed all trade restrictions with one crucial stipulation. If either Britain or France agreed to repeal its own discrimination, the United States would reimpose its trade restrictions with the other unless it followed suit before March 3, 1811.[8]

The bill was essentially an acknowledgment that the previous policies of economic sanctions had failed miserably. With Britain's blockade of Napoleonic Europe, Americans would end up trading with Britain rather than the continent. And that was exactly what Whitehall wanted. It was a humiliating retreat.

As if to underscore that smug British contempt for American impotence, another shooting incident took place in June 1810 when HMS *Mosette* fired on USS *Vixen*. Navy Secretary Paul Hamilton was enraged to learn that the American captain had not returned fire. He issued an order that henceforth every captain should fight back until he could fight no more.

While Whitehall could ignore Macon's Bill No. Two, Napoleon saw an opening. John Armstrong, America's minister to France, received an astonishing message on August 5, 1810, from Foreign Minister Jean-Baptiste de Nompère de Champagny, whom Napoleon had recently dubbed the Duke of Cadore. The emperor would cancel his Berlin and Milan decrees on November 1, 1810, but only if the British revoked their Orders in Council. Napoleon had dictated that message to Cadore three days earlier but had had his foreign minister sign it, which is why it became known as the Cadore Letter. Armstrong sent that letter to Washington before boarding, on September 12, 1810, a vessel bound for the United States.[9]

Once again the president faced a tough decision. Would Napoleon really end his predatory policies against American vessels and cargoes? He had put a huge condition on that act. Would he revoke his embargo only to reimpose it if Whitehall did not follow suit?

Madison did not care. At this point he was happy to grasp any passing diplomatic straw or fig leaf. He seized the Cadore Letter as an excuse to pressure the British to revoke their Orders in Council. So on November 2, the day after Cadore had said the Berlin and Milan decrees would be revoked, the president proclaimed that trade would be cut off with Britain within three months unless it also rescinded its Orders in Council.[10] Secretary of State Smith disputed the Cadore Letter's significance. He argued that it was too flimsy and vague a document to justify severing trade with Britain. Madison eventually replied to Smith's dissent with his dismissal.

The British strongly concurred with Smith. Foreign Secretary Wellesley dismissed the Cadore Letter as the latest of Napoleon's diplomatic tricks. William Pinkney, America's minister in London, dutifully reported that position back to Washington and then, after learning of Madison's November 2 proclamation, sent him a warning that the British would not change their position. Wellesley officially confirmed Pinkney's hunch on December 28. Whitehall modified that position on February 11, 1811 when Wellesley wrote Pinkney that Britain would revoke its Orders in Council only if France revoked its Berlin and Milan decrees.[11]

At this point, Pinkney gave up. His mission had failed on two vital counts—Whitehall refused either to yield on its Orders in Council or send a minister to Washington. He informed Wellesley of his intention to return to the United States. He would not get away as swiftly as he had hoped.

Congress overwhelmingly supported the president's policy. The House approved a renewal of the Non-Intercourse Act against Britain on February 27, and the Senate two days later. Madison signed the bill into law on March 2, 1811.

For once, the restrictions had some effect. The value of British exports to the United States plummeted from 10,920,000 pounds sterling in 1810 to 1,840,000 pounds sterling in 1811. The loss of that market pushed Britain's economy into a devastating depression that ruined countless businesses and countless more lives. That widespread misery was exacerbated by crop failures that brought the nation to starvation's brink. Desperate mobs vented their rage by invading factories and smashing the machinery. More constructively, ever more petitions calling for the repeal of the Orders in Council were delivered to Parliament. But Whitehall continued to hold firm to its policy.[12]

2 1

Florida Coups and Intrigues

If the results of Madison's economic warfare were ambiguous at best, he did preside over a clear foreign-policy victory elsewhere. The long-term goal of annexing the Floridas was partly realized in 1810. Americans had been immigrating to the region for decades and now greatly outnumbered the French and Spanish inhabitants. Madison secretly sent William Wyckoff and George Mathews respectively into West and East Florida to assess whether the American settlers were interested in mobilizing and revolting against Spanish rule and being annexed by the United States.[1]

In West Florida, the first overt attempt by the American settlers to organize themselves occurred at St. John's Plains in July 1810. Those who met debated how to define and assert their interests. The settlers split between those who sought reforms from the Spanish government and those who advocated independence and annexation by the United States. The meeting ended in deadlock. Then, in September 1810, a group of radicals overran the weakly defended Spanish fort in Baton Rouge and called for an American takeover.

That aggressive act presented the president with his latest dilemma. The United States had claimed West Florida with the Louisiana Purchase. Now a group of Americans had taken matters into their own hands, overthrown Spanish rule, and offered the region to Washington. Yet war with Spain and possibly Britain might erupt if Madison annexed West Florida. Conversely, if he did nothing, the Spanish, possibly aided by the British, would crush that revolt and with it America's claim to the region.

To the surprise of many, President Madison proclaimed on October 27, 1810, that as part of the 1803 Louisiana Purchase the United States owned West Florida between the Mississippi and Perdido rivers, and ordered Louisiana governor William Claiborne to secure the Baton Rouge region with troops. That act was an astonishingly bold act of imperialism for a president known for his timidity. Madison would complete the takeover of West Florida in 1813 when American troops occupied Mobile and marched east to the Perdido River.[2]

War did not erupt with Spain, let alone Britain. Both countries had mobilized nearly all of their forces for the war against Napoleon, who had been trying to conquer Spain since 1808. As a result, each government issued a stern protest and nothing more.

It seemed increasingly likely that Spanish East Florida would follow the same fate as West Florida. Tensions rose steadily between the United States and Spain over East Florida even though there was no direct American claim for the territory. For decades, slaves had escaped from the United States across the St. Mary's River into East Florida, while from there Spanish and, more recently, British traders sold arms, munitions, and other goods to Indians across the southern United States. This at once eliminated considerable American wealth while emboldening the southern tribes against the United States. The representatives and senators from Georgia and other southern states increasingly pressured the president to shut off that exodus of slaves and influx of goods, which were chronic problems. Then there was the fear that Spain might sell East Florida to Britain. This would allow the British to threaten the United States economically and militarily from three directions: Canada, East Florida, and the Atlantic Ocean.

President Madison sent a secret message to Congress on January 1, 1811, asking for authorization to act as he believed best with East Florida. Congress complied by appropriating $100,000 and authorizing him to occupy East Florida "if the local authorities were willing to deliver it up or if any foreign power attempted to occupy it."[3]

In East Florida, George Mathews exceeded his instructions and actually tried to provoke a revolt. Word of that effort horrified James Monroe, the new secretary of state. The administration wanted the peaceful transfer of East Florida from a willing Spain to the United States. Mathews's intrigues jeopardized that possibility. Monroe fired off a letter to Mathews terminating his "services." An enraged Mathews hurried back to Washington to protest and write an exposé on what he charged were the administration's inept policies. Soon he would be back in East Florida stirring up more trouble.[4]

22

The Struggle for the
Northwest Frontier

The 1795 Greenville and Jay treaties radically transformed the power balance in the Northwest Territory. The Treaty of Greenville rolled back the frontier to western Ohio and southern Indiana. The Jay Treaty required the British to evacuate their forts in American territory by July 1796. Settlers poured into those newly opened lands. Ohio's population exceeded sixty thousand and the region was granted statehood in 1803, while Indiana Territory between the Ohio, Great Miami, and Wabash rivers was rapidly filling up. Villages and farms sprouted closer and closer to the treaty line dividing Americans from Indians. Sporadic violence of each people against the other became more frequent. War appeared to be inevitable. The only question was when.

Indiana governor William Henry Harrison was the point man in trying to stave off that war. From 1802 to 1805, he had negotiated seven peace and land treaties with nearly all the tribes living in Indiana Territory, including the Shawnees, Miamis, Weas, Piankeshaws, Eel Rivers, Kaskaskias, Potawatomis, Sacs, and Foxes. The biggest cession came with the 1809 Fort Wayne Treaty by which the Indians surrendered another 3 million acres.

Under each treaty, the Indians ceded varying amounts of land in return for an initial payment in goods and annual annuities. The chiefs felt that they had no choice but to give in. The yield from hunting and trapping was dying steadily as the demand for food and furs outstripped supply. Land was the only commodity remaining to Indians, so they traded off portions in return for desperately needed supplies. But they could not sustain that forever.

Only one village refused to succumb. After 1795, the tomahawk of Indian resistance passed to a new generation. No leaders were more important from then through the 1812 War than the Shawnee brothers, Tecumseh and Tenskwatawa.[1] Their respective strengths complemented each other. Tecumseh was a brilliant orator, political leader, and warrior. Although his name means "Open Door," Tenskwatawa was better known as the Prophet. Since 1805, he had experienced visions in which the Master of Life told him that if all Indians united and purified themselves spiritually and culturally, they could forever halt the Americans. Many found that message enormously appealing. Disciples swelled their village of Prophetstown, sited near where the Tippecanoe River flows into the Wabash River. While the Prophet tended the flock at home, Tecumseh annually carried the message to as many villages as possible east and, at times, west of the Mississippi River.

Harrison was well aware of the Shawnee revival message and those missions. He met with Tecumseh in 1810 and 1811, but the two spoke past each other as each tried to talk the other into surrendering his people's land. Despite their differences, Harrison did not hide his admiration for Tecumseh, whom he described as "one of those uncommon geniuses which spring up occasionally to produce revolutions and overturn the established order of things."[2]

Tecumseh spent the fall of 1811 in a grand tour among the Creeks, Chickasaws, and Choctaws. His message of unity, tradition, spirituality, and an eventual uprising against the Americans was most enthusiastically received among the Creeks; that was not surprising since his mother was Creek, he spoke that language fluently, and the Creeks among the southwest tribes faced the worst threat from the aggression of neighboring Georgia. Tecumseh cited that year's earthquakes and a comet as omens warning the native peoples that they must drive away the Americans once and for all or be crushed and consumed by them.

Harrison took advantage of Tecumseh's absence to destroy Prophetstown. He sent a warning to the Prophet to abandon that village and take his people to live with the other Shawnees. When the Prophet refused, Harrison mustered about two hundred regulars and four hundred militia, and headed north up the Wabash valley toward Prophetstown, 180 miles upriver from Vincennes. On November 6, he and his army camped a mile from their objective. The Prophet ordered his warriors to attack shortly after midnight on November 7. The assault almost succeeded in breaking through the American lines and destroying Harrison and his army. Harrison managed to rally his men and repulse the attacks. The Americans lost 68 men killed and 120 wounded, and the Indians may have lost 50 dead and scores more wounded.[3] As dawn broke and the Indian defeat was clear, the Prophet ordered his people to gather their belongings and hurry to safety. Harrison marched his troops into the town, burned it, and then withdrew to Vincennes.

Despite his victory at Tippecanoe, Harrison's campaign was indecisive because the Prophet and most of his warriors had escaped. Unlike Gen. Anthony Wayne, who followed up his Fallen Timbers victory with a peace settlement, Harrison engaged in no diplomacy after Tippecanoe. Nor did Harrison plant a fort near Prophetstown and take over that region. The Prophet, Tecumseh, and their followers soon returned and rebuilt a town on the ruins of the old.

The gains for the United States were primarily psychological. Harrison was celebrated as a hero, and frontier folks could breathe a bit easier. Yet the impact reverberated far beyond the Northwest Frontier. The battle of Tippecanoe brightened a decade in which the United States had suffered one humiliation after another from foreign powers. As a pygmy among giants like Britain, France, and Spain, the United States could bitterly lament but not avenge those embarrassments. Harrison's victory emboldened the War Hawks in Congress and beyond. They believed that with the northwest tribes humbled, Canada would be an easy picking should war break out with Britain.

23

Down the Slippery Slope

The president replaced Robert Smith with James Monroe as secretary of state in April 1811. He did so because he wanted someone who could reflect, rather than challenge, his own beliefs and work for, rather than against, him. Monroe would serve as the acting secretary of state for more than seven months until the Senate unanimously confirmed his appointment on November 25, 1811.[1]

Meanwhile, Smith did not take his firing lightly. He vented his anger in a pamphlet entitled "Address to the People of the United States," in which he condemned Madison for mismanaging the nation's interests. The president's supporters shot back through Joel Barlow's series of essays in the Republican Party's chief newspaper, the *National Intelligencer*. The conflict widened the split within the Republican Party.

Monroe soon faced his first foreign-policy challenge as secretary of state. As always, issuing a decree proved to be much easier than enforcing one. Although the ban on British warships in American waters following the 1807 *Chesapeake* attack remained on the books, it was violated with impunity. Madison and his cabinet vowed to uphold that decree. Navy Secretary Hamilton dispatched orders to the captains.

That policy inspired an act that Madison and his men had not intended. For weeks HMS *Little Belt* had hovered off the entrance to New York Harbor. On the dark night of May 16, 1811, USS *President* approached the *Little Belt*, which responded by firing a warning shot. The *President* replied with a broadside that killed nine and wounded twenty-three British sailors. The death toll surpassed that suffered by the *Chesapeake* in 1807.

126

The Madison administration braced itself for Whitehall's reaction. But the British displayed restraint rather than belligerence when they learned of the incident. The reason was simple. Whitehall had reached the stark limits of national power. After seventeen years of nearly continuous warfare with no end in sight, Britain was exhausted financially and emotionally. The recent economic depression and crop failures had not only worsened the misery for most, but they had provoked widespread protests, some of which had turned violent. British troops and warships were stretched ever thinner around the world, in many places to the snapping point. Then there was the disturbing matter of King George's madness; he was declared permanently disabled on March 19, 1811, and the crown prince, who would eventually become George IV, was named the regent.

To varying degrees, those British weaknesses presented potential openings for the Americans to exploit. For instance, British conservatives condemned the Prince Regent for his political and personal license—he was notorious for cavorting with both Whigs and wenches. Seizing on that reputation, the Americans hoped that the Prince Regent would reverse his father's stern, unyielding policies. In that they would be disappointed. Whitehall rather than the Court of Saint James's held genuine power, and it was determined to stay the hard course against the Americans; the fact that George III thoroughly supported that policy merely made the cabinet's work easier.

In contrast, the knowledge that the British wanted to avoid war with the United States gave the Americans substantial bargaining power. William Pinkney wielded that by informing Foreign Minister Wellesley that he intended to return home if Whitehall did not make any concessions.

That threat did catch the cabinet's attention. The policy was to hold the Americans in abeyance and exploit them all the way to war's brink. Pinkney's departure might well pull both countries into a war that was in neither's interest. So Wellesley urged Pinkney to stay on and promised to appoint a new minister to the United States. That was not enough for Pinkney. He left London in February, but a long sail and a side trip home kept him from reaching Washington until June 1811. For the next crucial year America's most important relationship would be handled in London by the chargé d'affaires, John Smith.

Despite or perhaps because of Pinkney's departure, Wellesley did dispatch a minister to the United States. His choice of Augustus Foster was hardly a concession or improvement over his predecessor, Francis Jackson. Foster had reinforced a long-standing disdain for America and Americans while serving as the legation secretary in Washington from 1804 to 1808. The impact of his "diplomacy" would make war more, rather than less, likely.

Madison received Foster on July 2, 1811, and Monroe opened talks with him a few days later. The result was a dialogue of the deaf that persisted up to and beyond the war declaration. The gap between American and British interests and policies could not have been starker. The *Chesapeake* tragedy still festered. Foster insisted that reparations would come only if the Americans rescinded the ban on British shipping and condemned the *Chesapeake*'s captain. Monroe just as strongly called for Britain to renounce impressment while granting an appropriate monetary compensation. The United States forbade impressment; Britain championed it. As for the broader issue of neutral rights, Monroe asserted that the Non-Intercourse Act would remain in effect unless Whitehall rescinded its Orders in Council and its impressment policies. Foster firmly rejected that and instead demanded the unconditional resumption of trade. He argued that the Non-Intercourse Act actually violated Macon's Bill No. Two since Napoleon had not formally repealed his own restrictions on American trade.[2]

That latter point appeared to be valid. Napoleon had recently stated publicly that the Berlin and Milan decrees would remain in force as long as Britain's Orders in Council did. When Foster confronted Monroe with that evidence, the secretary of state dismissed it as inconclusive. Then Napoleon bolstered the American position when he decreed that all American vessels sequestered after November 2, 1810, would be released, and he welcomed all American vessels to his empire's ports.[3]

The emperor did not stop there. With his St. Cloud Decree of April 28, 1811, Napoleon announced the definitive repeal for the United States of the Berlin and Milan decrees that imposed a blockade on Britain and its colonies, and seized any ships sailing to those ports. Foreign Minister Hugues-Bernard Maret, the Duke of Bassano, presented that decree to Jonathan Russell, the chargé d'affaires.[4]

The trouble was that the document had been rather obviously and clumsily postdated. Russell sent the decree back to Washington with the warning that Napoleon's "great object" was "to entangle us in a war with England."[5] Russell's warning went unnoticed. The United States had lacked a minister in Paris ever since Armstrong abruptly left without authorization in September 1810. It was not until November 1811 that Madison nominated someone for that vital post. For once, he had found someone qualified. Joel Barlow unofficially headed the American community of several hundred merchants and artists, and was well liked and trusted by most prominent Frenchmen.[6]

Madison was as eager to believe Napoleon as he was thoroughly fed up with British stonewalling and arrogance. He felt that war with Britain was inevitable and feared it would come sooner rather than later. If so, he wanted Congress in session to rapidly approve any necessary measures. On July 24, he called for Congress to reconvene on November 4, a month earlier than its scheduled opening. At least one historian believes that this was a fatal step in the march toward war: "This proclamation, rather than the acceptance of the Cadore Letter in October 1810, was the most critical act of Madison's first term, for it amounted to no less than a decision to prepare the United States for war with Britain. This course now remained the only honorable one for the president."[7]

That may be an exaggeration. The actual war declaration was eleven months away. It was not inevitable, only increasingly likely, as the War Hawks dominated the political discourse with their loud, incendiary rhetoric and bullying tactics.

Every war has its own unique set of causes. Historians have identified a multitude to explain why the United States declared war against Britain in June 1812.[8] The reasons include two decades of festering, swelling rage against Britain for impressing sailors, seizing cargoes and vessels, denying trade reciprocity, aiding and inciting the Indians against the frontier, attacking American warships, and insulting the nation's honor, to name the more prominent. Some historians then and since have argued that these reasons were merely excuses cited by the participants to mask their true motive. The declaration resulted from an overwhelming greed by special interests to exploit the war's potential financial, territorial, political, and emotional spoils if America won. For the War of 1812 as for all wars, historians will forever debate just which causes were of primary and which of secondary importance, and the dynamic or vicious cycles among them.

While virtually all scholars explain the American war declaration as the result of events, policies, and decisions that took place when Madison was president, at least one scholar pins the blame on his predecessor. In his history of the war, Alfred Thayer Mahan concluded that its primary cause was Jefferson's inept policies: "We probably should have had no War of 1812; that is, if Jefferson's passion for peace, and abhorrence of navies, could have been left out of the account."[9] That may be too grand a stretch. Just because Jefferson refused to build up the regular army and navy does not make him responsible for the decision of Madison and Congress to declare war more than three years after he left office.

Madison sojourned at his plantation, Montpelier, during August and September, but it was probably not much of a vacation. For months he had been agonizing Hamlet-like over the ultimate political and moral question of whether to take the nation to war. As time passed, he felt more and more the prisoner than master of events and forces. That the politicians and the public were just as split complicated matters. Madison was perplexed by "the diversity of opinions and prolixity of discussion," which reveal that "few are desirous of war, and few are reconciled to submission; yet the frustration of intermediate courses seems to have left scarce an escape from that dilemma."[10]

If the nation was so bitterly split over the question, why did Madison finally favor war over other possibilities? British minister Augustus Foster was a close if biased observer of the American political and cultural scene. He concluded that Madison would not have asked for a war declaration without "the approaching presidential elections."[11] Did a man who suffered a lifetime of mockery for his frailties of will and body overcompensate on the eve of a presidential election? Did he seek to reunite the nation against a common enemy? If so, these motivations were most likely subconscious. No written evidence has emerged to back them.

The Twelfth Congress that convened on November 4, 1811, was noticeably different from the one that preceded it. Most obvious, about half the seats had changed hands, and most of those new faces were distinctly younger than those they replaced. But those were just the cosmetic changes. The substantive ones were so great that a historian described the Twelfth Congress as "a watershed in the history of the republic."[12]

The most important difference was ideological. The Republicans tightened their grip over Congress with shares of 72 percent of the House and 82 percent of the Senate. Within the Republican Party more than twenty War Hawks wielded a power far greater than their slender ranks. What they lacked in numbers they made up with zeal. They beat the drum for war through fiery speeches on the floor and incessant agitation behind the scenes. They were also able to chair and pack such key committees as Foreign Relations, Military and Naval Affairs, and Ways and Means.[13]

What explains that irrational exuberance for war? Virtually none of them had ever heard a shot fired in anger. And therein may lay the key. Their average age was barely thirty-something. From childhood they had listened enviously as their fathers, grandfathers, or other elders told Revolutionary War tales. The War Hawks were unbloodied and eager to heap glory and honor upon their own generation. Only through war could they emerge from beneath the shadow of the "greatest generation" cast by the nation's founding fathers, and stand in their own light. Yet there was a catch. They would lead America to war only from the safe confines of Washington. None among them would trade his cozy congressional seat for a commission at the front.

Most War Hawks hailed from the southern and western states. Although the representatives from Kentucky, Tennessee, and Ohio numbered only 10 of 142 members of the House, they were united behind the cause of warring against Britain. Of them, Henry Clay of Kentucky and Felix Grundy of Tennessee were the most vociferous. Among the southern states, none was more eager for war than South Carolina, with John Calhoun, Langdon Cleves, William Lowndes, and David Williams the leading voices. Elsewhere in the south, George Troup of Georgia was an outspoken advocate of war with Britain. But the War Hawks also had important allies in the north, including Peter Porter of New York, John Harper of New Hampshire, and Ezekiel Bacon of Massachusetts.

Not every Republican was hell-bent for war. The party was not as strong as it seemed despite its domination of Congress. The Republicans were beset with factions and rarely voted unanimously. The Old Republicans led by John Randolph of Virginia, the Clintonians led by George and DeWitt Clinton of New York, and the Invincibles led by Samuel Smith of Maryland, along with William Branch Giles of Virginia, and Michael Leib of Pennsylvania, would join in voting against the war and its related measures. Nearly all Federalists condemned any notion of going to war against Britain as akin to a death wish. Nonetheless, Madison would obtain solid votes in both houses of Congress when he asked for war.

No one more acidly opposed the War Hawks than Senator Randolph. He dismissed all the justifications for war as mere excuses. Payback rather than patriotism was the deciding factor. The War Hawks sought "to enrich the commissaries and contractors" to whom they were beholden. What better way to do so than to wage "a war not of defense, but of conquest, of aggrandizement, of ambition; a war foreign to the interest of this country."[14] Henry Clay for one did not deny that motivation but argued that it was one of many causes. Nonetheless, if "pecuniary considerations alone were to govern there is sufficient motive for war."[15]

No one in Congress was a more eloquent or effective War Hawk than Henry Clay.[16] Bored with what he believed was a somnolent Senate, he ran for and won a House seat in 1811. Because of his reputation for dazzling oratory, encyclopedic knowledge, and charismatic leadership, he was elected House Speaker as soon as he formally took his seat. It was Clay who had packed the committees with fellow War Hawks. Working with key colleagues, he decisively shaped nearly all the bills that led to and then ran the war. Clay issued a resounding call for war on New Year's Eve, 1811. While defending America's freedom of trade and the seas was important, there was an even more profound reason for war: "What are we not to lose by peace?" War would restore to the United States its commerce but above all "a nation's best treasure, honor."[17]

Perhaps the most comprehensive yet succinct justification for war came from Andrew Jackson when he called on Tennessee's militia to muster on March 12, 1812:

> For what are we going to fight? We are going to fight for the reestablishment of our national character, misunderstood and vilified at home and

abroad; for the protection of our maritime citizens, impressed on board British ships of war and compelled to fight the battles of our enemies against ourselves; to vindicate our right to free trade, and open a market for the productions of our soil, now perishing on our hands because the mistress of the ocean has forbid us to carry them to any foreign nation; in fine, to seek some indemnity for past injuries, some security against foreign aggressions, by the conquest of all the British dominions upon the continent of North America.[18]

The rush to war was spurred by promises of how easy victory would be. Clay boasted that "the conquest of Canada is in your power. . . . I verily believe that the militia of Kentucky are alone competent to place Montreal and Upper Canada at your feet."[19] John Calhoun echoed that notion: "I believe that in four weeks from the time a declaration of war is heard on our frontier, the whole of Upper Canada and a part of Lower Canada will be in our power."[20] From his mountaintop mansion, Jefferson voiced the most optimistic view of the War Hawks: "The acquisition of Canada this year, as far as the neighborhood of Quebec, will be a mere matter of marching."[21] Similar beliefs had helped fuel the invasion of Canada in 1775, although that campaign had not quite worked out as prophesized. None of the War Hawks dared look back to the lessons of the past, only forward at the mirage of their visions.

The swelling chorus of demands for war in Washington and beyond reached Whitehall and sobered the ministers somewhat. Prime Minister Spencer Perceval and his cabinet agreed that the time had come to offer a "concession" to the United States. For four years, Whitehall had stonewalled American demands for justice for the unprovoked attack on USS *Chesapeake*. On November 1, 1811, Foster informed Monroe that Britain would denounce the attack, pay compensation, and release the two surviving Americans who had been impressed.[22]

For most Americans that gesture was too little too late and salt rather than salve to a grievous wound. They viewed the concession as motivated by fear and weakness rather than a sincere effort for reconciliation. The lesson was that the British respected only strength of arms and will.

The president all but issued a war declaration when he addressed Congress on November 5, 1811. He denounced Britain for "trampling on rights which no independent nation can relinquish" and called on Congress to "feel the duty of putting the United States into an armor and an attitude demanded by the crisis, and corresponding with the national spirit and expectation."[23]

The Foreign Relations Committee issued a report on November 29, 1811, that essentially demanded war with Britain unless it yielded to all of America's demands.

It called on the United States to prepare for war by boosting the regular army to ten thousand troops, enlisting a volunteer force of fifty thousand to serve for three years, preparing all warships to sail forth against the enemy, and allowing merchant ships to arm themselves and resist any more depredations. By overwhelming majorities, the House adopted each of those resolutions between December 16 and 19.

The Senate was not to be outdone. On December 9, William Giles of Virginia introduced a bill that would raise the regular army to twenty-five thousand troops. Volunteers would be enticed with an enlistment bounty of $31, up from $12, and the promise of 160 acres of land. That same day, the House Ways and Means Committee sent a sensible request to the Executive Mansion—how much would the war cost? It would be another month before the committee received a reply.

Giles's bill passed on December 19 and was sent to the House Committee on Foreign Relations. There the number of troops was reduced to fifteen thousand. The House passed that troop bill on January 6, 1812. The Senate struck out that lower figure and raised the bid to thirty-five thousand troops. The bill was sent back to the House, which passed it on January 9.

Some congressmen feared that a regular army would take far too long to recruit, even with the higher enlistment money and land bonus. To fill that gap, a bill was introduced into the House on December 26 that would raise an army of fifty thousand one-year volunteers and authorized the president to call out a hundred thousand militia for six months' service. The bill passed both houses by large margins. The president signed the bill into law on February 6, even though he opposed parts of it. The bill gave control to the states, rather than the president, over appointing the officers. It also forbade the president from deploying the militia in Canada or elsewhere beyond the United States, an ideologically correct concession to states' rights that would prove to be a crippling imposition in the coming war. In April, that bill was amended to reduce the number of volunteers and their service to fifteen thousand men and eighteen months.

With most representatives sons of the soil, there was less appreciation for war at sea. Navy Secretary Hamilton issued a statement on November 19, 1811, calling for twelve 74-gun ships of the line and twenty 38-gun frigates for $4.5 million. The Executive Mansion submitted that plan to congressional committees on December 3. It took six weeks before the proposal emerged as a bill on January 17. That bill lost by the slender vote of 62 to 59 on January 27. Had it become law, the bill would have eventually developed a navy powerful enough to challenge any fleet the British could then muster against the American seaboard. A majority found two problems—it would require huge tax increases and would mostly benefit the commercial, manufacturing, and financial class in the eastern seaports.

So how much would a war cost America's taxpayers? Treasury Secretary Gallatin issued a report that called for a $5 million package of direct and indirect taxes and duties, along with a $10 million loan. But that was only a short-term down payment. Gallatin estimated that a two-year war would cost the nation at least $50 million. Although the war's actual direct and indirect costs would be more than twice as much, Gallatin's figure provoked outrage among the War Hawks, who called it a gross exaggeration. Their denial reveals that the conservative hatred of taxes and attempt to secure government services for nothing is hardly a recent phenomenon. Most Republicans enthusiastically clamored for war but resented having to pay for it. Felix Grundy expressed their worst nightmare: "What if we get taxes and do not go to war?"[24]

Regardless, the bills would come due sooner or later. On February 17, Ezekiel Bacon, the Ways and Means Committee chair, introduced a bill that would raise money for the war by a range of direct and indirect taxes. The House overwhelmingly crushed the tax bill by a vote of 22 to 96 on February 28. Bacon and his committee devised one less offensive. After three weeks of bitter debate, a bill narrowly passed on March 4, 1812, that would increase revenues with a direct tax of $3 million, to be levied on the states in proportion to their respective populations; raise taxes on salt; and borrow $11 million.

Throughout March, a series of revelations pulled the war question in opposite directions. The first occurred on March 9 when Congress received a bundle of letters from the president that seemed to reveal a British plot to break up the United States, involving a man named John Henry. Henry was born in Britain, immigrated to the United States in 1798, lived in various New England towns for several years, and then moved to Montreal. There Governor James Craig of Lower Canada recruited him to return to New England on a secret mission to assess and, if possible, promote the secession of those states.

The explanation accompanying the letters was that Henry did not uncover, let alone instigate, any genuine support for secession, but he instead found a new allegiance. In early 1812, he confessed his covert actions to the State Department and as proof furnished them with his correspondence with Craig and other British officials. His motive was to promote war or "confuse the opposition, arouse the spirit of the public, and unite all people against the enemy."[25]

With that spirit on March 9, Madison released those letters to Congress along with a condemnation of Britain for intriguing to sever New England from the United States.[26] The revelation had the intended effect. Virtually everyone across the political spectrum was outraged. Madison hoped to wield the Henry letters as a figurative sword with which to lead the nation to war.

Alas for the War Hawks, new information emerged that revealed the Madison administration's John Henry narrative to be largely a fiction. Whether he had worked for the British or now for the Americans, greed rather than principle had animated Henry. He had grown embittered when he received only 500 pounds sterling a year for his services rather than the 32,000 he demanded. At some point, someone who called himself Count Edward de Crillon, but was actually a French con artist named Paul Émile Soubiran, persuaded Henry to sell his letters to the American government; they would split the take. Henry and Soubiran journeyed to Boston, secured a letter of introduction from then governor Elbridge Gerry, and hurried on to Washington.

Secretary of State Monroe found far more value in those documents than Governor Craig. For those papers, he handed Henry the extraordinary sum of $50,000, which was the entire secret service fund budget and an amount that would be well over a million dollars today. That price alone shocked most members of Congress and the public. Then there was the problem of the content of the correspondence. Most of Henry's "intelligence" was nothing more than the sort of unfounded gossip bantered about in merchant houses, dockyards, and taverns. And compounding the disappointment for Republicans, Henry implicated no prominent Federalists in his intrigues.

A House of Representatives resolution called for Henry to appear before them. As if Monroe was not already embarrassed enough, he had to admit that Henry was not available. The spy and his sidekick had prudently taken the money and run.

The effect of the Henry-Crillon scandal was to delay rather than accelerate the war declaration. Monroe explained to the French minister that the administration had "made use of Henry's documents as a last means of exciting the nation and Congress."[27] It did, but not as the president and his men had intended. The Federalists in Congress and their newspapers heaped scorn on Madison as at once a dupe, a deceiver, and a spendthrift. Most Republicans were embarrassed and, for a while at least, kept lower profiles. Madison was so shamefaced that he would wait another two months before he sent Congress a war declaration.

The Henry-Crillon scandal hardly inhibited the War Hawks in Congress. On March 15, the House Speaker and Secretary of State met and discussed a range of vital issues concerning the preparations for war. Clay suggested a thirty-day embargo on shipping to allow merchants and captains to find a safe haven before the war began. But with the scandal still reverberating, Monroe admitted that politically the timing was not right to launch that policy.[28]

Then came the news that Gen. George Mathews was once again trying to mobilize American settlers in East Florida to revolt against the Spanish. It was an open secret that Mathews had once operated on oral orders from the Executive Mansion itself. Although Monroe disavowed Mathews's actions, few believed that early case of "plausible deniability." Critics denounced Mathews's not-so-covert action on two grounds. It was an act of unprovoked aggression against Spain and its ally Britain. It was also an act of hypocrisy on the part of the Executive Mansion that had condemned John Henry even though he had never actually attempted to stir any separatist movement among New Englanders.[29]

If the Henry and Mathews revelations briefly somewhat cooled the passions for war, word from Britain yanked public opinion in the opposite direction. A British ship bearing dispatches and news dropped anchor before Washington on March 20. It was soon known that Whitehall's official position was unchanged, but the cabinet's composition had actually become more anti-American as Robert Stewart, Viscount Castlereagh, replaced Richard Wellesley as foreign secretary.

Deftly played, that news could be wielded to reanimate the march toward war. Then, on March 23, came the word that a French frigate had captured and burned two American merchant ships. Either Napoleon's claim to have rescinded his own orders to seize American ships had not reached that frigate's captain, or else it was a deliberate lie designed to disadvantage the British. But, even if it were true, the War Hawks insisted that France posed a much lesser threat to the United States than Britain. Henry Clay explained that "I scarcely know of an injury that France could do to us, short of an actual invasion of our Territory, that would induce me to go to War with her, whilst the injuries we have received from Great Britain remain unaddressed."[30]

That bad news did not discourage Peter Porter, the Foreign Affairs Committee chair, but instead spurred him to redouble his efforts to promote war. The following day, on March 24, he met with Monroe and implored him to reconsider Clay's idea of an embargo, and also queried him on the Executive Mansion's war preparations. Monroe promised to attend to these matters. When they met again on March 30, Monroe explained that he had received the president's permission to appear before the Foreign Affairs Committee the next day.

Monroe told the committee that the president had expressed his hope that Congress would declare war before the session ended. An embargo would certainly be a sensible step to take before a formal declaration. Monroe did lament that "war measures had progressed tardily in Congress & also in the Executive branch" but blamed those shortcomings on "a condition inseparable from our System."[31]

Although he intended no irony in the timing, on April Fool's Day, Madison sent a message to the House Committee on Foreign Relations calling for a sixty-day embargo on all American shipping. Within hours, the committee introduced a bill with a ninety-day embargo to a closed session of the House, which promptly passed it by 70 to 41. The following day, in their own closed session, the Senate approved that bill by 20 to 13. Madison signed the embargo into law on April 4. With pointed symbolism, the embargo would take effect on July 4.

The response from the nation's newspapers, even the Republican ones, was less than enthusiastic. Another trade embargo meant more unemployment in the ports, lost sales for those who produced or handled exports, and higher prices for those who purchased foreign goods. Dismayed by the lack of support, Monroe instructed the *National Intelligencer* on April 14 to run an editorial championing the embargo and calling for outright war with Britain.[32] That wish would soon come true.

24

Into the Abyss

The success of pushing the latest embargo through Congress lifted the president's confidence. He got another boost when he learned that George Clinton, his vice president and the only Republican who was openly pondering a race for the party's nomination, had died on April 20, 1812. The Republican Party held its presidential nomination caucus on May 18. With about two of three congressional Republicans present, Madison received their unanimous support. While that was certainly heartening, Madison was well aware that eight congressional Republicans had boycotted the caucus in protest against the shoo-in for Madison.

Four days later, Pinkney's latest dispatches reached the Executive Mansion from London. Anyone who had hoped for some last-minute diplomatic breakthrough would be disappointed. Whitehall was as recalcitrant as ever. That message was reinforced when Foster shared with Monroe his latest dispatch from Castlereagh. The Republicans had agreed that war should be declared if the British did not yield. They had not.[1]

Yet Madison hesitated week after week to take that final plunge into the abyss. His embarrassment over the Henry-Crillon scandal partly explains his indecision. More important were the contradictions in logic, national interest, and morality behind a war declaration, which he expressed in a letter to Jefferson: "France has done nothing to adjust our differences with her. In the mean time, the business is becoming more than ever puzzling. To go to war with England, and not with France arms the Federalists with new matter and divides the Republicans. . . . To go to war against both presents a thousand difficulties."[2] Alas, the president left out another option: not warring against either.

Madison's hesitation exasperated Henry Clay. He was determined to stiffen the president's sagging backbone. On May 25 and 29, he strode at the head of delegations of congressional Republicans to the Executive Mansion, and together they urged Madison to compose and deliver a war declaration. The president turned over the drafting of the message to William Pinkney, who had returned from London to become the attorney general.

President James Madison secretly delivered the message to Congress on June 1. His argument for war cited the array of American complaints against Britain, emphasizing the impressments of sailors, seizures of cargoes and ships, illegal blockades, and incitements of the Indians against the American frontier. Yet he did not explicitly call for war. He would leave that to Congress.[3]

Congress debated Madison's message in a secret session. The House opened discussion on a war bill on June 3, and approved it by 79 to 49 on June 4, eleven Republicans joined thirty-three Federalists in voting nay.[4] The Senate took longer to debate the wisdom of going to war. After taking up the bill on June 9, the so-called malcontent Republicans joined with Federalists in denouncing the war as an inevitable disaster for American interests. Others called for limiting the war to sea, where most of the attacks on American interests had occurred. A few senators even called for fighting against Britain and France since both had harmed the United States. Those proposed amendments all failed. The Senate eventually approved the House bill, although the vote on June 17 was much closer, with 19 for and 13 against.

The votes reflected critical regional as well as party cleavages, with the south and west mostly favoring the war, while most dissidents were from the northeast. Republican support for the war was enthusiastic but far from unanimous. In all, 98 of 121 Republican members of the House and Senate, or about 82 percent of all Republicans, voted for war, while all 39 Federalists voted against it.[5]

Would those votes have differed had the debates been open rather than secret? What would have been the effect of reporters and concerned citizens crowding the galleries each day and then carrying on those debates in newspaper columns and taverns? Federalist Samuel Taggart believed that secrecy was essential to permit "a majority in Congress" to be "mad enough to vote a declaration of war." Had the proposal "been debated openly and fairly, the discussion probably would have been a long one and so many petitions would have come in from all quarters that [the War Hawks] . . . would not have dared to proceed."[6] Perhaps. Then again, although we will never know, probably few if any votes would have been cast differently. By then only a relative handful of people sat on the fence in or out of Congress.

In signing the bill into law on June 18, Madison called on all Americans to work together to win "a speedy, a just, and an honorable peace."[7] Most citizens undoubtedly found Madison's platitudes soothing and even inspiring. Throughout the nation's history, Americans have tended to shelve their disputes and rally around the flag when a war erupts. That initial burst of enthusiasm, however, tends to wane with the war's mounting toll in blood, treasure, and lost opportunities; it plummets when the nation appears to be losing and the original reasons for the war increasingly appear to have been either delusions or outright deceptions.

Not everyone surrendered all reason in that national rush for war. John Randolph typically rained reality on the War Hawk parade: "Go to war without money, without men, without a navy! Go to war when we have not the courage, while your lips utter war, to lay war taxes! When your whole courage is exhibited in passing Resolutions!"[8]

25

Second Thoughts?

As irony would have it, news arrived the next day that a lunatic had assassinated Spencer Perceval, the determinedly anti-American British prime minister. Would someone less hard-line and perhaps even conciliatory take his place at the cabinet's head? If that crucial question caused any of those who had voted for war to pause for thought, none publicly said so.

Over the next two months, more astonishing news reached Washington. Ships passed in the night as America's war declaration and Britain's concessions were sailed across the Atlantic. Whitehall had finally awakened to the reality that its policies enraged rather than intimidated the Americans. Castlereagh sent Foster a letter on April 10, instructing him to do everything he could to prevent war. On April 21, he announced that Britain would rescind its Orders in Council if France openly repealed its own. Napoleon obliged on May 11, 1812, by producing the St. Cloud Decree, dated April 28, 1811. Although that document was widely recognized as a fabrication on both sides of the Channel, Whitehall would eventually go along with it. But that process was disrupted by Perceval's assassination the same day of Napoleon's announcement. Precious time was lost as the British formed a new government.

It was not until June 6 that Castlereagh announced that the Orders in Council would be suspended. Ten days later, the government introduced to Parliament a bill that formally did so. After a week of debate, it passed on June 23. Word of that revocation would not reach Washington until mid-August.

141

Madison later admitted that had he known Whitehall had rescinded the Orders in Council, he "would have stayed" or shelved his war declaration. Instead he stayed the course. He rejected separate appeals for an armistice from both Adm. John Warren, the commander of the Royal Navy's North Atlantic fleet, and George Prevost, the commander of British forces in North America.[1]

Impressment was the sole remaining reason for the war and the president was clinging to it. A House resolution expressed the impressment issue with what today some might call "moral clarity" and others might denounce as a self-defeating "moral mirage": "While this practice is continued, it is impossible for the United States to consider themselves an independent nation. Every new case is new proof of their degradation."[2]

For Madison and his fellow War Hawks, the die had already been cast. There was no looking, let alone stepping, back. After years of advocating war, they had finally gotten it and they were going to keep it. They cited the spectrum of reasons for doing so, of which none was more vital than honor.

26

Mustering the Nation

I t was one thing for Congress and the president to pass resolutions declaring war and calling for a huge military buildup. It was quite another for them actually to begin to implement these goals.

The policies that Madison and Congress pursued to help pay for the war certainly struck observers then and since as contradictory and at times outright bizarre. They agreed that to raise desperately needed revenue, the United States would have to keep trading with the enemy. In other words, for nearly two decades, the Republicans had advocated various forms of trade sanctions against Britain and, for the last four years, had actually imposed them when the two countries were at peace. Now that America and Britain were finally at war, trade with Britain was essential to fighting and ideally winning a war against Britain.

There was a political motive as well. Jefferson explained that "open markets are the very first object toward maintaining the popularity of the war." Madison agreed, but to keep up appearances as well as revenue, he advocated issuing licenses to those who carried the trade, which would be neutral rather than American vessels. Jefferson concurred.[1]

Money to fight the war fell ever shorter of its need. By July, the treasury had only been able to borrow $6.5 million of the $11 million that Congress had authorized. To fill that enormous gap, Congress authorized the issue of $5 million short-term treasury bonds with interest rates of 5.4 percent. It also doubled average tariffs from 17 percent to 34 percent, issued a 10 percent surcharge on cargo carried by foreign vessels, and quadrupled the duties on those ships from 50 cents to two dollars a ton. The Republicans refused for the moment to raise domestic taxes. It would have been politically risky and ideologically incorrect to do anything other than print treasury bonds and raise tariffs to pay for their war.[2]

The worst blow of all to fiscal sanity had been the elimination of the Bank of the United States on March 3, 1811, the day its charter expired. By a single-vote, the bill to renew the bank was bottled up in committee. Here again ideological correctness trumped national interests. Claiming constitutional and even moral arguments, Jeffersonians in Congress and the press vitriolically assailed the bank. Federalists countered with very different concepts of morality and the Constitution.

Once again Madison was torn between his principles and practical needs. He understood that the bank was vital for developing the economy and would be essential for funding the war. He could have swung that crucial nay vote or more on the committee had he strongly supported the bill. But instead he filled the gap between his conflicting principles and practical needs with silence.[3]

The death of the Bank of the United States would be a disaster for America's economy and its ability to finance the war with Britain. After liquidating the bank, the government had to export $7 million dollars' worth of gold to foreign shareholders. Henceforth the government would have to borrow money from volatile markets at higher interest rates. That would force Treasury Secretary Gallatin to ask Congress to double all duties. The result was a vicious cycle of higher interest rates, inflation, joblessness, and debt, and lower economic growth than would have otherwise occurred.[4]

The United States went to war in 1812 with the army and navy that it had. Unfortunately, that did not amount to much given the nation was squaring off with the world's greatest navy and perhaps finest army man-for-man. For that the Jeffersonian antimilitary philosophy was to blame. During eleven years of Republican rule, the nation's defense was rooted largely in militia and gunboats.

The nation did have plenty of militia. The sole advantage in relying on militia was financial. They served without pay. But the military disadvantages were crippling. More often than not, politics rather than military prowess explained who was commissioned a militia officer; the men elected their leaders up to the rank of captain, while governors handpicked those from major to general. Regardless of who was in charge, militia could be balky as mules in marching to the front and then tended to flee at the first shots. Moreover, Congress had passed, and the president had signed, a bill preventing them from serving outside the United States, which would severely crimp American offensives against Canada.

As for regulars, enlistments fell far short of the designated 25,000-man, twenty-one regiment army. At least the troops were well armed. War Secretary Dearborn had the armories at Harper's Ferry, Virginia, and Springfield, Massachusetts, increase their annual production from seven thousand muskets in 1809 to ten thousand in 1810.[5]

The Royal Navy then had 640 warships in active service, of which 124 were ships of the line with 50 or more guns and 116 frigates with 30 to 50 guns, while another 250 were either being repaired or constructed. To fight this maritime Goliath, the United States had seven frigates and nine smaller warships. The nation did have plenty of gunboats—176 that altogether had cost taxpayers about $1.5 million. Although they were relatively cheap to build, man, and arm, they were militarily worthless. They were essentially a coast guard scattered in ports along the Eastern Seaboard. At best they might have been able to chase smugglers but would have been blasted to splinters had they ever tangled with a British warship. The money that was expended on the gunboat fleet could have bought and maintained several frigates, or even a 74-gun warship.[6]

Perhaps more usefully, Jefferson and Madison did spend $2.8 million on coastal fortifications from 1801 to 1812, three times the budget of the Washington and Adams presidencies. Alas, the twenty-four forts and thirty-two batteries from New Orleans, Louisiana, to Eastport, Maine, were almost all poorly constructed and garrisoned. Then there were privateers who enriched not only themselves but also the treasury, since the government took a cut of these profits.[7]

When Congress finally adjourned on July 6, 1812, the War Hawks at least could take pride in having passed 143 bills during their 246 days in session, nearly all of which attempted to ready the nation for war.[8] Yet that effort fell far short of what was needed.

The United States not only lacked enough troops, sailors, guns, and ships to fight Britain, the nation's civilian and military leadership was almost uniformly abysmal at every level from top to bottom. The United States was in desperate need of competent leaders who could muster vital resources and implement sound strategies.

The military bureaucracy was a tangled mess. Rather than work in harness, the components fought incessantly for more resources and duties. That tug-of-war was especially rife between the Ordnance and Military Store sections, whose powers and duties overlapped the most. Elsewhere, more rather than less administration was needed. Among Jefferson's economizing "reforms" was the abolition of the quartermaster and commissary departments in 1802. The American armies that marched from 1812 to 1815 did so with bellies pinched with hunger and bodies weakened from malnutrition. Then as now, the army depended on private contractors to supply the beans, bullets, and blankets. Often the result was shoddy equipment, rotten food, deficient muskets, and flash-in-the-pan gunpowder for the army, and always vast profits for the well-connected, often no-bid contractors.

All of that red tape was exacerbated by War Secretary William Eustis himself, who drowned himself in details rather than grasped the big picture, and led accordingly. On the war's eve, Eustis complained of exhaustion to Madison. He pleaded with the president for permission to hire two assistant secretaries to join the department's eleven overworked clerks, and to shed completely the overlapping duties for Indian affairs and land grants to the Treasury Department. Madison agreed but Congress rejected the request for the two assistants as an extravagance.[9]

James Wilkinson and Wade Hampton were the regular army's first- and second-ranking generals. They despised each other. Tragically, the American army has had its share of inept generals throughout history, of which Wilkinson was among the worst. Wilkinson just could not stay out of trouble. After his acquittal for treason, he was restored to command of American forces in the southwest. In early summer 1808, he encamped his troops at Terre aux Boeufs, a clearing in a malaria-ridden swamp south of New Orleans. The result lengthened the list of disasters shadowing Wilkinson. In only a few months, 816 men died and 745 were hospitalized.[10]

The subsequent demands of prominent officers and citizens for a court of inquiry put Madison in a bind. To heed that call would dredge up the old accusations against Wilkinson as a traitor and Jefferson as a dupe or worse. Yet to ignore the scandal might be politically worse if it did not go away. The president might be accused of covering up a dereliction of duty that killed or sickened over fifteen hundred soldiers.[11]

A court of inquiry was eventually convened. The investigation lasted nearly two years. Once again, Wilkinson was legally exonerated. But nearly all of the officer corps had turned against him and the Federalists evoked his name as the epitome of Republican skullduggery, corruption, and favoritism. Worst of all was the corrosive effect on army morale of retaining such an inept, callous, and treasonous general.

The northern army's commander would soon become as controversial. For that vital post, Madison sent Henry Dearborn's name to the Senate on January 20. Dearborn had served dutifully if not exceptionally in the Revolutionary War, was a representative in Congress during the 1790s, and then served as Jefferson's war secretary. He was in over his head as an administrator—the paperwork overwhelmed him. Exhaustion and ill health forced him to resign as war secretary in April 1808. Dearborn was a sickly and lethargic sixty-one years old when he reluctantly accepted the new command. While the president could publicly cite his military experience, privately he could take comfort that a loyal friend and Republican was in charge. Alas, Dearborn would prove to be utterly inept.

The president not only had to choose the generals but every officer down to lieutenant. By the end of 1812, Madison and Eustis had offered commissions to more than eleven hundred men, of whom 85 percent accepted, although 8 percent would resign within a few months. The officers then recruited men to the ranks of their units. As an incentive, an officer received two dollars for each recruit, who in turn received an enlistment bounty of thirty-one dollars, a uniform, five dollars a month, and 160 acres of land when he was mustered out.[12]

America's officer corps was largely filled by standards of ideological correctness and political loyalty. Among a handful who emerged from the war renowned for their skill, courage, and vision, Winfield Scott bitterly recalled that "party spirit of that day knew no bounds, and, of course, was blind to policy. Federalists were almost entirely excluded from selection, though great numbers were eager for the field. . . . There were but few educated Republicans. Hence the selection from those communities consisted mostly of coarse and ignorant men."[13]

Most of the new officers had little more than enthusiasm going for them, and some not even that. Congressman Peter Porter complained that "our army is full of men fresh from Lawyer shops & counting rooms who know little of the physical force of man—of the proper means of sustaining & improving it—or even the mode of its application."[14] Most of the older officers had little more than cynicism and debauchery to share with these younger men. Scott complained that the "old officers had, very generally, sunk into either sloth, ignorance, or habits of intemperate drinking . . . utterly unfit for any military purpose whatever."[15]

With a national population of 7.5 million Americans, filling the ranks of the army and navy should not have been difficult. The northwest alone had enough potential recruits to overwhelm any British forces in the region. According to the 1810 census, Kentucky and Ohio respectively had 406,511 and 230,760 inhabitants.[16]

Yet the army's regular and volunteer regiments were grossly understrength by the year's end. By November, the volunteer army officially numbered only 9,823 of its authorized strength of 25,000 troops. By December, the regulars numbered only 5,447 of its authorized 10,000 troops and were scattered in twenty-three posts across the country.[17]

There were good reasons for that shortfall. It was well known that army life was an oxymoron. Only society's dregs would prefer the poor pay, bad food, mind-numbing tedium, and cruel punishments for the slightest infraction to virtually any other work. The danger of combat was fleeting, but soldiers faced a daily enemy from the myriad diseases that festered in the filthy conditions of an army camp or barracks. Typhus, pneumonia, typhoid, malaria, and smallpox killed scores each year. Even more soldiers deserted before their time was up. Those that remained were plagued by bad morale and skills, while many engaged in "robbery, disorderly & Mutinuous Conduct."[18]

The army faced a chronic dilemma of how to retain old soldiers and attract new recruits. Although the monthly pay was raised from five to eight dollars, it was still below the ten or twelve dollars that an unskilled laborer made. Congress boosted the enlistment bonus from $31 and 160 acres of land to $124 and 320 acres of land. That extravagant offer did spur more men to line up before recruiting sergeants, but it also inspired many soldiers to desert and then reenlist in a different regiment under a new name.[19]

Planning for the war centered on President Madison, Treasury Secretary Gallatin, Secretary of State Monroe, War Secretary Eustis, and Navy Secretary Hamilton. To their credit, the president and his men tried to align their military and diplomatic strategies. The resulting strategy was straightforward enough. The Americans would defend the Eastern Seaboard against a British invasion while sending three armies into Canada from Lake Champlain, Niagara, and Detroit. The conquest of Canada would give the United States the bargaining power to win any concessions from Britain at the negotiating table. Henry Clay explained that "Canada was not the end but the means, the object of the war being the redress of differences, and Canada being the instrument by which that redress was to be obtained."[20]

Canada was seen as an easy picking, with only about a half million people, or one-fifteenth that of the United States, and could count only 7,000 regulars and 86,000 militia compared to 12,000 American regulars and 650,000 militia. The War Hawks reckoned that the American army would not only quickly rout the British but would also be greeted with open arms by those Canadians who dreamed of being part of the United States. After all, two of three people living in Lower Canada were of French ancestry and about a third of the entire population had emigrated from the United States. Cooler heads with longer memories reminded the War Hawks that their predecessors had bandied about the same predictions in 1775, but the results of that invasion of Canada had not turned out as they had so confidently predicted.[21]

For the Madison administration, Canada's conquest was crucial for two related reasons. Whitehall had steadily shifted its imports of such products as naval stores, timber, grain, livestock, and fish from the United States to Canada; by lessening its economic dependence, Whitehall strengthened its diplomatic power. So capturing

Canada would at once regain for the United States those lost sales along with a diplomatic trump card. Most War Hawks demanded Canada not as a bargaining chip but as part of the winning pot. And some would not stop there. Felix Grundy demanded that the United States "add the Floridas to the South . . . [and] the Canadas to the North to this empire."[22]

Those who trumpeted a quick and decisive victory would be mistaken. The war began disastrously for the United States.

27

The Great Lakes Front

The strategists believed that of the three campaigns, that in the northwest would be the easiest. This prediction would prove true from a British point of view. For the United States, however, the northwest campaign would be the most catastrophic. That region's command structure and leadership epitomized all the problems plaguing Washington and the rest of the United States. Military forces were split among the state of Ohio and the territories of Indiana, Michigan, and Illinois, governed respectively by Return Jonathan Meigs, William Henry Harrison, William Hull, and Ninian Edwards. During the war, cooperation among them would be as rare as rivalry for scarce supplies and troops was incessant.

The command of that crucial front would go to someone who proved to be utterly incapable. When William Hull was in Washington in April, Madison offered him the rank of brigadier general and command of the northwest's forces. Hull accepted and hurried back to Detroit to organize an army, mass supplies, negotiate a peace with the Indians, and plan for the invasion of Upper Canada. With varying degrees of ineptness, he failed in each of those duties. William Hull was among those aging, lethargic, dull-witted Revolutionary War veterans who could have spared the nation much grief had he retired from public service. He no longer cut the trim, energetic figure of his youth. At fifty-nine, he was overweight and feebled mentally, emotionally, and physically by a stroke. Much to the derision of his troops, he had trouble mounting let alone controlling his spirited horse. Many saw it as a metaphor for his command of the army.[1]

Yet commanding that front would have been an enormous challenge for anyone. Just gathering needed troops would be hard enough. When war was declared, the United States had only 625 troops scattered among six isolated forts in the northwest. Madison ordered Governor Meigs to muster and dispatch twelve hundred volunteers to serve at Detroit. Meigs protested that to do so would denude Ohio's defenses, but he eventually did as he was told. Hull arrived at Detroit on July 5 and took command of the two thousand armed men there. His orders to launch a swift invasion forbade him the time to begin to transform that armed rabble into soldiers.

Then there was Hull's related strategic and diplomatic situation. British forces in the region were concentrated at Amherstburg and nearby Fort Malden, a half day's march down the Detroit River. With Fort Malden commanding the lower Detroit River and a small flotilla on Lake Erie, the British could intercept any supplies moving by water. Hull learned that lesson the hard way when the British captured the vessel carrying his baggage and campaign plans on June 30. So supplies to Detroit had to be brought overland. Wagon trains slowly rumbled up that long, narrow, wretched road through the wilderness, vulnerable to Indian attacks.

Diplomacy was supposed to mitigate the threat of these attacks. Hull was unable to address that particular duty. After learning that the United States had declared war on Britain, the Shawnee leader Tecumseh and his followers joined about eighteen hundred Indians encamped around Fort Malden. Hull may have taken little solace that Tecumseh was now on his front rather than rear. The brilliant Indian leader would not stay there for long.

Hull launched his invasion of Canada on July 12. Although two hundred of his Ohio militia refused to cross the frontier, he still outnumbered the British at Fort Malden by two to one. Bad news stopped Hull and his army in their tracks. A British force of troops and Indians had intimidated Mackinac Island's small garrison to surrender. He would later learn that hundreds of Potawatomis had wiped out Capt. Nathan Herald, his fifty-five troops, and a score of camp followers after receiving his orders to abandon Fort Dearborn at Lake Michigan's south end. Indians would also attack Fort Wayne on the Wabash-Maumee divide, and Fort Madison and Prairie du Chien on the upper Mississippi River.

The worst news was on his front. Tecumseh had recrossed the Detroit River and routed a detachment on the supply road. The American army's rear was now cut off. Hull dispatched six hundred men back across the river to reopen that road. Tecumseh managed to spook them into Detroit. A thoroughly cowed Hull called an officers' council on August 1 and proposed withdrawing to Detroit. His officers instead demanded that he attack Fort Malden. Hull hesitated for four days and then ordered a retreat when he learned that British reinforcements under Col.

Isaac Brock were on the way. Once safely back in Detroit, Hull sent another force down the supply road. That too was defeated by a force of Indians and British.

Brock led his army of sixteen hundred regulars, militia, and Indians over the river, planted them astride Hull's retreat route, dug in his siege guns, and demanded that Hull capitulate or else. Without firing a shot, Hull meekly surrendered his twenty-five hundred men on August 16.

America's Northwest Frontier had receded from the Great Lakes to Fort Wayne at the Wabash River headwaters and Fort Meigs on the lower Maumee River. Madison was about to confer that region's defense upon Gen. James Winchester, when he learned that Kentucky governor Charles Scott had entrusted his own state's militia to William Henry Harrison. On September 17, the president officially designated Harrison the regional commander. War Secretary Eustis ordered Harrison to undertake "the conquest of Upper Canada which you will penetrate as far as you see fit."[2]

Winchester refused to cooperate let alone subordinate himself to Harrison, whom he dismissed as a militia general. Instead he convinced a reluctant Harrison to discard his planned joint spring campaign and support a winter campaign by Winchester against Detroit. On December 30, 1813, Winchester marched north with 850 troops from Fort Meigs. En route, he ignored a recall order from Harrison. The British blocked his way with eleven hundred troops at the River Raisin and badly beat him. On January 21, 1813, Winchester became the latest American general to ignominiously surrender his army. That humiliating defeat and the subsequent Indian massacre of at least thirty prisoners would later inspire the American battle cry "Remember the Raisin."

Madison's diplomatic strategy with the Northwest Indians collapsed with the series of surrenders on that front. The president had hoped that his envoys could keep the tribes neutral by dispersing big enough piles of gifts and promises at councils. But diplomatic victories could only come after military victories. Illinois governor Edwards recognized that fact and canceled a council scheduled to be held at Kaskaskia when he feared gathering all those Indians among the relatively small number of settlers and troops. A council with more than a thousand Indians was meeting at Piqua, Ohio, when word arrived of Hull's surrender; the Indians' attitude shifted from conciliatory to confrontational. Although they were never in any danger at the council, the three commissioners, Governor Meigs, Thomas Worthington, and Jeremiah Morrow, and their small guard felt lucky to escape back to the settlements. They could report that the Shawnees and Delawares appeared mostly committed to peace, while the Wyandots, Potawatomis, and Winnebagos were hostile. The Miamis had refused to join the council.[3]

The campaign on the Niagara front was only slightly less disastrous. Stephen Van Rensselaer had no military experience other than militia duty before he was commissioned a general and given command there. His sole qualification was that he was from one of New York's most politically and economically powerful families. He would make an utter mess of things.

His force of six thousand men outnumbered the two thousand British and Indians across the river by three to one, the ratio considered by students of military history as essential for a successful attack. That maxim assumed that the leader of the attack knew what he was doing. Van Rensselaer would be the victim of not just his own ignorance but of politics. Gen. Alexander Smyth, who commanded the region's regular forces, refused to take orders from a militia general. Nor would most of Van Rensselaer's militia. Fearing they would be surrendered, they stayed on the Niagara's south side when Van Rensselaer crossed over in early October. So Van Rensselaer had only three thousand men when he launched his attack at Queenston Heights. Smyth and his troops had followed at a distance but were sitting in camp rather than obeying Van Rensselaer's orders to assault Fort George about six miles away. Van Rensselaer faced one last challenge, perhaps the toughest of all. The British army was commanded by Isaac Brock, who was promoted to general and had hurried down to Niagara after capturing Hull at Detroit. The small but expertly led British army routed the Americans and captured 950 men. It was Brock's last battle; a bullet killed him. Van Rensselaer, Smyth, and the remnants of their troops managed to escape back to the American side of the Niagara River.

Madison accepted Van Rensselaer's resignation and replaced him with Smyth as commander on that front. Smyth did not last long. In November, he tried to mount an attack on Fort Erie on the Canadian side, but once again the militia refused to cross over. Smyth resigned in disgust. That front was soon buried beneath the winter snows, rendering raids impossible.

The decisive thrust of the three offensives was supposed to be targeted on Montreal. Gen. Henry Dearborn took personal command of that campaign. He proved to be as able as Hull, Winchester, Van Rensselaer, and Smyth. It was not until November 8 that he headed north from his headquarters at Greenbush, near Albany. A week later he found only about five thousand men gathered at Plattsburgh. Despite the paucity of troops and the onslaught of winter, Dearborn felt compelled to do something. He sent a raiding party into Canada and tried to follow with the rest of the army. Once again, the militia balked at crossing the frontier. Dearborn called off the campaign, dismissed the militia, and sent most of his other troops back to winter quarters in the Hudson River valley.

28

The War at Sea

Ironically, only the American navy scored any victories during that first year of war. The United States enjoyed an overwhelming advantage in numbers on land yet had been repeatedly humiliated by smaller but better-led and better-trained British forces. At sea the Americans were a pygmy to the British giant, yet they managed to inflict some stinging blows.

Initially, the administration was divided over how America's handful of frigates should be best deployed. Monroe preferred to keep them in port to help fend off British attacks. Gallatin wanted them to concentrate on guarding convoys of merchant ships whose trade provided revenues vital to financing the war. Paul Hamilton was typically noncommittal. Madison, who knew nothing of such matters, kept silent. The sea captains naturally wished to sail forth and square off against their British counterparts, although they differed over whether to operate separately or as a squadron.[1]

Hamilton finally decided to divide the frigates into two forces, with each to prowl the seas in search of British convoys and their frigate escorts. Word of that strategy eventually reached Vice Adm. Herbert Sawyer, who at Halifax commanded the naval effort against the United States. He had initially intended to blockade America's ports and capture any vessels coming or going. Instead, he concentrated his warships and sent them on a fruitless search for the American frigates. That in itself was a crucial victory for the United States, as financially lucrative as it was bloodless. With the blockade diminished, more trade vessels could sail to and from American ports.

The American navy scored some direct victories during the first year of the war. In 1812 alone, American warships "defeated or captured three British frigates, two sloops, a brig, and a transport, while losing only two vessels of its own."[2] The greatest coups were those of the 54-gun USS *Constitution* captained by Isaac Hull over the 49-gun HMS *Guerriere* on August 19, 1812; that of the *Constitution* captained now by William Bainbridge over the 49-gun HMS *Java* on December 29, 1812; that of the 56-gun USS *United States* captained by Stephen Decatur against the 49-gun HMS *Macedonia* on October 15, 1813; and that of the 18-gun USS *Hornet* over the 18-gun HMS *Peacock* on February 18, 1813. Hull's triumph retrieved some measure of honor for his family as well as his country; he was the nephew of the man who surrendered an army at Detroit.

Superior American seamanship, gunnery, and daring were the decisive elements in those triumphs. The navy also captured about fifty merchant ships. That figure was overshadowed by American privateers, which took more than 450 vessels in the war's first half year. In contrast, British warships and privateers took 150 American privateer and merchant ships. The word of these victories at sea were salve to an American public reeling from the humiliating defeats on land.[3]

29

Staying the Course

James Madison would win reelection in 1812 despite all the bad news from the distant fronts and growing doubts among thoughtful Americans about whether the war had been a good idea. Two decisive related forces contributed to his victory. No strong candidate opposed him within the Republican Party or in the general election. And then there were those comforting clichés that guide most people in any crisis, especially wartime, such as "not changing horses in mid-stream" and "staying the course."

The 1812 presidential campaign opened in February when Virginia's Republican-controlled legislature nominated electors committed to Madison, which inspired Republicans in seven other states to endorse him as well. In May, more than two-thirds of a caucus of congressional Republicans agreed to support Madison's reelection, along with Elbridge Gerry as vice president. That unbroken string of endorsements ended when New York's Republican Party championed DeWitt Clinton, New York's mayor, the scion of one of the state's most powerful families, and the nephew of the recently deceased vice president who had served both Jefferson and Madison.

The backing for Clinton presented a dilemma for the Federalist Party. Given the political climate, any candidate running under their banner would surely lose. But if they threw their support behind Clinton, who had opposed the war, would it further weaken the Federalist Party? Favorite sons were nominated by several states, such as Virginia with John Marshall, New York with Rufus King, and South Carolina with Charles Pinckney. The question was decided at a convention in

New York in September. The result was a deadlock in which the Federalists did not officially nominate anyone. Most delegates championed Clinton, but they agreed that to openly do so might bestow upon him the kiss of political death. So instead the Federalist convention encouraged electors to back the candidate "who was most likely to effect a change in the present course of measures," meaning the war.[1]

As the country moved toward the general election, the War Hawks ratcheted up their smear campaign against DeWitt Clinton. He was eviscerated as "the modern Cromwell," "the sprig of upstart nobility," and akin to a "Judas Iscariot" who would betray the nation, sell out to the British, and establish a military dictatorship. That there was not an iota of truth behind any of those accusations made no difference. What mattered was that the fear and smear campaign worked.

Nonetheless, Madison's popularity had fallen sharply from 1808. Of 217 electoral votes cast, Madison garnered 128 and Clinton 89, with the south and west along with Pennsylvania backing the president while his challenger took New York and every New England state except Vermont. That was below Madison's 1808 victory of 122 to Charles Pinckney's 47. In Congress, the Republicans gained seats in 1812. They did so despite, or perhaps because of, that year's humiliating surrenders and defeats. When the political dust settled, the War Hawks had routed the Cassandras. The Republicans had 114 representatives to the Federalists' 68 in the House and, although they lost two seats in the Senate, retained a solid majority of 28 to 8. John Randolph was the most prominent antiwar critic who lost his seat. The War Hawks won by wielding the same strategy of "rally around the flag" emotionalism for themselves and attacks against their foes.

30

Paying the Piper

The reelection of James Madison and a Republican majority in Congress was a fleeting distraction from the war, but not the only one. In December 1812, as the president and Congress were trying to figure out what went wrong in that year's campaigns and were preparing for those of 1813, an exhausted and discredited William Eustis resigned as war secretary. Finding someone qualified for that thankless job would be no easy task.

James Monroe advised the president to assign Henry Dearborn that post. Who then would command the northern army? Monroe eagerly offered himself in return for a lieutenant general's commission. Madison hesitated. He feared that Dearborn would be just as lackluster a secretary as he was a general, which does not explain why the president kept him in place as a field commander. So instead Madison asked Monroe to accept a second portfolio as war secretary. After all, his diplomatic duties as secretary of state were relatively light given the severance of relations with Britain.

Monroe did not take long to make up his mind. He accepted the job, but only until Madison could find someone else. He was looking ahead to 1816 when he intended to run for president. His prospects would be greatly boosted if he were renowned for winning glory at the head of an army rather than getting entangled in the war bureaucracy's red tape.

Monroe got to work mapping out how many troops were needed for the coming year. A major hurdle was the president's insistence that the country be divided into nine military districts, with each allocated a commanding general and enough troops to defend itself. Theoretically that would drain about ten thousand troops from the thirty-five-thousand-man army Congress had authorized. But the number of men actually in the ranks was only about fifteen thousand. To fill that vast gap, Monroe hoped to ask Congress for permission to raise twenty thousand one-year volunteers solely for the northern frontier, which would bring the army's authorized strength to fifty-five thousand. But recruitment was tougher than ever. The initial burst of enthusiasm among hot-blooded young men for the war had dwindled steadily with the string of seemingly endless defeats.

As for the navy, both sides of the aisle hoped that secretary Paul Hamilton would resign. Hamilton had proven to be utterly inept in that post. He had been a purely politically choice, a sop to South Carolina. It was hard to imagine anyone less qualified. He had no knowledge of seafaring. Alcoholism exacerbated his natural sloth. He made a fortune skimming money from naval contracts. He shrugged off all pressure to resign from the president on down. He had no intention of walking away from his golden goose.

Those below him in the naval hierarchy may have deplored his corruption and mismanagement, but they applauded his proposal to build a dozen 74-gun ships of the line. Congress whittled down that ambitious plan. The bill that passed on December 23, 1812, would add to the fleet four 74-gun and six 44-gun warships for $2.5 million. However, to the outrage of the Jeffersonians, Hamilton advocated scrapping the 176-vessel gunboat fleet, which he dismissed as "receptacles of idleness and objects of waste and extravagance without utility."[1] The guns, munitions, provisions, crews, and appropriations from those gunboats would be transferred to the warships. Madison reacted to the proposal by vowing to retain the gunboats and dump Hamilton. The president gave his naval secretary the choice of either resigning or being fired. Hamilton grudgingly rendered the post.

The president tapped William Jones of Pennsylvania as the new navy secretary. Jones was a good choice. During the revolution he had fought on land and sea and had later mingled a congressional stint with amassing wealth as a Philadelphia merchant. He was as energetic and competent as Hamilton was the opposite, and was a vigorous advocate of a blue-water navy capable of squaring off with Britain's.

It was up to Treasury Secretary Gallatin to somehow scrape together the money for the army and navy budgets. That would require all his bookkeeping and diplomatic skills. Most members of Congress and the public desired the glory of war, which so far had proven elusive, but resented having to dig into their pockets to pay for the glory. The previous year, Gallatin had barely been able to convince enough congressmen to borrow the money needed for current expenses. Congress had adamantly rejected his proposal to raise internal taxes.

Gallatin's first step was to convince Monroe to cut back an overly ambitious scheme that inevitably would fall far short of both the recruits and funds. In the end, Monroe and Gallatin compromised. Rather than boost the army's authorized but unfulfilled numbers, they would ask Congress for more generous enlistment bonuses to fill existing ranks. In return, the War Department would have to adhere to a very tight budget of no more than $1.4 million a month. The bill became law on January 25, 1813. Having accomplished that crucial job, Monroe then stepped down as war secretary.

All along, Gallatin had been trying to draft and promote revenue schemes that Congress might approve. The treasury appeared to be enjoying a revenue windfall from one source, although it proved to be a mirage. Merchants who violated the non-importation law suffered the seizure of their goods and vessels. By the end of 1812 alone, the federal government had impounded $18 million of shipments that would be released only after the owner paid a penalty. It was a quick and easy way for the government to reap $5 million of desperately needed revenue that enabled Gallatin to bridge that year's spending gap. The trouble was the political cost it inflicted on the Republican Party by alienating those rich and powerful merchants. In the end, most Republicans joined with the Federalists in passing a bill that remitted all of that money to those who had violated the law. Madison's war would not be the last in American history when so many of those who were the most vitriolically "patriotic" appeared so unwilling to make any genuine personal sacrifices.

Gallatin was back at the beginning. Looking ahead to 1813, he foresaw expenses of $36 million and revenues of only $17 million. To pay for that $19 million shortfall and raise extra money for the next fiscal year, he submitted to Congress a plan for borrowing $16 million, raising tariffs by $5.5 million, and initiating an internal tax for an as yet undetermined amount.

Congress approved the borrow and tariff policy but adamantly rejected the internal tax proposal. That certainly made ideological and political sense but would over the long-term inflict far more damage on America's economic development than if taxes rather than loans had paid for the war. The Republican Party's spend-and-borrow policies for the war would simply burden future generations, thus robbing them of wealth they might otherwise have gained.

Financiers initially spurned that $16 million bond sale. Gallatin managed to peddle $50,000 of bonds in Boston and another $500,000 across the rest of New England. That anemic response further boosted the bargaining position of two overlapping circles of investors in New York and Philadelphia led by America's first millionaire, John Jacob Astor; Stephen Girard; Alexander Dallas; and David

Parish. They agreed to buy two-thirds, or $10 million, of the treasury bills but at a 12 percent discount rate, which meant that they paid $88 for each $100 of bonds. They also persuaded Gallatin to raise the interest rate from his initial offer of 6 percent to 7.48 percent. The New York and Philadelphia groups respectively bought $5.72 million and $6.8 million of bonds. Thus would those already rich men pile up yet another vast fortune.[2]

Astor was sporting enough to explain to Gallatin that the government would not have to borrow so much at such bad terms if the Republicans had not abolished the Bank of the United States. No one in Madison's inner circle understood that better than the treasury secretary. Alas, however sensible that restoration would be, Congress remained controlled by strict Jeffersonians who put ideological correctness over practical needs.[3]

Gallatin had no choice but to accept their demand for a discount and higher interest rate. Otherwise he would not have found anyone willing to risk their money on such a scale. However, word of that deal animated financial circles. If Astor and his associates were confident enough to lend so much money, the risk must be small and the rewards enormous, or so the reasoning went. Other investors swiftly bought up the remaining bonds. And with that infusion of treasure, the war ground on.

31

Truth and Consequences

By the end of 1812, the War Hawks were deeply rooted across the political landscape despite their disastrous leadership of the war and the exposure of their delusional rationales for starting it. So why did voters reward them? The Republicans may have been babes in the woods when it came to running a war, but they were brilliant at political demagoguery; they championed themselves at the epitome of Americanism and smeared their opponents as unpatriotic and even worse. And most Americans unquestionably and enthusiastically believed them.

As for their assertions about how justified the war was and how easy victory would be, what went so horribly wrong? To New York mayor DeWitt Clinton, it was quite simple—Jefferson and Madison had grounded their foreign policy in "too much theory" and "too little practical knowledge."[1]

The flawed assumptions began with the belief that Britain was more economically dependent on the United States than the United States on Britain. Thus a cutoff of trade with Britain would sooner or later bring that nation to its knees. This theory was a fantasy, as those who actually studied the trade statistics, like Alexander Hamilton and his followers, pointed out. But the fantasy was no less politically potent. It appealed to two powerful, related constituencies. One was those who wanted to "get tough" with the British. The other was those whose income depended on local rather than international markets, and thus would not be noticeably hurt by the embargo.

The embargo proved the simple truth that the Hamiltonians had spent nearly two decades exposing. While the United States suffered a severe economic depression along most of the Eastern Seaboard, Britain was barely touched by cessations of trade with the United States.

A couple of months after the war declaration, word arrived that the war's justifications no longer existed. Why then did Madison and the War Hawks not try to end the war? What stopped the president from simply ordering his troops to stand down? He could have done so as he fired off a letter to Whitehall with the face-saving message that had he known that the Orders in Council would be revoked, he would never have asked for a war declaration in the first place.

Perhaps the best explanation is that the War Hawks were infected with one of humankind's worst afflictions—hubris. Those with hubris are the last to admit they have made a mistake. Indeed, the more grievous the mistake, the more fiercely they cling to the delusion that it was not one at all, but the right thing to do; they shut their ears and closed their eyes and recited more loudly all their discredited justifications. Madison and his fellow War Hawks had persuaded a majority in Congress and the public into supporting a war that had already cost the United States hundreds of lives and millions of dollars. Would that lost blood and treasure be shed in vain?

Atop of all that was a glaring practical problem. By then the facts on the ground had changed dramatically, and not in America's favor. Hull had surrendered his army at Detroit and the British had punched back the American frontier from the upper Great Lakes to the upper Wabash and Maumee rivers. Would the British simply give back their winnings or demand them and more in compensation for the American war declaration and invasion of Canada? Throughout the war, Madison and the War Hawks acted like novices among sharpies at a poker table; they believed that if they just kept playing double or nothing, they would eventually win back all they had lost.

There were those, however, within the Madison administration who doubted the wisdom of their actions. Secretary of State Monroe privately explained that the administration was "sincerely desirous of an accommodation with Great Britain."[2] But Madison and his men feared that any communication of that desire to Whitehall would be seen as a sign of weakness. So, for now, they did not make one.

Instead, the War Hawks refused to look back, let alone admit that reality. They condemned their critics as being unpatriotic and cowardly. Dissent was treasonous in wartime. All Americans had to unite without question behind the Madison administration or the war would be lost. But the Republican strategy did not rely on simply condemning their critics alone. Shouting down the dissenters was not enough. Somehow the War Hawks had to reanimate those who had originally supported the war but who were now discouraged and having second thoughts after America's series of humiliating disasters.

President Madison tried to bolster this support with his State of the Union address on November 4, 1812. He argued that the United States had no choice but to stay the course. After all, the British had spurned his efforts to settle the problems diplomatically. Instead they had taken over the Michigan territory, threatened America's hold over the entire northwest, and unleashed the Indians against the frontier. He made no mention of the reality that the British had done so in response to America's war declaration followed by three invasions of Canada. Nor did he reveal that Whitehall had actually revoked the Orders in Council, which were the War Hawks' most important justification for the war declaration. He ended his speech by asking all Americans to unify behind a war that threatened their very existence as a nation and whose end could not be foreseen.[3]

And most Americans did just that.

PART 4
Madison, 1813–1815

Those who are not for us are against us, and will be dealt with accordingly.
ANDREW JACKSON

We have met the enemy, and they are ours.
OLIVER HAZARD PERRY

The war, with its vicissitudes, is illustrating the capacity and the destiny of the United States to be a great, a flourishing, and a powerful nation.
JAMES MADISON

You may thank old Madison for this. It is he who has got you into this scrape.
ADM. GEORGE COCKBURN

32

The Politics of War

Having determined how much the nation would have to spend and borrow that year, President James Madison and his men had to figure out what to do with their expanding army and navy. John Armstrong, the man whom Madison chose to replace William Eustis as war secretary, had specific ideas. Armstrong was a rich New York merchant who had served as minister to France for six years and had written a treatise on war called "Hints to Young Generals from an Old Soldier."

Despite those qualifications, Armstrong was Madison's latest controversial choice. Although he was a Revolutionary War veteran, he was most remembered for having helped pen the mutinous Newburgh letter in 1782, which tried to rally unpaid army officers to march against Congress. He had a well-deserved reputation for being abrasive and obstinate, a disposition aggravated by such maladies as gout, rheumatism, and poor eyesight. The president hoped that Armstrong's domineering ways would shake up the war bureaucracy. They did but in a way that worsened rather than lessened its red tape, chaos, and corruption. After taking over the War Department on February 4, 1813, Armstrong shamelessly wielded his patronage and contracts in payback to his political cronies.[1]

War planning for the Madison administration involved a two-step process of first getting Congress to muster and pay for a certain number of troops, and only then figuring out what to do with them. With the first step accomplished, Madison and Armstrong quickly sketched out a plan to hold the Lake Erie and Lake Champlain fronts while launching twin offensives across Lake Ontario against

167

Kingston and York as soon as the ice melted, around the first of April. Flotillas would convey four thousand troops from Sackets Harbor against Kingston and three thousand from Fort Niagara against York.[2]

On paper the plan seemed reasonable enough. Rather than disperse troops and supplies among three fronts, the effort was concentrated on one front. The key element was to strike as soon as possible before British reinforcements and supplies reached those enemy positions.

However, Gen. Henry Dearborn and Cdre. Isaac Chauncey noted some potential flaws. Most crucially, there were only enough troops, supplies, transports, and warships on Lake Ontario for a good chance of capturing one of those towns. Trying to take both at once might lead instead to twin defeats. They suggested the easier target of York rather than Kingston. But leapfrogging Forts George and Erie and striking York directly was too risky. It would be better to mount a methodical campaign that captured those two forts before marching on York. Madison and Armstrong worried that the campaign would stall before the forts. So instead, they ordered a thrust from the army and flotilla at Sackets Harbor directly against York.

Yet that alternative also provoked criticism. It made much more strategic sense to take Kingston at Lake Ontario's east end rather than York, the capital of Upper Canada, on the northwest side. Kingston stood on the north shore where Lake Ontario drained into the St. Lawrence River. If the Americans could take and hold Kingston, they would cut off all reinforcements and supplies moving up the St. Lawrence to British posts on the Great Lakes. Those posts would then wither on the vine and eventually be easy pickings for opposing American forces.

Regardless of the target, the emphasis on the Lake Ontario front prevailed for a very good reason—political rather than military strategy lurked behind it. The president hoped to announce a smashing victory before April 27 when the voting for New York's governor and assembly began. In the 1812 election, antiwar Republican mayor DeWitt Clinton had won his home state in the presidential campaign, while Federalist Rufus King captured a Senate seat from Republican John Smith. The Republicans feared that if Clinton won reelection as governor and Federalists won a majority in the assembly, New York would be firmly replanted in the peace camp. And that could encourage other states with war-weary populations to follow. The Republicans hoped that a quick and glorious victory could reverse that political tide.

Weather would defeat the administration's ambitious plan. The winter was unusually severe and ice still covered most of Lake Ontario when the polls opened in late April. Good news would eventually arrive, but only after a majority of voters decided who would be the state's governor.

The York campaign aside, Armstrong was actually prudent in picking when, where, and how to attack. His strategy was to build up a professional army capable of trouncing the finest veteran British regulars, and only then going on the offensive. To that end, he instructed his generals to drill their troops until they could sleepwalk the formations. He also sent word that the militia should not be called into the field. Historically, with rare exceptions, they tended to hinder rather than help America's war efforts. Like most commanders, Armstrong complained that the militia mostly got in the way, devoured scarce provisions, bellyached, and turned tail at the least danger. As for the one-year volunteers, Armstrong's attitude was that they should either join a regular regiment or stay home as well.

That goal of building a professional army was easy to decree, but proved harder to implement. Even with a generous enlistment bonus and land grant, recruits were a trickle of those needed. A common laborer still made more than a private and could go home at night. There was no want of patriotic men willing to serve their country in war. But they would do so by volunteering only for a year.

All the regional commanders but one backed that plan. Gen. William Henry Harrison protested Armstrong's orders that he hold tight at Fort Meigs and forswear reinforcements of militia and even volunteers. With only several hundred regulars, he might be routed by a British offensive. His strength would be further diluted by Armstrong's plan to send troops to the village of Cleveland where the Cuyahoga River flows into Lake Erie. Capt. Oliver Hazard Perry was to hurry to Presque Isle and there construct and lead a fleet powerful enough to capture control of the lake. While Harrison clearly recognized that a successful campaign against Detroit depended on American naval superiority on Lake Erie, he protested camping an army at Cleveland, which faced nothing but that lake's widest expanse. The only sensible strategy was to concentrate all troops in the region under his command at Fort Meigs, just fifty miles south of Detroit where a British army was massed under Gen. Henry Procter.[3]

When Armstrong ignored the general's protest and advice, Harrison just as pointedly disobeyed Armstrong's orders. He called on the governors of Ohio and Kentucky to send him all the militia and volunteers they could gather. He would march on Detroit as soon as his ranks reached seven thousand armed men. That would be no easy matter. Governor Meigs asked Harrison to pay the Ohio volunteers in advance. Harrison had neither the money nor authority to do so. So most Ohioans stayed home. Kentucky, however, came to the rescue with thirty-five hundred volunteers under Gen. Isaac Shelby. Harrison's insubordination would pay off. That year's only decisive American victories would be scored on the Lake Erie front.

33

The Lake Ontario Deadlock

The York campaign may have missed the New York election but nonetheless got under way with surprising speed. Capt. Isaac Chauncey and Gen. Zebulon Pike respectively commanded a flotilla and seventeen hundred soldiers at Sackets Harbor. On April 23, they sailed forth, and four days later, Pike's army disembarked near York. The British under Gen. Roger Sheaffe put up a fierce fight, but Pike's men finally routed them. Casualties soared when a powder magazine blew up and killed or wounded several hundred people; Zebulon Pike, the hero who had journeyed on a secret mission all the way to the Rocky Mountains was among the dead. The Americans were already outraged enough by that carnage. When a scalp was found in a home, they reacted by looting and burning the town. The British would avenge that atrocity by torching Washington City's public buildings the following year.

The York campaign was simply a large-scale raid. The Americans withdrew to Sackets Harbor, and the British reoccupied the town's charred ruins. In May, a British flotilla commanded by Capt. James Yeo disembarked 750 troops under Col. Edward Baynes near Sackets Harbor. With about 400 regulars and 500 militia, Gen. Jacob Brown repulsed the attacks. Although the Americans inflicted nearly three times as many casualties on the British as they suffered, a panicky officer who feared all was lost set fire to the warehouses and destroyed most of the supplies.

At the other end of the lake, Gen. Henry Dearborn crossed his 5,800-man army over the Niagara River in May. The initial object was Fort George, defended by 1,100 British regulars under Gen. John Vincent. While a force under Lt. Col.

170

Winfield Scott besieged that fort, Commodore Chauncey's fleet pounded it from the lake. Vincent managed to escape on May 27 with most of his army, although he suffered 350 casualties to the American losses of 150 men. That unhinged the entire British position. Vincent ordered his troops to withdraw from forts Chippewa, Queenston, and Erie, and mass at Burlington Heights.

With the enemy on the run, a decisive commander would have hurried on his army to hound the enemy until they stopped either to fight or surrender. That was certainly what Scott urged, but he was not in charge and could not find anyone who would listen to, let alone act, on his advice. Immediately above him were Gens. William Winder and John Chandler, whose lofty ranks reflected their political rather than military prowess. They squabbled with each other and paid no heed to Scott's pleas. The command was further tangled when Dearborn fell so violently ill that for days he seemed at death's door. With no clear substitute, Gen. John Boyd at Fort George and Gen. Morgan Lewis at Fort Niagara split the army between them like a wishbone.

The army did advance, but slowly if not cautiously. On June 5, the lead American regiments were camped at Stoney Creek when an elite British force under Col. John Harvey attacked and captured Winder and Chandler along with 150 others before withdrawing. The American advance slowed to a crawl. General Boyd ordered Lt. Col. Charles Boerstler to attack a British force hovering on a flank. Boerstler ran into an ambush at Beaver Dams and surrendered with his 600 troops. From his sickbed, Dearborn panicked and ordered the entire American army, except for a garrison at Fort George, to withdraw behind the Niagara River. By midsummer, other than the tenuous grip at Fort George, the Americans were strategically back at the beginning on the Niagara River front.

Once again, an incompetent but politically prominent general had led an American army into a humiliating defeat. Armstrong sent Dearborn orders on July 6 to retire, but he then replaced him with someone far worse. James Wilkinson had been a turncoat, a spy for Spain and possibly Britain, and for years had conspired to detach the western states and territories from the United States. Although a jury had acquitted him of treason for his role in the 1807 Burr plot, most of his fellow officers despised him for being inept, disloyal, corrupt, and, as Winfield Scott put it, an "unprincipled imbecile."[1]

When the war broke out, Wilkinson commanded American forces in the southwest, with his headquarters mostly at New Orleans. In the five years since, he had arrived in Louisiana, his heavy-handed and self-serving policies had alienated nearly all of the state's elite and much of the populace against him. Most of the militia refused his summons to muster. Louisiana's two senators demanded his recall.

Yet he scored a significant, bloodless victory on the front. Following orders, he marched his troops to Mobile. The Spanish commander surrendered his eighty-man garrison without a shot being fired on April 15. The United States now controlled all of West Florida between the Mississippi and Perdido rivers.

For that coup, Armstrong transferred Wilkinson to command the Lake Ontario front. His orders were to take Kingston with his seven-thousand-man army and then descend the St. Lawrence River valley. Meanwhile, Gen. Wade Hampton was to lead his forty-five hundred men north up the Lake Champlain valley. Ideally, the two armies would trap the British army in a vise, crush it, and then capture Montreal.

Once again, an ambitious plan ran aground on the shoals of nasty rivalries and befuddled generalship; Wilkinson and Hampton were plodding leaders who despised each other. It took Hampton until October before he had readied his army for the advance. Wilkinson dallied even longer and tried to persuade his officers to postpone the campaign until the next spring; they voted unanimously to proceed even though the late October sky had begun to unleash snow flurries.

Hampton attempted to outflank the British stronghold at Île aux Noix by advancing down the Chateauguay River. Once again, the militia refused to step across the frontier. That hurt the morale of the regulars who feared they would be outnumbered by the enemy before them. Although the officers objected to proceeding with so few troops, Hampton goaded his small army forward. Blocking his route were fourteen hundred French Canadian militia. This time Hampton did not try to end run the enemy. He ordered a direct assault on October 26. When that attack was repulsed, he retreated to Four Corners far up the Chateauguay.

Wilkinson's first mistake was to sidestep rather than sail across and capture Kingston. That misstep gave the British commander the opportunity to advance either against Sackets Harbor or his own rear. With eight hundred troops, Col. Joseph Morrison crossed to the St. Lawrence's south shore and shadowed Wilkinson's expedition eastward. Wilkinson turned on his pursuer at Crysler's Farm on November 11 but did not direct the battle. Ever larger doses of laudanum to ease a range of emotional and bodily ills had rendered him even more erratic and irritable than usual. He put Gen. John Boyd in charge. Boyd ordered a frontal assault that cost the Americans 340 casualties and 100 captured, to British losses of 180. Wilkinson retreated east fifty miles and went into winter quarters at French Mill.

Wilkinson needed a scapegoat to obscure his own dismal leadership. Hampton rebuffed his insincere demand to join him for an advance on Montreal, allowing Wilkinson to claim that Hampton's failure had cost them Montreal's capture within ten days. He attributed his rival general's inaction to a "beastly drunkenness," and called for his arrest and court-martial. Hampton vented his own rage and accusations against Wilkinson. Cooler heads prevented a duel. Armstrong would eventually relieve them both.

Late that year, the British decisively shifted the power balance on the Niagara River front. A series of raids around Fort George convinced its commander, militia general George McClure, to abandon that position and withdraw across the Niagara River on December 10. Then, on December 18, Gen. Gordon Drummond ordered 550 elite troops to cross over the ice and launch a surprise attack on Fort Niagara. While suffering only a dozen casualties, they inflicted over eighty and captured the fort along with 350 troops and vast stores of munitions and provisions. The British would hold Fort Niagara for the war's duration. Another British force routed two thousand militia near Black Rock, and then torched Black Rock, Lewistown, and Buffalo on December 30.

Virtually all that year's American efforts on the Niagara, Ontario, and St. Lawrence fronts had been humiliating disasters. Americans, however, could lift heads bowed by those dreary defeats with word of victories capped by two dazzling triumphs elsewhere.

34

"We Have Met the Enemy and They Are Ours!"

The initial reports from the Lake Erie front were troubling. In May, Gen. Henry Procter marched with 900 regulars and 1,200 Indians from Detroit and besieged Fort Meigs, defended by General Harrison and 550 men. The British killed or captured more than half of 1,200 Kentucky volunteers under Gen. Green Clay who were marching to reinforce the fort. Harrison, however, refused all demands to surrender. With his supplies and munitions dwindling, Procter broke off the siege on May 9. It was a Pyrrhic victory for the Americans. They had suffered more than 300 killed and 600 captured, while the British lost only a hundred men. But at least that front had held steady.

After replenishing his supplies, Procter marched south again two months later, this time with 5,000 troops and Indians, and besieged but failed to capture Fort Meigs. He dispatched a 400-man force to take Fort Stephenson on the Sandusky River. Maj. George Croghan and his 160 troops defeated that assault. Procter finally gave up and retired to Detroit in early August.

A decisive naval victory on Lake Erie that year led the way for a decisive land victory. Capt. Oliver Perry performed wonders at Presque Isle. Somehow he managed to scrape up enough shipwrights and tools on the east coast and deploy them at Presque Isle. By late summer, he had a small flotilla of six warships. Having completed one Herculean task, he faced another even more formidable. The British fleet under Capt. Robert Barclay outgunned his own and was manned by experienced seamen. Undaunted, Perry set forth with his warships in search of Barclay. On September 10, the two fleets met near Put in Bay on one of a cluster of islands in southwestern Lake Erie. It was among history's fiercest naval battles as most sailors on each side were killed or wounded. In the end, Perry sent Harrison the triumphant message: "We have met the enemy and they are ours."[1] The entire British fleet of two warships, two schooners, one brig, and one sloop had struck its colors.

That stunning victory enabled Harrison to march north. He set forth in September with 5,500 men, mostly Kentucky volunteers. Procter abandoned Detroit and withdrew across the river into Canada. When Harrison followed, Procter abandoned Fort Malden as well and withdrew northeast up the Thames River valley. Harrison caught up to him at Moraviantown on October 5. Although his army had dwindled to 3,000 men as the militia refused to cross into Canada, he still outnumbered Procter's 800 regulars and 500 Indians. The result was a rout in which Tecumseh was killed along with 33 known Indian dead, and the British lost 634 troops, of which 477 were captured, at cost of 15 Americans killed and twice that wounded. Huge stores of provisions and munitions fell into American hands.

While news of that victory electrified the nation, at least one person found fault with Harrison. Jealous that Harrison had defied his orders on strategy, volunteers, and militia, War Secretary Armstrong loosened a barrage of criticisms and accusations against him. Harrison could finally endure that abuse no longer. In May 1814, he resigned because of "the most malicious insinuations . . . made against me."[2] Thus did the United States lose its most consistently successful general of the war alongside Andrew Jackson and Jacob Brown.

35

The Red Stick War

A new front opened in 1813.[1] As with nearly all tribes, the Creeks were split between traditionalists and accommodationalists, and proponents of war or peace against the United States. These divisions widened with a spiritual revival led by several prophets and an inspiring visit by Tecumseh in 1811. Those who favored returning to their own cultural roots and driving off the Americans were known as the Red Sticks, because of the color they painted their war clubs. However appealing the Red Stick message, most Creeks still favored peace for a very practical reason—they knew that warring against the United States would be suicidal; defeat and the loss of their land was inevitable. In reply, the Red Sticks recited the litany of American broken promises, land grabs, and aggression. The latest insult was the effort to build a road through the heart of the Creek nation to link Nashville, Tennessee, with the port of Mobile on the Gulf Coast. As if those were not reasons enough to rise against the United States, America's war declaration against Britain presented a perfect opportunity. Their Indian brothers to the north had joined the British against the United States. Honor and interest demanded that the Creek nation and the other southern tribes join that confederacy.

Events would split rather than unite the Creeks. When the Red Sticks murdered several whites in 1812, the peace chiefs banished them. The Red Sticks moved their families to a cluster of villages along the Coosa and Tallapoosa rivers in what is today central Alabama.

American administrators and settlers in the region were well aware of the divide within the Creek people and the Red Stick danger. They debated whether diplomacy or war was better for overcoming the Red Stick threat. Those who advocated war won. On July 27, 1813, militia fired on a group of Red Sticks return-ing from Pensacola where they had bought huge stores of corn, munitions, and other vital supplies. Although the Red Sticks drove off the militia, most of their supplies were ruined or carried away. The Red Sticks retaliated by attacking and destroying Fort Mims on August 30; it was a bloody battle in which more than 100 Indians and 250 militia and settlers died.[2]

The Madison administration and most of the Republican Party welcomed the outbreak of war with the Red Sticks as an opportunity rather than a calamity. It was expected that the United States would not only defeat the Creeks and expel them from their land, but also march on and drive the Spanish from the rest of Florida. The nearly two generations of struggle between the United States and Spain for that region would be settled once and for all.

The only trouble was that American forces were already stretched to the break-ing point and had been beaten on nearly all fronts. Madison had hoped that Georgia governor David Mitchell would take overall charge of the Creek cam-paign by coordinating offensives of militia from his own state, Tennessee, and the Mississippi Territory. But the eyes of the governor and most other prominent Georgians were riveted not west against the Creeks but south against the Spanish in East Florida. They eagerly awaited any provocation the Spanish might give them as an excuse to attack and annex the long-sought land.

Instead Madison delegated that war to Tennessee governor William Blount and militia generals Andrew Jackson and John Cocke, who respectively commanded the western and eastern districts. Jackson quickly mustered 2,500 militia and marched south. He modeled his strategy on that of Anthony Wayne against the northwest Indians in 1794 and 1795. As he advanced, he left behind troops to build and defend fortified depots, the last of which was Fort Strother on the north-ern fringe of Red Stick territory. With his supply line secure, he then quick-marched his troops into the enemy's heartland and inflicted bloody defeats on them at Tallahatchie on November 3 and Talladega on November 9. But he was forced to withdraw to Fort Strother as supplies and the enlistments of nearly all his men expired. By January, Jackson's command was reduced to 130 armed men.

Jackson's thrust could have been decisive had it been coordinated with two other expeditions, those of Gen. Ferdinand Claiborne from Mississippi and Gen. John Cocke from east Tennessee. But, as on other fronts, poor communications and even worse animosities characterized relations among the three militia gen-erals. The result was that the other two expeditions only partially penetrated the territory and stung the enemy in a few skirmishes before turning back.

36

"Don't Give Up the Ship!"

A t sea, the American navy did not win the laurels in 1813 that it had the previous year. The British were determined to crush that pygmy fleet. To that end, they boosted their forces in American waters to 10 ships of the line, 38 frigates, and 52 smaller warships under the command of Adm. John Warren.[1]

The American naval strategy for 1813 was to split the warships into three squadrons of a heavy frigate, light frigate, and sloop led by Cdres. John Rodgers, Stephen Decatur, and William Bainbridge. Those squadrons simply were not strong enough to square off against such overwhelming odds. The warships in port when the blockade was reinforced had to remain. Those at sea continued to prowl for British merchant ships. But that prey had become more elusive since the Admiralty had begun organizing convoys protected by numerous frigates.

Whitehall's blockade strategy was rooted in the classic maxim of divide and conquer. Well aware of the economic, political, and ideological factions among the Americans, the Admiralty imposed a blockade from New York south to Savannah while permitting New England's ports to conduct business as usual. They also let trade continue across the Canadian border.

Try as they might, the British could no more inflict a decisive economic defeat on the United States than the American navy could decisively defeat the British navy. Although prices of goods and ship insurance soared, Americans either went without or found substitutes. Indeed, the war actually proved to be a blessing for at least one sector of the economy. American manufacturing boomed as competitive imports dwindled to a trickle just as government contracts for a range of manufactured goods soared. However, most of the muskets, shoes, blankets, uniforms, cartridge boxes, cannons, and so on churned out by domestic workshops and factories were shoddy and overpriced.

Whitehall did not confine its naval strategy to blockading American ports and convoying British merchant ships. It launched a series of devastating raids along the coastline. The worst of 1813 came with Adm. George Cockburn and his armada. In a circuit of much of the Chesapeake Bay, he landed troops to rout the local militia, and then loot and burn not just ships, warehouses, and factories, but entire towns like Frenchtown, Havre de Grace, Georgetown, Fredericktown, and the Principio Works Foundry. The worst attack was on Hampton, Virginia, where 2,000 redcoats disembarked, quickly scattered the 450 militia, and then committed "every horror . . . with impunity, rape, murder, pillage: and not a man was punished!"[2] The Americans were only able to defeat a British attack on Norfolk where USS *Constitution* was refitting.

That year, the United States suffered the loss of two frigates, the 50-gun *Chesapeake* and 46-gun *Essex*—each against two enemy warships—as well as the 10-gun *Argus*. James Lawrence, the *Chesapeake*'s captain, muttered the dying words that became one of the war's rallying cries for Americans: "Don't give up the ship."[3]

But the naval news was not all bad. The 16-gun USS *Enterprise* fought and captured the 14-gun HMS *Boxer*. The privateer *True-Blooded Yankee* racked up the war's greatest naval success when, during a thirty-seven-day cruise around the British isles, it took twenty-seven prizes, burned seven vessels in a Scottish harbor, and occupied an Irish island for six days. Operating together, the privateers *Sourge* and *Rattlesnake* took twenty-three prizes. Those vessels and their cargoes would fetch a fortune when sold at auction. At least some Americans were benefiting from the war.[4]

37

Groping for a Way Out

Of the reasons cited for going to war, only impressment lingered. Madison believed he had found a face-saving compromise on that issue but could not convince the British to consider it. Three times between July and November 1813, Whitehall rejected his attempts to open talks on the basis of the United States agreeing to bar foreigners from its ships if Britain gave up the practice, if not principle, of impressment. There was ample irony in that proposal. The Jefferson and Madison administrations had repeatedly rejected that same proposal from Whitehall in the years leading up to America's war declaration against Britain.

So the president had Treasury Secretary Albert Gallatin craft a bill to that effect and submit it to Congress. The bill had both diplomatic and political purposes. Ideally, the British would accept it as the foundation for ending the war. If not, politically, as Gallatin explained, it would "take from England and from our domestic enemies any pretext" to denounce the war.[1]

The proposal was criticized from two very different directions. War Hawks blasted it for appeasing the British. Shipowners and merchants protested that barring foreign seamen would sharply raise labor costs and prevent many ships from finding enough men to set sail. Nonetheless, in both houses a coalition of moderate Republicans and Federalists hoped that the measure might end the war. What they called the Seamen's Bill, their opponents derided as the Impressment Bill. The bill passed the House on February 12 by 103 to 31, and the Senate by 18 to 12 on February 27. The bill did not live up to the hopes that inspired it.

Whitehall ignored the bill as contemptuously as it had Madison's previous attempts at diplomacy.

Madison's most important diplomatic initiative was to seize an offer that Czar Alexander had made in September 1812 to John Quincy Adams, America's minister in Saint Petersburg, to mediate a peace between the United States and Britain. The czar had both practical and lofty reasons for doing so. Around the same time that Washington had declared war on Britain, Napoleon had invaded Russia with more than 600,000 troops, of whom half were French and the rest cobbled together from his conquests and allies. Britain's war with America was a severe drain of troops, ships, supplies, and money away from its alliance with Russia, which was dedicated to destroying Napoleon once and for all. But Alexander was also a visionary and a humanitarian. He greatly admired America's experiment with liberal democracy and free enterprise, even if he believed that such values and practices were alien to Russia and should be kept firmly at bay.[2]

The message was not received until March 7, 1813. Madison authorized Secretary of State Monroe to inform Andrei Dashkov, Russia's minister to the United States, that the czar's mediation would be greatly appreciated. Ideally, Whitehall would accept via Russia the deal that it had rejected directly from Madison. And if not, the president hoped that he might use the opportunity to forge a trade treaty between the United States and Russia.[3]

Dashkov was able to obtain a diplomatic pass from Adm. John Warren, who commanded the blockade of America's coast, and followed that up on April 3 by requesting an armistice while the diplomacy unfolded. Warren promised to ask Whitehall for permission. Unfortunately, the conciliatory diplomacy at the local level would not be matched at the top of the command chain.

The War Hawks were doing all they could to undercut that delicate diplomacy. William Duane, the *Aurora*'s publisher, wrote a series of articles condemning Russia as a despotism with which the United States should spurn any association. The essays so offended Dashkov that War Secretary Armstrong warned Duane to desist.[4]

Madison wanted to send a bipartisan delegation to Saint Petersburg. From the Federalists he chose James Bayard, a Delaware senator. He first considered nominating Henry Clay, the House Speaker. He eventually decided that Albert Gallatin was just as brilliant but was completely loyal and far more even-keeled than the fiery Clay. Dashkov himself had encouraged Madison to pick the wise, courtly Gallatin as the man most likely to impress Alexander. But who would mind the treasury while Gallatin was away? Madison asked William Jones, the navy secretary, to add the treasury portfolio to his duties.

The instructions for Gallatin, Bayard, and Adams were to ground any settlement on the trade-off contained in the Seamen's Bill. In practical terms, barring foreign seamen from American ships would impose significant costs on American shipowners, while Britain would lose little from giving up impressment. Atop that, the envoys were to negotiate a trade treaty between the United States and Britain that conferred reciprocal rights and access.[5]

The president then added an even more ambitious goal to the mission—Upper Canada. That was an extraordinary demand given that the British had by then overrun the Michigan territory and pushed back America's frontier to upper Indiana and northwestern Ohio; the battles of Put in Bay and the Thames were months away. But Madison's call for Upper Canada was no mere bargaining chip. He was dead serious. How else could he appease the War Hawks who demanded a "victory" that aggrandized the United States? Among their rationales for war was the chance to take Upper Canada, and thus at a stroke quell the Indian threat and open the resources of that vast region to American entrepreneurs and settlers. Anything less would be peace with dishonor.[6]

Then, as almost an afterthought, Madison included yet another item on the wish list. Should Florida come up, the commissioners were to insist that West Florida was an integral part of the United States, and demand East Florida as compensation for Spanish depredations against American shipping. Gallatin and Bayard drew the line at the Floridas. They argued that to include the issue would be inappropriate, complicated, and probably self-defeating. The president agreed to keep the Floridas off the table.[7]

Madison's appointment and dispatch of Gallatin and Bayard to Russia took place while Congress was out of session; the commissioners set sail on May 9. When Congress reconvened on May 24, 1813, many senators took umbrage that Madison had acted without their approval. The more die-hard Republican senators despised Gallatin for his lukewarm support of the war and insistence that taxes be raised to pay for it. Evidence suggests that War Secretary Armstrong was egging on Gallatin's enemies from behind the scenes; his motive was to rid the cabinet of what he believed was his worst ideological and political rival.[8]

Madison tried to soften that anger with a conciliatory speech before Congress on May 25. Then, on May 31, he sent the nominations of Adams, Bayard, and Gallatin as peace commissioners, and of Jonathan Russell, then the chargé d'affaires in London, to be the minister to Sweden. Three days later, he undercut his nominations when he allowed William Jones, the acting treasury secretary, to present to Congress Gallatin's proposal for nine direct and indirect taxes that would help finance the war by raising $6,365,000.[9]

The Jeffersonians exploded in wrath at that proposal. Those in the Senate inflicted a stinging rebuke to the president for daring to violate such a key Republican principle. In July, the Senate approved the nominations of Adams and Bayard, but rejected Gallatin's by 18 to 17 and Russell's by 22 to 14. Russell's foes accused him of inept diplomacy in London and protested the cost of deploying a minister to a relatively unimportant country such as Sweden. Ironically, a majority in both houses would eventually approve a modified version of Gallatin's tax hikes.

Meanwhile, the Federalists got in their own licks against Madison and his men. In their respective houses, Daniel Webster, then a freshman congressman from New Hampshire, and Sen. Robert Goldsborough of Maryland, proposed a resolution on June 10, 1813, that the president release all documents on French claims of having revoked the policy of seizing American merchant vessels sailing to Britain and its colonies. If that were true, Federalists then asked rhetorically, why were French warships and privateers violating that very decree? The answer, as another congressman put it, was "that Napoleon has inveigled us into the war. . . . But for his arts, intrigues, and duplicity, the United States would not now [be] at war with Great Britain."[10]

Hard-line Republicans typically turned their rhetorical guns against the Federalists. Felix Grundy, that era's leading Republican attack dog, disparaged anyone who supported the request for information as against the war and thus "moral traitors."[11] But such smears ruined rather than won the debate for the War Hawks.

The Senate resolution passed as moderate Republicans joined Federalists in wanting answers to such a crucial foreign-policy question. The Senate then appointed a committee of Federalists, Goldsborough and Rufus King, and Republican Joseph Anderson, to investigate the question. The House debated the issue for five days before a majority passed five resolutions, each with a request for specific information.[12]

Secretary of State Monroe put off providing the information until Congress pointedly reminded him to hurry up. On July 12, 1813, he submitted a long report along with documents. The essence of his argument was that there was no substantial difference between the Cadore Letter of August 5, 1810, and St. Cloud Decree of April 28, 1811. Both announced that France would no longer seize American ships bound for Britain and its colonies. Thus under Macon's Bill No. Two, the Madison administration was justified in reimposing the non-importation policy against Britain when it did not follow suit. Monroe admitted that the St. Cloud Decree did render "definitive" what was "conditional" about the Cadore Letter.

Regardless, it was not until more than a year later that the United States declared war on Britain.[13]

The mix of incessant work, exposure to diseases, and the stress of fighting both the British and a spectrum of domestic enemies finally broke Madison down. What was then known as bilious fever, a diagnosis for any prolonged fever accompanied by nausea and vomiting, laid him up for a month beginning June 15, and during that time, he could or would not see anyone. That same mysterious disease felled Vice President Elbridge Gerry around the same time. Armstrong and Monroe essentially ran the government during the president's absence.

It was not until July 16 that Madison felt well enough to discuss issues with anyone, although he did so from bed. His first policy decision was to call for the latest embargo on all American exports. He was provoked to do so by reports that American merchants were trading with the enemy, especially at the island of Bermuda several hundred miles east of the Carolinas. Although that measure passed the House on July 22, it died in the Senate on July 27.[14]

The Thirteenth Congress had inflicted upon Madison a string of embarrassing setbacks during its first session from May through August. Although Republican majorities dominated each house, many dissidents joined with Federalists to vote against the president. As Sen. Jesse Bedloe of Kentucky put it, "The friends of this administration will put it down faster than its enemies."[15] Many reasons accounted for that opinion, but the bottom line was that Madison's weak leadership and poor political skills inspired Congress to vote against him.

Bad news arrived from overseas. Whitehall rejected any notion of having Russia mediate peace. That rejection dashed hopes for a quick diplomatic settlement of the war. Indeed any British motive for wanting peace with the United States receded steadily with the threat Napoleon posed. The Russian army, endless steppes, and icy winter had destroyed Napoleon's vast army. He had escaped back to Paris, raised another army, and in the spring of 1813 marched into central Germany in a desperate attempt to reassert control over his empire. But Prussia had joined Russia against France in March, and Austria would join their ranks in September. In June, Wellington had crushed Joseph Bonaparte's army at Vitoria, Spain; that brother, whom Napoleon had crowned the king of Spain, fled back to France.[16] Napoleon's empire was crumbling.

On both the military and diplomatic fronts, the annual report that Madison sent to Congress on December 7, 1813, had two bright spots: Perry's capture of Britain's Lake Erie fleet, and Harrison's recapture of Detroit and advance into Canada where his army routed Procter and killed Tecumseh. Elsewhere, however, the best that could be said was that the United States had not lost any ground. As for diplomacy, Whitehall had spurned Alexander's mediation offer. Despite that mostly gloomy report, the president put his best spin on a disastrous dilemma: "The war, with its vicissitudes, is illustrating the capacity and the destiny of the United States to be a great, a flourishing, and a powerful nation."[17]

Two days later, the president called on Congress to impose a near total embargo on American exports and British imports. Neutral ships could not trade in the United States unless three of four crew members were natives of that country. The practice of ransoming ships captured by the British would be banned. The coastal trade was forbidden. Fishing boats could sail to the horizon only after posting a bond.[18]

Congress promptly enacted Madison's proposals into law. The penalties for violating any aspect of the law were harsh. Even tougher was the policy for treasury and navy officials to first seize a suspected violator's cargo and vessel, and later investigate. Once again, that policy provoked an uproar across New England's seaports that the Republicans gleefully ignored.

Meanwhile, Gallatin and Bayard arrived in Saint Petersburg on July 21. Three days later, Adams presented them to Foreign Minister Nikolai Rumiantsev. That and subsequent meetings were mere formalities since Whitehall had rejected Russian mediation. Gallatin convinced his colleagues to open a direct channel with the British. He wrote Alexander Baring of the mercantile firm Baring Brothers and asked that he informally see if the cabinet would be willing to talk. Baring did as requested and was able to convey the favorable reply of Whitehall's interest, and suggested meeting either in London or Gothenburg, Sweden. Eventually they would meet in neither of those places, but after months of diplomatic maneuvering, a breakthrough in Ghent would finally end the war.[19]

38

Politics as Usual

New faces joined Madison's administration. Managing both the Navy and Treasury departments had exhausted William Jones; he begged the president to confine his dwindling energies solely to naval affairs. Madison relented. To find a new treasury secretary, he typically put political loyalty before technical competence and chose Sen. George Campbell of Tennessee. Then William Pinkney resigned as attorney general to return to his lucrative law practice. Madison replaced him with Richard Rush, a prominent Philadelphia lawyer. Finally, Madison convinced the utterly corrupt Gideon Granger, a Connecticut Republican, to resign as postmaster general. Return Meigs eagerly accepted the post; apparently the financial benefits of being Ohio's governor were not as advantageous.[1]

War Secretary Armstrong was becoming ever more bellicose. He threatened to resign when the president appeared to favor peace over victory with Britain. With eyes on the 1816 presidential race, he opened secret talks with prominent Federalists for a coalition with breakaway Republicans that he hoped would win him the nation's Executive Mansion.

Animosities were worsening between the Republican majority and Federalist minority. The Federalists demanded investigations into the reasons for the defeats and allegations of widespread corruption, and called for a purely defensive war. The Republicans responded in two ways. Those in Congress had no trouble killing any investigations into the administration's incompetence and corruption. Meanwhile, the Republican press lambasted anyone who raised any questions about the military campaigns or contracts as certainly unpatriotic and possibly treasonous. But even that was not enough for some Republicans. Sen. John Calhoun of South Carolina was so infuriated that anyone would question the war's morality or management that he came close to challenging the two most outspoken critics to duels.[2]

William Jones could not have been more relieved to pass the ball to George Campbell, whose appointment the Senate approved on February 9, 1814. As yet another year of war loomed, one question above all dominated the Treasury Department—who will pay for it? Jones submitted his budget to Congress on January 10. Most members of Congress must have gasped when they read it. The war's direct financial costs had soared to $45,350,000, 50 percent more than the previous year's bill. That included $24,550,000 for the army, $7 million for the navy, and the rest for the sundry costs of running a wartime government and interest payments to service the swelling national debt. With the year's likely revenues amounting to only $16 million, the budget deficit would be at least $29.4 million.[3]

How would that gap be filled? The hodgepodge of higher trade duties and consumption taxes enacted the previous year would pay only a fraction of the bill. Any suggestion to the president and nearly all of his fellow Republicans that internal taxes be raised was ideologically dead on arrival. As heretical was the notion that a revival of the Bank of the United States could alleviate much of the government's financial calamity. Once again, Washington would have to paper over that vast chasm by going, hat in hand, to a small coterie of extremely rich and powerful financiers and promising them even higher interest rates and deeper discounts for the money.

The Madison administration's bill provoked outcries and line-by-line scrutiny when it reached Congress. The debate lasted nearly two months. Federalists angrily denounced the Republican spend-and-borrow policy as the epitome of irresponsibility. Congressman Alexander Hanson captured that policy's essence: "To float new loans to pay the interest on old ones . . . was to adopt a most desperate system of fiscal gambling."[4] But, in the end, what choice was there for Republicans other than to keep funding the war? By March 3, the bill had passed both houses by large majorities.

Even then the struggle to finance another year of war had only just begun. The bottom line was whether enough people would be willing to buy $25 million of government "IOUs." In May, the Treasury Department offered $10 million of bonds at a 12 percent discount and sold only $7.9 million's worth. It then offered $6 million of bonds at a 20 percent discount but only sold $2.5 million. Clearly

America's richest men lacked the money or confidence to buy more. The U.S. government hovered at bankruptcy's brink.[5]

Once again, misguided, ideologically driven policies had plunged the economy into the abyss. As prices soared, fewer goods were sold, less money changed hands, and people had even less money to spend. The economy was in a tailspin and the government lacked the means to yank it skyward. Revenues contracted with the economy. Even the rich became more careful about their purchases, including treasury bonds. As revenues plummeted, the government had to borrow more money at higher interest rates from financiers, which in turn squeezed out more entrepreneurs who otherwise would have borrowed and invested, and thus boosted the economy.

The embargo sharply reduced but hardly eliminated trade. Smuggling was rife. Many took advantage of the loophole that allowed privateers to set sail. The government's costs of trying to enforce the embargo soared as more money, men, equipment, and energy were diverted to the seacoast. That meant, of course, fewer resources with which to fight the British on other fronts.

Those smugglers who were not caught massed vast fortunes. And very few were caught. Smuggling was easy along a thousand-mile coastline dotted with countless coves and islands. And revenue officials palmed ever larger bribes to look the other way. The biggest loser was the treasury, and thus the soldiers who lacked proper equipment, provisions, munitions, and pay.

No one was more aware of the embargo's financial and military burden than Navy Secretary William Jones. That mission impossible utterly exasperated him. On March 9, 1814, he sent a memorandum to the president, advising him to abandon the embargo and channel the scarce resources committed to the war against smuggling into building, arming, and manning more warships to fight the British.

Madison's initial reaction was to dismiss the memorandum out of hand. He replied with silence to his navy secretary. But, try as he might, the advice echoed within his mind. The embargo debate was intricately tied with all the related dilemmas and disasters that characterized the War Hawk crusade against Britain.

39

First the Good News

Good diplomatic news arrived with the new year of 1814. Whitehall was willing to talk directly with the United States either at London or Gothenburg, Sweden. That word came directly from Castlereagh to Monroe.[1]

During a cabinet meeting on January 8, Madison forged a swift consensus on accepting the proposal. He wrote Castlereagh that envoys would be dispatched to open talks. The president asked the Senate to add Henry Clay to the previously approved team of John Quincy Adams, James Bayard, and Jonathan Russell. Shortly thereafter Madison learned that Albert Gallatin was still in Europe. On February 8, he asked the Senate to include Gallatin among the commissioners. This time Gallatin received the Senate's approval since Madison had lined up William Campbell to take his place as treasury secretary. Both confirmations came the next day.[2]

The next step was to define that delegation's ends and means. In a series of letters, Monroe elaborated the instructions he had issued to the mission the previous year. Impressment must end. Blockade and neutral rights must be clearly defined. An appropriate indemnity must be received for British depredations on land and sea. Upper Canada must be ceded.[3]

It would take months before the team assembled. Gallatin and Bayard sailed from Saint Petersburg for London on January 25, 1814. Clay and Russell departed from New York on February 25 and stepped ashore at Gothenburg, Sweden, on April 13. Adams was still at Saint Petersburg but would eventually join them.[4]

Those who wanted peace had little time to savor the hope that those envoys might find a way out of the labyrinth of war. Word arrived that the United States had suffered a devastating defeat on April 11, 1814, although it took place far across the Atlantic and cost no immediate loss of American blood or money. Peace returned to Europe when Napoleon abdicated on that day.

Ever since June 1812, the United States and France had fought Britain in parallel wars. That month's American war declaration and Napoleon's invasion of Russia were simultaneous and complementary, although coincidental, events. Thereafter the president, along with anyone else who understood the importance, acidulously followed Napoleon's campaigns. As always, the news lagged a couple of months or so behind events. They had rejoiced at word that Napoleon had captured Moscow in September 1812. Since then the news from Europe had provided them nothing but despair. Napoleon's 1813 campaign in Germany had ended in debacle when he lost most of his army at Leipzig in October and had retreated with the remnants to eastern France. There he made a last stand against allied armies that outnumbered his forces by three to one. Throughout February and March 1814, he fought one of his most brilliant campaigns, but he was eventually overwhelmed.

What was seen as a godsend to virtually all Europeans was a potential disaster for Americans. The British could now mass the full weight of their battle-hardened army and navy against the United States. And the envoys would be playing with a feeble diplomatic hand after negotiations opened. As if Napoleon's abdication were not troubling enough, the military news from North America would be almost uniformly dismal.

In anticipation of Napoleon's defeat, Madison convened a cabinet meeting on March 30. Peace in Europe would bring an end to impressment and thus the most important excuse for originally going to war. Acknowledgment of that reality could be a face-saving way to end the war. But that was not what the president wanted to discuss. Instead he put the embargo at the top of his agenda.

The blockades of Britain and France against each other would end with the war. Perhaps America's embargo should end as well, at least with the European countries. That would at once enrich American merchants and the treasury. With more money, the United States could finance more troops, warships, and campaigns.

But those revenues would not be enough to cover the budget deficit. That gap could be closed only by borrowing. America's financial giants had little money to lend and even less desire to do so. Thus the United States would have to borrow that money from foreigners. No country that emerged from the ruins of Napoleon's empire was more important to American national interests than the Netherlands. Over the decades, Dutch bankers had lent the United States the equivalent of tens of millions of dollars, much more than any other country except Britain. The more the United States borrowed from Holland, the less financially dependent it would be on Britain.

So once again Madison temporarily set aside his principles to make way for political realities. The latest flip-flop occurred on March 31, 1814, when he asked Congress to rescind the embargo bill, pass a new bill that continued to forbid British vessels and goods, and ban exports of hard currency; if foreigners wanted to trade in the United States, they had to do so for products rather than coin. While the Federalists enthusiastically embraced the idea, it widened the split between the Republican Party's ideological majority and pragmatic minority. In the end, the Republican moderates joined with the Federalists in repealing the embargo.[5]

40

The Rock of Sisyphus

As usual, military planning lagged far behind budget battles and debt issues. It was not until early June that Madison and his cabinet met to map out a strategy for the rest of 1814. Until then the president and each department head had mostly reacted to ongoing problems, and had done so by looking backward rather than forward.

Madison had discouraging news to share with his cabinet when he convened it on June 3, 1814. Britain's negotiating position had naturally hardened with Napoleon's defeat. The United States undoubtedly faced invasions with battle-hardened veterans of Europe's wars. The only way to win was to decisively strike first.

But before that, Armstrong had to sack the latest set of failed generals, James Wilkinson and Wade Hampton, and replace them with George Izard and Jacob Brown. American forces would attack Canada from two directions, Izard from Plattsburgh toward Montreal and Brown from Sackets Harbor toward York. Brig. Gen. Edmund Gaines would defend Sackets Harbor against a possible British attack during Brown's campaign.

A key question was whether enough troops could be mustered to fulfill that plan. The good news was that more generous economic incentives had spurred recruitment. During the first four months of 1814, 9,588 men had enlisted. That brought the army's official strength to 31,000, although only 27,000 were considered fit for duty, while the rest were laid up in sick quarters or absent without leave.[1]

192

The trouble was that behind those impressive numbers lurked some chronic problems. The troops were scattered across many fronts and districts. They were poorly equipped, trained, and motivated. They were led mostly by generals and officers who were inept and lethargic. Worst of all, those numbers were not considered adequate enough to defend America's frontiers, let alone conquer a Canada defended by twelve thousand British regulars and twice as many militia.

So to fill the depleted ranks, Armstrong proposed drafting 55,000 militia into the regular army. Madison nixed that as a politically disastrous notion. Instead the enlistment bonus was raised to $40 in cash, of which the recruit could immediately palm $24, along with 160 acres of western land once he mustered out. The army's official troop number was raised to 62,500. But that enticed relatively fewer men into the ranks; most of those who might have been inspired by such an offer had already joined up. So the gap between the army's paper and actual strength widened all the more.[2]

It would take many weeks before the generals and their troops would be ready to stir from their cantonments to fulfill the latest plans issued from the Executive Mansion. Yet the war had ground on even though the president had dallied for nearly half a year before figuring out what to do.

For better or for worse, the south's campaign season was year-round. Shortly after the new year began, Jackson resumed his offensive against the Red Sticks, fought two inconclusive battles on January 22 and 24, and then withdrew back to Fort Strother to replenish his supplies and troops. By February, he had massed over 3,500 armed men, including 600 regulars and several hundred friendly Creeks and Cherokees, and enough supplies for a sustained campaign. Once again, he marched south. After about fifty miles, he briefly halted his army and built Fort Williams. From there it was only a few days' march to the Creek stronghold at Horseshoe Bend on the Tallapoosa River. Upon reaching Horseshoe Bend on March 27, he had his troops encircle the village and attack. The Americans slaughtered more than 800 Creeks while suffering 200 casualties. He constructed Fort Jackson just downstream and sent envoys to demand that the Red Stick survivors surrender.

The Creek War was among the bloodiest in American history. More than 1,400 Creeks, or more than 40 percent of the population, perished. Of those who survived, many fled to East Florida to join the people known as the Seminoles. The rest asked for terms.

The diplomatic results of the Creek War were even more stunning. Jackson imposed a treaty on all Creeks, not just those who fought against him but also those who fought with him. Under the Treaty of Fort Jackson signed on August

9, 1814, he forced the Creeks to cede half of their land, or over 20 million acres, to the United States.

The threat to the southern frontier did not come only from the Creeks. A British armada attacked Fort Bowyer, which guarded the entrance to Mobile Bay, on September 12, 1814. As warships under Capt. William Percy opened fire on the fort, 225 marines and Indians landed to snipe at the defenders. The British flagship, the 22-gun HMS *Hermes*, ran aground when it tried to close for an effective bombardment. The American guns blasted it to splinters. Maj. William Lawrence, who commanded the 160-man garrison, curtly rejected the demand to surrender. After three days, the besiegers reembarked and the armada sailed away. But they would eventually return in far greater numbers.

On the Canadian front, Wilkinson, who had yet to be recalled, launched his own brief campaign in March. He marched down the St. Lawrence valley until he halted before a British garrison at Lacolle Mill. The general ordered the all-too-typical reckless direct American assault. The result was just as typical. The British repelled the Americans, inflicting 150 casualties while suffering only 60.

On Lake Erie, Col. John Campbell landed seven hundred troops to attack Port Dover and then loot and torch that town. In a war of escalating brutality, Campbell would justify doing so in retaliation for the British's burning of Buffalo, Lewistown, and Black Rock the previous winter. Later that year, the British would cite Port Dover, along with a list of towns that the Americans had torched, as justifications for burning not only Washington City but other towns around the Chesapeake Bay region. It was that kind of war.

That year, an effort was made to retake Mackinac Island in the straits where the waters of Lakes Superior, Michigan, and Huron mingled. Capt. Arthur Sinclair sailed with several warships and about seven hundred troops from Detroit and reached Mackinac in late July. The island's defense appeared so formidable that he hesitated for a couple of weeks before disembarking his troops on August 4. The Americans were routed when they walked into an ambush by two hundred British and Indians. Sinclair gave up and sailed away. The British would hold Mackinac Island, like Fort Niagara, for the war's duration.

The Lake Ontario front was stalemated. Both sides engaged in a naval race that produced more warships packed with more firepower. Topping the list was the 112-gun HMS *Lawrence*, which was launched in the summer of 1814. The Americans, meanwhile, were constructing two 100-gun ships of the line, the *New Orleans* and the *Chippewa*. The power balance was so tight that neither side wanted to risk a decisive naval battle. So those warships were mostly used to help protect their own ports. When they sailed at all, it was in support of land operations.

In May, the British tried to break the stalemate on Lake Ontario when Gen. Gordon Drummond and 750 troops packed aboard a flotilla commanded by Capt. James Yeo and sailed against Fort Oswego. They succeeded in capturing and destroying that fort before departing.

The Americans scored a minor victory later that month. Capt. Melancthon Woolsey was conveying an American flotilla packed with thirty-four naval guns, munitions, and supplies to Sackets Harbor when British warships appeared. He sought shelter in nearby Sandy Creek and deployed his troops in the forest near Lake Ontario. Capt. Stephen Popham, the British commander, sailed into that trap and suffered more than seventy casualties before withdrawing.

That year's only other waterborne expedition would be the most successful. Since the 1783 peace treaty, the Americans and British had squabbled over where exactly Maine ended and Canada began. In charge of asserting Britain's position by arms was Nova Scotia governor John Sherbrooke. He commanded the twenty-five hundred troops under Lt. Col. Andrew Pilkington and fleet under Adm. Edward Griffith. The expedition advanced methodically along the coast, captured the eighty-five-man garrison of Fort Sullivan at Eastport on July 11, scattered Castine's defenders on September 1, and occupied Machias without a fight. Sherbrooke presented a cruel choice to the inhabitants of that hundred-rugged-mile stretch of Maine coast—they could swear allegiance to the king or leave. Most stayed. They were tied more closely by trade to Nova Scotia than to New England. That swath of coastal Maine would be the third patch of American territory along with Fort Niagara and Mackinac Island that Britain would hold until the war's end. All along, American and British warships had prowled the seas in search of easy prey or escape when they were outgunned. The war at sea was as indecisive as the war on land. In 1814, three American sloops, the 20-gun *Hornet*, 22-gun *Peacock*, and 22-gun *Wasp* captured among them the 19-gun *Penguin*, 19-gun *Reindeer*, 18-gun *Avon*, and 18-gun *Epervier*. Meanwhile, American privateers took scores of merchant vessels as prizes, while the 15-gun *Chasseur* captured the 13-gun *St. Lawrence*. The news was not all positive. British warships forced the 22-gun *Frolic*, 16-gun *Syren*, and 16-gun *Rattlesnake* to strike their colors in 1814.

During the frequent and prolonged lulls on the various fronts, opposing generals had at times conducted their own diplomacy, such as prisoner exchanges during the first two years of the war. An agreement signed at Halifax on May 12, 1813, elaborated an earlier deal on November 28, 1812. Each side was to enforce the same rules: prisoners were to be treated humanely, corporal punishment banned, daily rations fixed, places for exchanges designated, and the value of ranks for exchange established.[3]

But Whitehall never ratified that agreement, and reports that British guards brutalized American prisoners filtered back to the United States. Word that the British had cut back rations to American prisoners in Halifax, Barbados, and Jamaica prompted a policy of retaliatory measures against British prisoners held by the United States.

The worst incident was when the British captured twenty-three Irishmen, who had enlisted in the American army, and shipped them back to Britain to stand trial for treason. Madison was appalled. He had Monroe send a stern warning to Whitehall to desist and ordered twenty-three British troops to be held as hostages. George Prevost, Canada's governor general, then had forty-six Americans picked out as hostages. Madison retaliated by placing all captured British officers literally under the noose.The British followed suit.

A diplomatic effort to resolve that standoff began when Gen. William Winder, who had himself been captured and exchanged, received permission from Madison to journey to Canada and negotiate directly with Prevost. Unfortunately, the deal that he signed on April 15, 1814, excluded the original twenty-three Irish and the hostages on either side. Madison refused to accept that agreement and ordered that a new one be negotiated. A final deal was cut on July 16, 1814, that provided for the exchange of the hostages. The twenty-three Irish, however, would be held in England until the war ended.

The president acceded to a request by General Winder that he be allowed to negotiate a prisoner-of-war exchange with General Prevost, the commander of British forces in Canada, and Vice Adm. Alexander Cochrane, who commanded the fleet in North American waters. The British had no reason to negotiate. Since they held more enemy soldiers and sailors, an exchange could only aid the United States, which could not recruit enough men for its regiments and warships. Prevost thus dragged out the talks in order to distract the Americans, while Cochrane announced in April a blockade of the entire coast. Meanwhile, ever more prisoners died from disease, starvation, and despair.[4]

41

Moral and Diplomatic Dilemmas

James Madison never once publicly expressed any doubts about going to war. Simply because the president was highly intelligent and socially shy does not mean that he was introspective. If he ever harbored any uncertainties about his decision, they have been lost to history.

Yet two years after having led the nation to war, he was clearly struggling over how to end it as soon as possible. In late June 1814, he convened his cabinet to discuss various diplomatic options. Impressment remained the sole reason left for America's war declaration. Should it remain a deal breaker? The British had consistently maintained that they would never give up the principle, although they had hinted at curtailing its practice. If so, would it not make more sense to leave impressment off the table altogether? Perhaps the war should be separated from its causes. Why not agree to peace now and then sort out those perplexing questions of impressment, freedom of the seas, and commerce later? But to do that would call into question the rationale for going to war in the first place. Had the United States expended thousands of lives and tens of millions of dollars over the previous two years in vain?

The cabinet was split over Madison's choices. Secretary of State Monroe, Treasury Secretary Campbell, War Secretary Armstrong, and Navy Secretary Jones agreed that impressment should be a negotiable rather than absolute bargaining position. Perhaps a face-saving compromise similar to that posed by the British should be accepted. Only Attorney General Richard Rush insisted that American honor could solely be satisfied if the British rendered the principle as well as the practice of impressment. As for making no reference to impressment in a treaty, it was Jones and, surprisingly, fire-eating Armstrong who agreed, while the rest were opposed. Everyone but Rush supported the idea of simply signing an armistice that ended the fighting and called for commissions to negotiate the issues of impressment and commerce.[1]

That last option was the one Monroe wrote up and sent off to the envoys. He had no sooner done so when dispatches arrived from Albert Gallatin and James Bayard on June 26. They had paid a private visit to London and met informally with numerous officials—to no avail. With France's empire destroyed and Napoleon banished, the British would spurn serious negotiations and instead mass their forces for a knockout blow against the United States. As for Whitehall's position, impressment not only remained off the table, but the Americans would have to give up their fishing rights in Canadian waters and navigation on the Great Lakes, adjust the boundary southward to reach the Mississippi River, and return Louisiana to Spain.[2]

The following day, Madison called the cabinet to formulate their next move. They unanimously agreed to shelve the impressment issue completely with no reference to it in any treaty. With that, the Madison administration gave up the war's last justification. But they would dig in their heels on Britain's other demands. That latest position was forwarded to the envoys.[3]

What else could be done? With America's armies stalled on various fronts, the only chance was to appeal to the goodwill and offices of other European powers. On June 29, Madison declared that the British extension of their blockade to the entire American coastline was illegal, and he called upon all other states to defy that blockade with their trade. He then had that proclamation printed along with America's grievances against Britain and had it sent to the capitals of Europe. He had Monroe ask Russian minister Dashkov whether Alexander would be willing to again mediate peace between Britain and the United States.[4]

Other than those gestures, there was nothing more of substance to do. The Madison administration had scraped up funds and plans for its armies and a stance for its diplomats. Clearly any diplomatic victory depended on a decisive military victory. Later that summer, a humiliating peace appeared to be all but certain after the United States suffered its most devastating defeat of the war.

Although Madison had managed to forge a consensus on the issues of military and diplomatic strategy, his cabinet was rent by bitter disputes and intrigues. With his abrasive personality and presidential aspirations, Armstrong was the worst offender. He cut Madison down behind his back as incompetent, weak willed, and ignorant of military matters. He also attacked Monroe for trying to assert control over duties that belonged to the War Department. He had earlier blasted General Harrison for sloppy and, he implied, corrupt bookkeeping. Harrison resigned on May 11, 1814. Having appointed Gen. George Izard to command the army, Armstrong began hounding him on various issues until they openly vented their mutual hatred.

Despite all this, Madison rejected the advice of Monroe and others to fire Armstrong. As usual politics was the most important reason. Madison feared that the political damage Armstrong could inflict on him outside the cabinet was worse than what he was inflicting inside it. Instead he subtly began investigating Armstrong's own bookkeeping practices at the War Department. Ideally, if he found enough dirt, he could wield it to force Armstrong into retirement. It would take Madison until late summer before he had amassed enough evidence against Armstrong. The timing of his condemnation could not have been worse. He would present his case against his war secretary on the eve of the British invasion.

On April 25, Navy Secretary Jones pleaded to be allowed to resign for reason of exhaustion. Madison begged him to stay on until he could find an equally qualified substitute. Jones reluctantly agreed.

42

Indian Summer Campaigns

A merican army rolls listed about forty thousand troops by midsummer 1814. Impressive as that number may appear, it was undermined by three crucial problems. First, the troops were scattered across the country's nine military districts rather than concentrated at Plattsburgh, the frontier's closest staging post for a campaign against Montreal. Second, the usual gap between the paper and actual strength of those troops persisted, with desertion, disease, and padding explaining the difference. Third, there was the question of quality—nearly all of those men were poorly led, equipped, disciplined, and motivated.

With thirty-five hundred troops, Gen. Jacob Brown led the latest invasion across the Niagara River on July 1. He crossed just below Fort Erie whose commander capitulated on July 3. Brown then pointed his army north. His goal was to rout all enemy forces and capture Forts Chippewa and George along the Niagara River until he reached Lake Ontario. There he would join with Capt. Isaac Chauncey's flotilla for joint operations around the lake, and capture in turn Burlington, York, and Kingston. The ambitious plan might have succeeded had not Chauncey lingered at Sackets Harbor rather than threatened the British rear at Fort George.

Spearheading the advance was Winfield Scott's regiment. Through incessant drill and meticulous care, Colonel Scott had honed his troops until they were as professional as the finest redcoats. His first chance to prove them came at the Chippewa River, where Gen. Phineas Riall blocked his way with 1,500 troops on July 5. Scott quickly scanned the situation and then ordered a flank attack that routed the British and inflicted 500 casualties while his troops suffered 325. The

American maneuver and discipline caught Riall by surprise. "Those are regulars, by God," he exclaimed.[1]

With only a thousand troops, Scott hurried after Riall, whose army absorbed reinforcements as he retreated. The British turned to fight at Lundy's Lane on July 25. It was a desperate seesaw battle of attack and counterattack. Both opposing generals, Brown and Drummond, marched their troops to the sound of the guns and took over the battle from Scott and Riall, respectively. The British outnumbered the Americans by 3,000 to 2,100 men. Those odds were bad enough, but Brown lost heart when he was wounded along with Scott. He ordered a retreat. Each side lost about 850 men. Tragically for the American cause, Scott's injuries were so severe he would be sidelined the rest of the war. Drummond followed up his victory by dispatching Lt. Col. John Tucker with six hundred troops across the Niagara to destroy the American supply depot at Black Rock. With three hundred troops, Maj. Lodowick Morgan drove off Tucker's advance at Conjocta Creek. Meanwhile, Drummond advanced after the American army, now commanded by Gen. Edmund Gaines. On August 13, he cornered the Americans at Fort Erie with their backs to the lake and river. He would have bagged Gaines and his army had he brought up heavy artillery and conducted a methodical siege. Instead, during a rainstorm on August 13, he ordered a bayonet attack. The Americans killed or wounded 350 British and captured 540, while losing only 150.

Drummond now dug in his troops and brought up his guns. Although gravely weak, Brown took back the army's command. He resisted calls from most of his officers to retreat across the Niagara River during the dead of night. Instead, on September 17, he ordered a night attack on the British batteries. It was a vicious battle of bayonets puncturing bodies and musket butts crushing skulls. The Americans spiked the guns and killed or wounded 600 British to their own losses of 500. The result was a deadlock. Drummond lacked the guns and troops to batter the Americans into surrender; Brown lacked enough troops to drive off the British. With winter coming on, Brown evacuated his troops back to Buffalo on the night of November 5, and blew up Fort Erie behind him. Once again, the Niagara front ended in a deadlock.

War Secretary Armstrong had intended Lake Champlain to be a quiet front that year. He actually transferred General Izard and four thousand troops from Plattsburgh to Sackets Harbor to prepare for what turned out to be an aborted campaign against Kingston. That left Plattsburgh defended by only thirty-five hundred men under Gen. Alexander Macomb, along with four warships and ten gunboats under Cdre. Thomas Macdonough, which would prove to be a nearly fatal mistake for the American effort.

Governor General Prevost set forth on August 31 with ten thousand troops toward Plattsburgh, while a flotilla of four warships, a dozen gunboats, and as many supply vessels commanded by Capt. George Downie followed offshore. Although faced with overwhelming odds, Macomb and Macdonough rejected the pleas to retire by their more fainthearted officers. Each man would perform wonders in Plattsburgh's defense. Downie sailed his flotilla straight at Macdonough's flotilla guarding the port on September 11. The American warships pounded the British vessels and captured three of them; Downie was killed. Prevost, meanwhile, launched a limited attack on the American position, which was repulsed after he lost 35 killed, 47 wounded, and 72 captured. To those losses were another 234 men who deserted after Prevost ordered a retreat upon learning of Downie's defeat. His withdrawal was so hasty that he left behind many of his supplies. In all, Prevost had proved to be nearly as inept as the worst of his American counterparts. He would be exceeded only by the criminal incompetence of those who commanded Washington City's defense.

43

Is Washington Burning?

The United States suffered its most stinging defeat when the British captured and burned Washington City on August 24, 1814. Although the loss of life in the short campaign leading to that disaster was light, the cultural and psychological blow was incalculable. The British torched public buildings holding archives whose loss historians have lamented ever since. Emotionally, the war came home to the president and most of the others who had so zealously championed it. The conflagration that devoured the Executive Mansion, Capitol, and nearly all other government buildings in Washington was deeply seared into the national psyche, compounded by more recent traumas like Pearl Harbor and September 11. And like those two other disasters, the burning of Washington provoked a desire for vengeance rather than submission among most Americans. The British campaign's goal had been to devastate rather than conquer.

Word that the British were preparing an armada to attack Washington and the region reached the capital a couple of months before it actually appeared. The commander in chief delegated local defense to the secretary of war. John Armstrong had a combative, domineering, intimidating personality, but none of that meant he was militarily fit for such a critical command. The first of numerous and reinforcing mistakes that he made was not to take the rumors seriously. Arguing that the capital had no military significance, he dismissed any notion that the British would attack Washington City. To him, just as derisive was the notion that fortifications protected cities. He insisted that "bayonets are known to form the most efficient barriers."[1]

Alas, Armstrong did not act on that belief. Only five hundred regulars with bayoneted muskets would plant their boots on the ground when the British invaded. However, there would be plenty of militia, which Jeffersonians insisted were superior to regulars. The militia, however, lacked not only bayonets for their hodgepodge of weapons but also experienced officers, training, discipline, and élan. Like their counterparts on other fronts and in other wars, the militia before Washington would break and run without firing more than a few shots.

Militia was only half of the Jeffersonian concept of national defense. Scores of gunboats were tied up in various Chesapeake ports. They were worse than militarily useless since their construction, equipping, manning, and maintenance had diverted scarce resources from the warships and regulars that were crucial for defending the United States. Capt. Joshua Barney, who was renowned for his naval exploits in previous wars, commanded a flotilla of gunboats. When the British fleet appeared, all that Barney could do was hole up in the Pawtuxet River to avoid being destroyed. Then, when the British finally advanced on his position, he would order his boats and supplies burned before fleeing inland with his men.

Madison complicated the command structure for defending Washington when, on July 1, he created a tenth military district embracing the region, and put General Winder in charge. Armstrong and Winder despised each other. Armstrong would issue a stream of orders that Winder did everything possible to sidestep.

The urgency for preparing Washington's defense heightened on July 28 when reports arrived that a British armada had anchored off the Pawtuxet River in the Chesapeake Bay, only twenty miles as a crow flies from Washington. Crammed aboard Admiral Cochrane's fleet were forty-five hundred soldiers and marines under Gen. Robert Ross. Despite that formidable force, Ross and Cochrane were cautious. They imagined that the Madison administration would mobilize every fit man within marching distance to defend the capital. Cochrane's most aggressive subordinate was Adm. George Cockburn, who had devastated towns and shipping throughout the region the previous year and was eager to wreak even more havoc. For another two and a half weeks, Ross and Cochrane resisted Cockburn's plea for action.

Meanwhile, Madison could no longer endure the bickering between Armstrong and Winder. On August 13, he strongly reprimanded the war secretary for mismanaging his department, although he stopped short of outright accusing him of corruption. And rather than ask for his resignation, the president implored his war secretary to do better. For Madison, this was no time for a cabinet shake-up.

Ross landed his army at Benedict, Maryland, on August 19. Moving cautiously up the Pawtuxet River, he did not reach Upper Marlboro until August 22. Until the last moment, both Armstrong and Winder clung to the belief that the British had targeted Baltimore rather than Washington for capture. When reports revealed that Ross was advancing on the capital, few preparations had been made for defending that route. Winder ordered all available troops to converge at Bladensburg. Eventually a horde of 7,000 armed men massed there, with a sixteen to one ratio of the 6,500 militia to the 420 regulars.

Cochrane became increasingly nervous given reports that reinforcements were swelling American forces to invincible odds. He ordered Ross to retreat on August 24. Ross was torn over what to do. Cockburn convinced him to ignore the order and push on against the American army just a few miles up the road at Bladensburg.

The British army appeared before Bladensburg early that afternoon. What followed was not much of a battle. Ross ordered a massive attack along the line. The Americans held for as long as they could, inflicting 249 casualties and suffering 177, before breaking.

A courier galloped up to the Executive Mansion with word of the rout. The president ordered the capital evacuated. The British marched into the city that evening. Soon almost all the public buildings, the navy yard, the 44-gun *Columbia* and 22-gun *Argus*, and many private homes had been looted and torched. To a group of ladies who pleaded with him to stop the arson, Admiral Cockburn replied, "You may thank old Madison for this. It is he who has got you into this scrape."[2]

The following morning, Ross ordered his men to march back to the fleet. America's humiliations did not end with the sack of Washington. Twelve miles down the Potomac, Fort Washington guarded the river approach to the capital. When a flotilla under Capt. James Gordon appeared on August 27, the commander, Capt. Samuel Dyson, ordered Fort Washington abandoned without firing a shot. Gordon captured huge stores of provisions and munitions and destroyed those he could not carry off. But, mercifully, he sailed away rather than continuing upriver to destroy the prosperous town of Alexandria in Virginia.

The attack on Washington had not satiated the British desire to devastate the region as much as possible. The next objective was Baltimore, then the nation's third-largest city. On September 12, Ross landed with 4,500 troops at North Point and began to march toward Baltimore, fourteen miles away. Halfway there, Gen. John Stricker and 3,200 militia stood defiant. The Americans put up a fight before giving way after losing 215 men. The British losses were worse, 320 troops, including Ross, who was shot dead. Col. Arthur Brooke took command, resumed the march the next day, and appeared before Baltimore on September 15.

The plan that Cochrane and Brooke devised was simple. Brooke would attack after Cochrane's warships subjected Baltimore to a devastating bombardment. The water approach to Baltimore was defended by Maj. George Armistead, who commanded the thousand men garrisoning Fort McHenry and a battery on Lorenzetto Point across the harbor. Neither fort had cannons with ranges as long as those of the British. During September 13 and 14, British warships fired over fifteen hundred rounds at Fort McHenry, but Armistead refused to strike his colors. Cochrane launched twelve hundred troops in whaleboats against Lorenzetto Point, but the defenders drove them back. Cochrane had had enough. After Brooke and his army reembarked, the armada sailed away.

As the British marched to Washington, the president and his cabinet had scattered, and it took a while for them to trickle back. Upon learning that the British were safely away, Madison returned to the capital's charred ruins on August 27. His first significant act was to turn over command of the region's defense to Monroe, since Armstrong was still at his refuge in Frederick, Maryland. The president had no sooner settled into temporary quarters at the Octagon House, a mansion spared by British arsonists, when he fled again at word of the British attack on Fort Washington roughly twelve miles down the Potomac.

When Armstrong finally showed up, he exploded in wrath that Madison had given Monroe his duty for directing the region's defense. With typical understatement, the president expressed his disappointment at how the war secretary had handled the job. Armstrong threatened to resign. Madison begged him to stay and must have winced inwardly as he cited his dependence on Armstrong's strong leadership.

Why did Madison respond that way after he had been privately lamenting Armstrong's incompetence and bullying ever since he became war secretary? As usual, politics and fear trumped the most elementary principles of leadership. Madison was terrified that New York's War Hawks would blister him for letting their leader go and that Armstrong himself would lash out at him.

Those fears would be realized. After Armstrong resigned on September 4, New York's War Hawks did indeed lambast the president, while Armstrong joined the ranks of disgruntled former administration members who penned tell-all exposés of the president's weak leadership.

A House congressional committee investigated just who was responsible for letting the British burn the capital. The report appeared in late November. Those hoping for a strong condemnation of the Madison administration's incompetence would be disappointed. Instead the nation was treated to a classic Washington whitewash. Blame was spread so widely that everyone and no one were implicated. The Republicans dominating the committee were reluctant to point the figure at those culpable, who happened to be their own party leaders. There was also the near-universal feeling that full exposure was not appropriate when the nation was at war since it might undermine America's effort and strengthen the enemy's will.[3]

Madison's administration was crumbling beneath the strains of war and weak leadership. After Armstrong's resignation, Monroe served as the secretaries of both state and war. Pleading exhaustion, Navy Secretary Jones and Treasury Secretary Campbell respectively bowed out on September 11 and 28. Although Madison buttonholed plenty of potential candidates, there were no immediate takers. Who would board what appeared to be a sinking ship?

Federalists called for a bipartisan cabinet that could end the war and advocated Rufus King for the treasury post. They pointed out that the president had already appointed a bipartisan peace commission. But Madison feared further alienating his own party. Eventually he found Republicans willing to head those departments— Samuel Smith for treasury and Benjamin Crowninshield for navy. Then the latest vacancy appeared when Vice President Elbridge Gerry died on November 23.

Madison sent his annual message to Congress early that year, on September 21. He padded his speech with patriotic platitudes and wishful thinking rather than hard analysis and plans. No matter how hard he tried, he could not gloss over the reality that the war was now in its third year with no end in sight, the Americans had lost far more battles than they had won, the British had burned the capital, and the cost in blood and cash soared.

On September 28, the same day he resigned, Treasury Secretary Campbell reported that next year's deficit would be $23,327,586. The Republican creed of no internal taxes and no national bank meant that once again the government would have to borrow the money. The trouble was that the financial barrel of willing American lenders had been scraped bare. That money could be raised only by turning to foreigners and then paying a hefty price for the bailout. The nightmare of gleaning that money fell on the shoulders of Campbell's successor, Alexander James Dallas.[4]

Dallas threw off Jeffersonian dogma and boldly called for tax hikes and a new Bank of the United States. His bank plan involved an initial subscription of $50 million, with the government retaining one-fifth of the shares. The bank would be headquartered in Philadelphia and have branches of discount and deposit throughout the United States. Once established, the bank would lend the government $30 million at 6 percent interest. To those who condemned such an institution as unconstitutional, Dallas justified the bank as essential for fulfilling the Constitution's "necessary and proper" clause "for carrying into execution" the duties of government.

Congress received Dallas's tax and bank proposals on October 18. By this time, the die-hard Jeffersonians ranks had dwindled before the relentless financial and moral demands of war. Without debate, the House passed the tax package on October 27 and addressed Dallas's bank proposal the following day. It was here that the Jeffersonians, led by John Calhoun, attacked and won. Jeffersonian Samuel McKee proposed his own bank bill, which would strip the institution of autonomy, power, and professionalism. Had that version been enacted, it would have been a money fountain for corruption and cronyism. To his credit, Madison vetoed that bill on January 30, 1815. Senate pragmatists put together a face-saving compromise that retained the essence of Dallas's version. Calhoun again led the charge against the bill in the House and won an indefinite postponement after word of the peace treaty arrived.[5]

44

Conformists and Dissidents

The news that the embargo would end was certainly good for those who depended on international trade. But many people saw reason to end the war as well. In no region was that opinion more outspoken than in New England. Most folks there had opposed the war from the very beginning. That view had only hardened after two years of mostly defeats in an endless war. The peace movement began at the political grassroots level, as citizens in one town meeting after another rallied against the war.

Although the Federalist Party and newspapers amplified the peace movement, churches may have been even more influential.[1] Then as now religion and politics meshed. Across the nation, ministers preached very different sermons over the war's wisdom or folly. Those sermons at once reflected and shaped the prevailing local sentiments. The Congregationalist churches of New England and the Quaker churches of Pennsylvania protested the war as fervently as most other denominations elsewhere promoted it. Those who demanded peace did so most commonly through town meetings, petitions, and protests.

The Republican Party itself was not free of internal dissent, and some of it was quite tough.[2] There were the "we told you sos" from those who had voted against the war. Then there were those who still believed that the war was just but condemned the Madison administration for thoroughly bungling the job. The ever outspoken Henry Clay assailed the commander in chief for being "wholly unfit for the storms of war. Nature has cast him in too benevolent a mould. Admirably adapted to the tranquil scenes of peace . . . he is not fit for the rough and rude blasts which the conflicts of Nations generate."[3] He undoubtedly saw himself as the right man for that duty. John C. Calhoun found the roots of the failures much further back "deep and coeval with the existence of Mr. Jefferson's administration."[4]

War Hawk anger and frustration grew as the toll in deaths, deficits, and defeats mounted year after year. Rather than admit their own responsibility for the debacle, they sought a scapegoat. They vented rage on the peace advocates as unpatriotic and even treasonous. Attorney General William Pinkney and Supreme Court Justice Joseph Story were among the leading voices calling for repressing dissent by reviving the 1798 Sedition Act. They had condemned the law at the time because it was unconstitutional and because they were on its receiving end. But now, somehow, that law was justified.

The pressure on Madison to crush the dissent increased with the volume and diversity of those condemning the war. To his credit, Madison discouraged the Sedition Act's revival and would consider marching troops into dissident New England towns only in "an extreme case."[5] Yet the president could do nothing to quell the extreme backlash against those who advocated peace.

Few extremists were more zealous than Vice President Elbridge Gerry. John Calhoun quoted Gerry as accusing the Federalists of plotting "for a secession of the Northern states and the erection of a Hanoverian monarchy." For Gerry, there was only one solution to that problem: "If we do not kill them, they will kill us."[6] Although, mercifully, the Republicans never acted on that extreme paranoia, they apparently never repudiated it.

Elbridge Gerry will be forever remembered for inspiring the invention of the term "gerrymandering" for the political practice of rigging elections by redrawing the districts to advantage one party over another. He might also be cited for personifying the concept of "projection." People with deep character flaws that they refuse to acknowledge, let alone overcome, tend to project their vilest characteristics onto hated others. By rigging elections, Gerry was subverting the Constitution and the founders' intentions. At the same time, he imagined himself an outstanding patriot. Rather than admit that his behavior sullied his self-image, he instead accused others of trying to destroy the Republic. Such pathologies are hardly rare in American political history.

The peace movement climaxed with the Hartford Convention.[7] By a vote of 260 to 90 on October 18, 1814, the Massachusetts state assembly approved a resolution calling for all the New England states to send delegates to a constitutional convention in Hartford. When the convention opened on December 15, there were only twenty-six delegates from Massachusetts, Rhode Island, and Connecticut. They met in closed session until January 5, 1815. Unfortunately, no one kept a record so exactly what they discussed will remain forever a mystery. The delegates did issue a report on January 12.

Those who feared or hoped that the convention would call for peace and separation would be either relieved or disappointed. As for the war, after three weeks of intense debate, the delegates simply condemned the Madison administration for incompetence and failing to defend New England. More generally, they criticized being ruled by "Virginians" with their policies of embargoes, slavery, and imperialism. Their most important achievement was to propose constitutional amendments that would eliminate the three-fifths-of-a-person tenet that allowed slaves to be counted in a state's electoral population; require a two-thirds vote to declare war, regulate trade, or admit new states; deny foreign-born citizens the right to hold public office; limit the president to one term; and prohibit a president from being from the same state as his predecessor. And then, with their work done, the delegates adjourned indefinitely. None of the proposals would ever be seriously considered by other states, let alone become amendments.

Republicans condemned the Hartford Convention as an act of sedition. The more extreme demanded that the military break up the convention and arrest the delegates. Madison was only slightly less harsh. He condemned the deserters as suffering from a "delusion" akin to "the reign of witchcraft."[8]

The most important sign that those who favored peace were a minority were the results of the 1814 midterm elections. The Republicans retained overwhelming strength in Congress, with 119 to 64 in the House, up from 114 to 68, and 28 to 8 in the Senate, down slightly from 30 to 6. Nearly all of them would continue to support the war, although with increasing criticism about how it was being run and doubt over whether it was justified after all.

45

The Treaty of Ghent

As more and more Americans concluded that the war had been a terrible mistake and should be ended as soon as possible, diplomats on the Atlantic's far side were trying to achieve just that. The first agreement was negotiated by Gallatin with Castlereagh in London. The site of the talks was switched from Gothenburg to Ghent, a far more convenient location for communication and transportation across the English Channel and the Atlantic Ocean. Letters chased down the other envoys at their far-flung locations. Each settled his affairs and made his way to Ghent. Adams and Russell arrived on June 24, Clay the following day, Bayard on June 27, and Gallatin on July 6. They lodged at the Hôtel des Pays-Bas.

Having assembled, they discovered that there was no one to negotiate with. Whitehall's strategy was to put off any serious talks until after British armies had chalked up decisive victories. The British could then dictate rather than negotiate a peace. So the commissioners cooled their heels in Ghent for nearly six weeks until the British delegation arrived.

On paper, Madison had assembled an excellent diplomatic team. Each man was highly intelligent and accomplished. No one at that time and few since had amassed more diplomatic experience than John Quincy Adams. In 1778, as a lad of eleven years, he had accompanied his father to Paris where John Senior served as an American envoy. At only fourteen, he served as the secretary to Francis Dana at Saint Petersburg; thereafter, he was minister to the Netherlands from 1794 to 1796, Portugal in 1796, Prussia from 1797 to 1801, and Saint Petersburg from

1809 to 1815. In comparison, Albert Gallatin had only a fraction of the experience but, with his natural graciousness, wielded greater diplomatic skills than the acerbic Adams. After Adams, Jonathan Russell had served the most time as a diplomat; he had been the chargé d'affaires at Paris in 1811 and at London from November 1811 to September 1, 1812. John Bayard was most famous for having cast the decisive vote in Jefferson's favor during the deadlocked 1800 presidential election. With eight years in the House and nine in the Senate, he was a skilled politician. Of the five envoys, Henry Clay may well have had the most intellectual gifts after Adams, and he loved to parade them.

Unfortunately, as the weeks passed, they increasingly got on one another's nerves. Personalities clashed, especially between such titanic egos as Adams and Clay. Adams was a unifying force for the other four envoys but not in a positive sense. They reviled Adams for his snobbery, aloofness, and condescension.

The Americans felt enormous relief when the British team finally showed up and settled into the Hôtel du Lion d'Or on August 6. By all accounts, the three envoys— James Gambier, Henry Goulburn, and William Adams—were Britain's diplomatic second-stringers. Gambier was an admiral and the team leader, Goulburn was a member of Parliament and had served as undersecretary for war and home affairs, and Adams was a prominent lawyer. They lacked both diplomatic experience and full negotiating authority. Foreign Minister Castlereagh, who was the ghost at the diplomatic table, made up for that deficiency. The envoys would continually have to refer back to him for instructions on often the most minor points.[1]

The inadequate skills and powers of the British team were not a calculated Whitehall ploy to insult the sensitive Americans. Britain's best diplomats were assembling in Vienna. A congress of all the European states was convening that fall to settle a quarter century of revolutions and wars that had ravaged the continent. In comparison, the negotiations at Ghent were a diplomatic sideshow.

The American and British delegations met for the first time at the Hôtel des Pays-Bas on August 8. Speaking for their respective teams, Adams and Gambier exchanged courtesies and agreed that thereafter they would alternate meetings between their residences. Over the next four and a half months, the negotiations would be as tough and unyielding as they were mostly civil. On his way to Vienna, Castlereagh dropped by from September 18 to 20 to stiffen the diplomatic backbones of his envoys. The British seized the diplomatic initiative by insisting that any treaty be based on the right of impressment, the inclusion of their Indian allies in the United States in any settlement, and a revision of the boundary favorable to Canada. Those demands forced the Americans to play defense. A series of long memorandums were exchanged in which each side asserted its own position and refuted the other's. They would then elaborate on those written arguments during their sessions.[2]

The Americans succeeded in getting the British to yield on the Indian ally issue when each side finally agreed to enjoy the exclusive right to negotiate and trade with Indians in its own territory. That dashed British hopes of erecting an Indian buffer state between the United States and Canada. The American case rested on two key points. All Indians in American territory were subject to American law and would be dealt with by treaty with the United States. Britain's conspiracy with those tribes had been among the reasons for the war and would not be tolerated.

On impressment, however, the British refused to budge on their "right" to stop ships of any kind and search them for subjects of the king and deserters from the Royal Navy. What's more, the war's end in Europe had rendered the issue moot. The two sides eventually agreed to disagree on the issue and took it off the table.

The boundary question was the trickiest for two reasons—their positions were far apart and much of the territory in question had yet to be explored let alone mapped. They disputed where the line should be drawn west of Lake Superior and between Maine and New Brunswick. On the western frontier, the British demanded a line that included the Mississippi River's headwaters and thus the right to navigate the river. As for the eastern boundary, the 1783 Treaty of Paris had drawn the line from the middle of the St. Croix River to its source and then westward until it reached the source of the Connecticut River. British troops now occupied the Maine coast as far as Castine. Whitehall wanted a line drawn as far south into Maine as possible. They finally agreed to extend the boundary along the 49th parallel westward from Lake Superior. They could not, however, agree on an eastern boundary and left its fate to a future commission.

Then there was the fisheries issue. The 1783 Treaty of Paris had allowed Americans to fish in Canadian waters off Newfoundland and dry their catch ashore. The British tried to revoke that right. The Americans offered a compromise whereby America's fishing rights and Britain's navigation rights on the Mississippi would both be accepted, but the British spurned that notion. The two sides shelved that issue as well.

The Americans did not press for the cession of any part of Canada. Given the humiliating failures of America's northern campaigns, to have insisted on even part of that land would have provoked an angry response. Instead, the Americans called for the Great Lakes to be demilitarized. The British disagreed and that proposal also died.

The British had initially favored grounding a peace in *uti possidetis*, or allowing each to keep what it had taken. That deal would have been slightly to Britain's advantage. After more than two years of fighting, neither side had gained more than toeholds of the other's territory. The Americans occupied Forts Erie and Amherstburg just across the Niagara and Detroit rivers, while the British held Castine and Machias on the Maine coast, Fort Niagara on Lake Ontario, and Fort Michilimackinac. The Americans insisted on status quo ante bellum by which each was restored those lands it had before the war. The British finally gave in on that crucial point.

After news of Washington's burning on August 24 reached Ghent, the British tried to capitalize on that latest and most demoralizing defeat. On October 8, they submitted a memorandum that essentially demanded the Americans bow to their positions or else the talks would end.[3]

The Americans took five days to debate and draft a reply in which they stood their ground. News of American victories at Baltimore and Plattsburgh, however, did little to alleviate their poor diplomatic hand. When the British were just as obstinate, the Americans sent back a dispirited letter to Monroe on October 25, in which they wrote that any peace treaty was currently unlikely. The British were deliberately prolonging talks so that they could send over more military forces for a decisive victory.[4]

The British suffered their own constraints. After two decades of nearly continuous warfare, the national debt had soared, the treasury was nearly empty, and the public had no stomach for any more death, taxes, or other sacrifices. With Napoleon's defeat and exile, Britain faced no foreign threat. What was the point of warring against the United States? The great Duke of Wellington himself had refused to command a campaign against the United States and advised against trying to conquer any American territory. The virtually universal sentiment favored a face-saving peace in which both sides could declare victory and then return home. At Vienna, Castlereagh's diplomacy was undercut by the distractions and demands of the American war.

Castlereagh finally broke the deadlock by calling a draw. The treaty would be founded on the status quo ante bellum, and was silent on the war's causes, including impressment. The delegates signed the Treaty of Ghent on Christmas Eve 1814. Before the envoys went their separate ways, the Americans hosted a public dinner at the Hôtel de Ville for their British counterparts and local officials. Adams and Gambier toasted each other's country. A band played "God Save the King" and "Hail Columbia."[5]

The relief at having finally signed a treaty was overshadowed by the fear that Madison either would not submit it for ratification or, if he did, that the Senate would reject it. For those reasons, Whitehall refused an armistice and insisted that the war would continue until ratifications were formally exchanged in Washington. The more belligerent in the cabinet hoped that the Americans would not ratify the treaty. That refusal would allow a British armada sailing toward the gulf coast to seize Mobile and New Orleans, and thus radically transform the strategic and diplomatic calculus. They also planned to offer a separate peace with the New England states and perhaps an association with Britain.

George IV, the Prince Regent, would have none of that. He had always opposed fighting the Americans and welcomed the chance to end the war. He ratified the treaty on December 28, only five days after the signing. Beyond that action, he could do nothing else. The armada could not be recalled. The fate of the treaty, along with the armada, was now in the hands of the Americans. And one man would be crucial in deciding both questions.

46

The Battle of New Orleans

Of all the warriors that the English fought over their long history, perhaps none would exceed and few would match Andrew Jackson in fierceness and hatred.[1] His antipathy to the English was deeply rooted. He bore scars across his face and left hand where a British officer had slashed him with his sword because Jackson, then thirteen years old, refused to blacken his boots. By the time he was fourteen, his entire family had died of malnutrition and disease, most in a British internment camp in South Carolina during the Revolutionary War. Those tragedies ignited within him an inextinguishable rage. Thereafter he was driven to seek out and destroy a series of enemies against whom he could vent some of that hatred before it devoured him. Fighting and dueling were enormous releases for him; a pistol ball was embedded in his chest from the one man he killed.

While he was renowned for his hair-trigger temper and unflinching courage, he made his fortune as a lawyer and land speculator. After the Revolutionary War, Jackson supported himself as a saddlemaker's apprentice and schoolteacher before passing the bar in 1787 and moving to Jonesborough, then in western North Carolina. His success as a frontier lawyer probably owed more to his power to sway a jury with the sheer force of his personality than from any legal arguments. He was named the Solicitor of North Carolina's Western District in 1788 and retained the post after that land became the Tennessee Territory in 1791. He served as a delegate to Tennessee's Constitutional Convention, as that state's representative to Congress in 1796, and as a U.S. senator in 1797. He then resigned a year later to be a judge on Tennessee's supreme court.

Given Jackson's insatiable thirst for battles of all kinds, it may be startling to realize that he was a latecomer to the profession of war. Although at age thirteen he was a courier during the American Revolution, he saw no battles and was soon a prisoner. His first military command did not come until 1801, when he was made a militia colonel at age thirty-four. It would be another twelve years before he actually led troops into battle in the Creek War; he was then forty-six.

Jackson proved to be as relentless at diplomacy as he was at war. He devoted most of the summer of 1814 to conducting diplomacy with the Creeks at Fort Jackson. Under the Treaty of Fort Jackson, signed on August 9, the Creeks ceded 20 million acres of their land in return for peace. After he vanquished the Creeks, his next objective was clear. He could finally begin to seek vengeance against the nation that was responsible for the death of his family three decades earlier.[2]

For years, British agents had used Pensacola as their base for arming and inciting the Creeks and other southeastern tribes against the settlers. That support became open when, on August 14, Maj. Edward Nicolls disembarked with a hundred troops and dispersed them into forts ringing Pensacola Bay. Jackson wrote Governor Manrique González that he must either expel the British or else face American retribution and possibly war between the United States and Spain.[3]

When González replied defiantly, Jackson resolved to capture Pensacola and finally rid the southern frontier of that nest of Spanish, British, and Indian intrigue. Jackson sent word of his plan to the Madison administration and then marched off to Pensacola. The president and his cabinet viewed his plan with alarm. The last thing they needed was war against both Spain and Britain. Monroe sent him orders to desist, but they reached him too late.[4]

Jackson acted with typical decisiveness. He marched his forty-one hundred regulars, militia, and Indians into Pensacola on November 7. Faced with overwhelming odds, the Spanish governor surrendered the city and his five hundred troops. The British blew up their forts defending the bay and withdrew to a position on the Apalachicola River. Learning that the British would soon attack Mobile or New Orleans, Jackson then turned his army's back on Pensacola and marched west.[5]

The British were indeed approaching. In September, Admiral Cochrane received orders to muster seventy-five hundred troops and a flotilla, and capture Mobile and New Orleans. Unlike the Washington campaign, this would be no mere large-scale, destructive raid. Cochrane was to take and hold both cities. Leading the invading army was Gen. Edward Pakenham, the Duke of Wellington's brother-in-law. Nearly all the regiments had fought in the Spanish campaign. Having repeatedly defeated the French, the redcoats were highly confident that they would swiftly rout any ragtag Americans who opposed them.

Jackson reached New Orleans on December 1. He found a city nearly denuded of defenses and the population panicky and even fatalistic. His arrival spurred Governor William Claiborne into action. Together they set to work fortifying the approaches to the city and mobilizing the militia for duty. On December 16, Jackson declared martial law with the stern words: "Those who are not for us are against us, and will be dealt with accordingly."[6]

No American army had ever before been so diverse. There were regular infantry regiments; militia from Kentucky, Tennessee, Mississippi, and Louisiana; a battalion of free blacks; several score Choctaw Indians; and more than a hundred "pirates" led by Jean Lafitte, who for years had conducted a massive smuggling operation from his lair deep in the bayous near the coast.

Pakenham first landed his army at Cat Island, eighty miles east of New Orleans, on December 13. That position gave him three approaches to New Orleans: from the east via Lake Borgne, overland from the northeast via the Gentilly Plain, and from the north via Lake Pontchartrain. Pakenham chose the direct approach through Lake Borgne.

Lt. Thomas Jones blocked that route with 185 men and five gunboats. The British attacked on December 14 with twelve hundred troops led by Gen. John Keane. Against overwhelming odds, Jones and his men put up a spirited fight and inflicted a hundred casualties before surrendering.

Pakenham established a base on Pea Island and began bringing up supplies to launch his campaign's next stage. Then, as luck would have it, nature aided the Americans. A freak winter front plunged temperatures below freezing for nearly a week. The British could merely huddle shivering in their tents and ships before resuming their slow advance. It was not until the morning of December 23 that the lead force of sixteen hundred troops under Col. William Thornton reached the Jacques Villeré plantation, on the Mississippi River eight miles downriver from New Orleans.

That night, after learning of Thornton's appearance, Jackson mustered eighteen hundred men and marched against him, while two warships, the 22-gun *Louisiana* and 14-gun *Caroline* slipped quietly downstream. The warships opened fire when they were adjacent to the British camp. That signaled the troops to launch a frontal attack. It was a bloody free-for-all of shooting, clubbing, and stabbing in the black night, illuminated only by campfires and gunshot flashes. In the confusion, many of the 275 British and 213 American casualties were undoubtedly inflicted by their own respective sides.

After routing the British, Jackson collected his scattered men and withdrew to a canal running between the river and a cypress swamp five miles from the city.

There he had breastworks constructed of earth, cypress logs, and cotton bales. He also prudently had two other lines built behind his army just in case.

Reinforcements brought British forces up to four thousand on Christmas Day, when Pakenham himself arrived and established his headquarters in the Villeré mansion. On December 28, he led his army forward but soon ordered a withdrawal after a sharp skirmish against the entrenched Americans and bombardment from the warships. He would wait until all his troops and siege guns were in place before attempting another attack.

By New Year's Day, his army was in place, and he had four batteries behind barricades. The British guns opened fire and soon the American guns were firing back. The artillery duel lasted two and a half hours. With more skilled gunners and stronger defenses, the Americans knocked out all four batteries and killed or wounded about seventy-five gunners while losing only thirty-five of their own.

Pakenham and his men were increasingly discouraged and frustrated. The Americans had checked their every move. At a council of war among his leading officers, Pakenham agreed that an all-out assault was the only option other than a withdrawal. He would hurl fifty-three hundred troops against Jackson's line, while Thornton would cross the Mississippi with six hundred men and attack seven hundred Kentucky and Louisiana militia and a battery under Gen. David Morgan.

Fog appeared to be a British ally as the redcoats marched or rowed into position on the morning of January 8. Ideally they could advance nearly to the American line before being spotted and then rush with lowered bayonets toward the breastworks. That was what Thornton and his men did. They crossed the river and attacked through the fog, routing the Americans and capturing the battery.

The eruption of gunfire alerted the four thousand Americans along the canal. They packed the breastworks and peered intensely into the fog before them. Pakenham waited too long before launching his attack. The morning sunlight devoured the fog as his troops marched forward in three broad columns and became clear targets around five hundred yards from the American line. The American cannons opened fire and tore through the massed British ranks, leaving scores thrashing and screaming. Within three hundred yards, the riflemen lowered their barrels, squinted down the sights, and gently squeezed triggers. Scores more redcoats were knocked back dead or with gaping wounds. Within a hundred yards, those with muskets opened fire. At that point, most of the British broke and ran; some rushed forward and fired at the breastworks; only a handful splashed across the canal and tried to climb over the wall before being shot or clubbed to death. As the British fled or milled in confusion, hundreds of Americans

scrambled down and advanced. Over five hundred redcoats dropped their muskets and held high their hands.

The battle of New Orleans was America's greatest victory and Britain's worst
defeat of the war. When the guns finally fell silent, the British had suffered 2,037
casualties, including Pakenham, who was shot dead, while Jackson lost only 13
men on his line and 55 on the other side of the river. Throughout the entire campaign, the 2,450 British casualties included 400 killed, 1,500 wounded, and 550
captured or missing, while the approximately 350 American casualties included 50
killed, 200 wounded, and 100 captured or missing.[7]

Gen. John Lambert took command. A council of war decided against an immediate retreat. It would be suicidal to withdraw from their fortified camp with the
victorious Americans on their heels. Instead the British strengthened their
defenses, began sending the wounded back to the coast, and awaited the arrival
of Cochrane who was sailing up the Mississippi. If that powerful fleet arrived, it
could bombard Jackson into either retreat or surrender.

Sixty-five miles downstream, Fort St. Philip blocked Cochrane's advance. The
British warships opened a massive bombardment, but the fort held and Cochrane
was forced to withdraw downstream and out to sea. Learning of that latest defeat,
Lambert withdrew his battered army toward the transports on Lake Borgne on
January 18.

The campaign was not yet over. The British tried again to take Mobile. The
armada anchored beyond cannon shot of Fort Bowyer in early February. General
Lambert landed with a thousand troops and a half-dozen siege guns. Faced with
overwhelming odds, Maj. William Lawrence surrendered his fort and 370 men on
February 11. The next day, Lambert was preparing to take Mobile when he
received word of the peace treaty.

The war would continue at sea for months as America's intrepid frigate captains were among the last to learn of the Treaty of Ghent. In victory and defeat,
they proved that American sailors were as valiant and skilled as the very best of
the Royal Navy. The American navy suffered its worst defeat at sea on January
15, 1815, when the 52-gun *President*, commanded by Stephen Decatur, was over-
taken by three smaller and faster frigates, the 40-gun *Endymion*, the 38-gun
Pomone, and the 38-gun *Tenedoes*. Although the *President's* broadsides damaged
the enemy warships, Decatur finally struck his colors after his ship was disabled.
Capt. Charles Stewart scored the greatest American victory when his 52-gun
Constitution squared off with the 34-gun *Cyane* and 20-gun *Levant* on February 20,
1815, and blasted both into surrender. Perhaps appropriately, the war at sea ended
in a draw.

Upon receiving a copy of the treaty on February 14, Madison convened his cabinet to decide whether to accept it. That took three days of hard debate. The treaty was barren of any of the grandiose promises with which the War Hawks had marketed their war. Over two and a half years of a disastrous and brutal struggle had banished the fantasies and delusions from all but the most extreme Republicans. Now nearly all Americans just wanted the war to end. The stunning victory at New Orleans provided a fig leaf for getting out. On February 17, 1815, Madison sent the Treaty of Ghent, along with all relevant documents to the Senate, which unanimously approved it that day. The treaty was sent by a fast vessel to London, where it arrived on March 13, and was duly accepted by the Prince Regent and Whitehall. The War of 1812 was now officially over.

47

A Distant Mirror?

U ntil the more recent chimeras of Vietnam and Iraq, no war in American history was more reviled than Mr. Madison's. There was certainly ample cause to question its wisdom then and since. Although the War of 1812 has been called a draw, in reality both countries lost heavily, especially the United States.[1]

The war was an economic disaster for America. Trade enriched the nation with desperately needed hard money and products that could not be made as well or at all. War deprived the United States of that vital source of wealth and thus power. American exports plummeted from $61.3 million in 1811 to $6.9 million in 1814, and imports from $53.4 million to $13 million. Much of what trade did occur was carried by America's rivals. American ship tonnage drastically fell from 948,000 to 60,000. That trade collapse slashed government revenues from $13.3 million to $6 million.[2]

The war's total official cost reached $68,783,122 in 1815. The real cost was more than double that, $158 million, which included $93 million in military expenses, $49 million for veterans benefits, and $16 million for interest on the national debt. To pay for the immediate war, the Madison administration borrowed $80 million. The national debt skyrocketed from $45 million in 1812 to $127 million in 1815.[3]

While it may have been ideologically correct, a kind of collective madness let the Bank of the United States charter expire on the war's eve. State-chartered banks proliferated after the Bank of the United States died, with the number nearly doubling from 112 in 1812 to 202 in 1814. Virtually none were guided by government oversight or national interests. Nearly all operated under the principles of "anything for a buck" and "let the buyer beware." In that Darwinian marketplace, get-rich-quick speculations rather than cool-headed, long-term investments prevailed. The result was a severe misallocation of scarce capital that undercut both the nation's wealth and power to finance and fight a war. And, when it came to borrowing money to wage its war, the Madison administration ended up paying much higher interest rates from private investors and state banks than it would have if the Bank of the United States had not been destroyed.[4]

The impact of the Madison administration's spend-and-borrow policies inflicted harsh blows on the American economy and people. Higher interest rates and the diversion of that much money from productive to paper investments reduced spending. Of course, that would be somewhat offset as the government used paper to buy goods and services. But the net effect would be a depressed and distorted economy in which the prices for scarcer goods, services, and capital soared higher, leaving most people worse off.

The war imposed a classic economic trade-off on Americans between guns and butter. While contractors and insider traders made out like bandits, most people had to make do with less and pay more for it. Atop that was the economic devastation inflicted by the looting and burning by British soldiers around the Chesapeake Bay and along the frontier, as well as the losses of American vessels and cargoes at sea. Those losses will never be adequately calculated.

The war inflicted economic damage on the nation's development far beyond the vicious cycle of worsening budget deficits, national debt, interest rates, and growth. When nations or individuals live beyond their means, they will have to harshly cutback their lifestyles and forgo opportunities in the years and decades ahead. By borrowing rather than taxing, the War Hawks heaped the financial burden onto the shoulders of future generations, and thus robbed them of economic opportunities and wealth they might have otherwise enjoyed.

Did the United States get anything from the war other than death, debt, and destruction? Not from the British, who ceded no land or reparations. The Spanish, however, did not resist as American troops marched first into Mobile and then into Pensacola; although the Americans would withdraw from the latter, they would permanently hold all land west of the Perdido River. The respective northwest and southwest Indian campaigns of Harrison and Jackson shattered the power of the surviving eastern tribes. Thereafter the Indians had no choice but to sign a succession of treaties that let the United States devour ever more of their land and finally expelled them west of the Mississippi. Those territorial gains in the northwest and southwest could have been achieved without a war against Britain.

The war cost the United States a critical toehold on the Pacific that had been established in 1811, when John Jacob Astor's Pacific Fur Company set up a trading post at the mouth of the Columbia River, near where Lewis, Clark, and their men had wintered five years earlier. That year, two expeditions converged there, one by sea and the other, led by Wilson Hunt and Robert Stuart, overland all the way from St. Louis. For the next two years, they traded and trapped furs throughout the region. Then, in 1813 amid the war with Britain, the Pacific Company surrendered all of its trading posts, furs, and equipment to the North West Company. It would take more than three decades before the United States could oust Britain from the northwest and take over that territory.

The War Hawks shrugged off all the lost wealth and blood that America had suffered during the war. They believed that the nation had won something far more critical, if impossible to measure. Henry Clay insisted that before the war the United States had suffered "the scorn of the universe, the contempt of ourselves" compared to "our present situation—security and confidence at home."[5] Those who opposed the war retorted that a fleeting boost in national pride and prestige was a meager prize compared to the enormous loss of life and treasure.

A few bright spots glittered in the Madison administration's otherwise dismal handling of the war. The United States was able to mobilize, organize, and sustain far more men, money, and material more quickly in the War of 1812 than in the Revolutionary War, while the scale of the fighting, number of battles, and casualties during the former nearly equaled those of the latter.

This greater military power was grounded in the nation's greater economic and political power. A central government; diversified, unified, and dynamic economy; and sophisticated financial markets made a crucial difference. Most money, arms, munitions, and provisions were massed at home and were far more ample during the War of 1812 than the Revolutionary War, when most of those important sources of power came sporadically from overseas. Nonetheless, the record of how well those men were trained, supplied, and led is charitably mixed. Certainly the Americans who fought in the War of 1812 suffered less than those of the Revolutionary War.

On paper an astonishing 528,000 men, or 47 percent of men between sixteen and forty-six years old, mustered during the War of 1812, although only 14 percent of them were actually in units under federal control. During the war, 62,674 men served among forty-six regular infantry regiments, four rifle regiments, three regiments each of artillery and light dragoons, and one of light artillery. The rest were state volunteers or militia, of whom nearly half never marched beyond their village greens. Another 20,000 men served in the navy or marines.[6]

For the 286,000 men who reached a front, the chances of getting home in one piece were actually quite good. In battle, the Americans lost 2,260 killed, of which 1,950 were soldiers, 265 sailors, and 45 marines, and 4,505 wounded, of which 4,000 were soldiers, 439 sailors, and 66 marines, for a total of 6,765 casualties. Disease killed perhaps as many as another 17,000 men.[7]

Leadership was the army's Achilles' heel. The record of army generals like Hull, Dearborn, Izard, and Wilkinson were varying levels of disastrous. They lacked even the most rudimentary of command skills, knowing little of logistics, training, strategy, tactics, and, most importantly, how to inspire men to face death without question or hesitation. A few were simply cowards. The biggest reason for these failures was a lack of rigorous standards and training that could weed out the worst from their betters. The army's leadership expanded to eight major generals and sixteen brigadier generals; few of them had ever before commanded a regiment, let alone an army. The officer corps soared from 674 to 3,493; few of those men had ever headed more than a militia company, and a fraction of that a regular company.[8]

Mercifully for the American cause, three generals—William Henry Harrison, Jacob Brown, and Andrew Jackson—proved to be outstanding commanders by any measure. The respective victories of Harrison and Jackson at the Thames and New Orleans were decisive in securing fronts at opposite ends of the nation. Jacob Brown is hardly a household name today, but he won four of America's nine major victories of the war.[9] The victorious battles of those three generals were the culmination of carefully planned and executed campaigns fought by well-trained, supplied, and motivated troops.

Winfield Scott was a brilliant regimental commander who trained and inspired his men to such professional heights that they could square off with and defeat the finest British regiments. Unfortunately, first politics and then a severe wound prevented him from joining Jackson, Brown, and Harrison as a first-rate army commander in that war. He would have to wait a generation before he would prove his gifts leading an army in the Mexican War.

It was the American navy rather than army that displayed consistent professionalism at all levels. Although outnumbered fifty to one, the navy performed wonders by emerging victorious from two of three sea battles, and American warships and privateers captured over seventeen hundred British merchant vessels. The strategy of loosening the frigates against British shipping forced the Royal Navy to weaken its blockade of the American coast and caused British insurance rates to soar. The strategy's only flaw was for American frigates to fight rather than

flee British frigates. That policy was potentially disastrous given the vast dispar-
ity in naval forces. The British could afford to lose naval battles that the
Americans could not afford even to win. A British or American frigate represented 1 percent and 20 percent of the two nations' respective total number. So
for the United States, the sinking or capture of just one frigate represented a major
defeat, while victory was inevitably Pyrrhic since the frigates were often so battered that they would be sidelined in port for months of repairs.[10]

Overall, the War of 1812 was an utter failure of American power. For that, no
one deserves more blame than President James Madison, whose defects of leadership and ideology exacerbated each other. He was intellectually gifted but much
more at the theory than practice of politics. His ideal calling was a classroom
rather than the Executive Mansion, or even the legislative chamber. Given his
shyness and poor oratory skills, his students might have remarked that his lectures
were as dull as they were profound. As a politician, he had certainly won well-
deserved praise both at the Convention and in Congress. Yet somehow the skills
he had earlier displayed eluded him when he was president. He was overwhelmed
by the demands of his office and the consequences of his policies. Then there was
his ideology. The essence of Jeffersonism is the catchy but self-defeating slogan of
"the government that governs least governs best," with its attendant notions of
state's rights, home defense, representation without taxation, and liberties without duties. The result was a vicious cycle of American power by which gross inad-
equacies of leadership, government, revenues, diplomacy, troops, warships, and
national will eroded one another.

Underlying all the rationales cited by Madison and his fellow War Hawks was
an overweening, false sense of "honor," "pride," and "manhood." The most zealous advocates for war were mostly thirty-somethings who sought to match or surpass the battle and frontier tales of their elders. The War Hawks were ecstatic as
they led the nation to war. Then, perversely, few actually volunteered for the front
and most were stingy when the bills came due. Nearly all were content either to
run the war or criticize those who did, far from any actual fighting. They
adamantly refused to call off the war after news arrived that Whitehall had
revoked its Orders in Council and was willing to give up the practice if not the
principle of impressment. They insisted on staying the course even as America
suffered one humiliating defeat after another while the toll in blood and treasure
soared. The ideology of the War Hawks at once reflected and shaped their emotional needs and demands.

An understanding of why the War of 1812 was fought at all, and so incompe-
tently, only begins with James Madison and the War Hawks. The psyches of the

president and his men at once reflected and shaped a national psychosis. Contrary to the assertions of the War Hawks, the United States faced no imminent British threat in 1812. It was well known that Whitehall had no desire for war with the United States, was certainly not preparing an invasion, and had not even seized more American vessels, cargoes, or sailors than in previous years. But the War Hawks rejected any information that conflicted with their comforting ideological nostrums. Ultimately, the War Hawks took the United States to war to protect abstract principles and enflamed feelings rather than hard economic and strategic interests. Tragically, that would not be the last American war fought for those reasons.

The Art of American Power
in the Early Republic

It is impossible not to look forward to distant times, when our rapid multiplication
will expand itself beyond those limits, and cover the whole northern,
if not southern continent, with a people speaking the same language, governed
in similar forms, and by similar laws.

THOMAS JEFFERSON

I must study politics and war, that my sons may have the liberty to study
mathematics and philosophy. My sons ought to study mathematics and philosophy,
geography, natural history and naval architecture, navigation, commerce and
agriculture, in order to give their children a right to study painting, poetry, music,
architecture, statuary, tapestry, and porcelain.

JOHN ADAMS

Wealth and Power

National wealth and power are inseparable. By 1815, America was a far wealth-
ier and thus potentially more powerful country than it had been in 1775. In the
beginning, thirteen colonies broke free of a British straightjacket that determined
what they could make and with whom they could trade. Four decades later, a
national market unified seventeen states. That progress was not a smooth, steady
climb. Along the way, the economy contracted sharply several times. The government was the culprit in the two most severe depressions with its embargo from
1807 to 1809 and war against Britain from 1812 to 1815. Yet, overall, Americans
would have been astonished at how much better off most folks were had they
somehow been whisked from that era's start to its finish. The population more

than quadrupled from 2.5 million to 10 million people, while an ever larger proportion of the people were of the "middling sort" who led comfortable and often affluent lives.

Jeffersonians could take little credit for those accomplishments. Indeed, that remarkable economic transformation of the United States mostly happened despite rather than because of how Jefferson, Madison, and the Republican Party wielded power.

The vision and policies of Alexander Hamilton largely fueled this economic revolution. Underlying Hamiltonism was a partnership between the public and private sectors that worked together to expand the nation's wealth, and thus power. The government's role was to nurture infrastructure, industries, and capital markets that are the skeleton, muscle, and mind of a dynamic modern economy. His most vital specific policies included selective tariffs; fiscal sanity; the assumption of the state debts; a hard, fixed national currency; and, above all, the Bank of the United States. The result was a stable, expanding, unified capital market that financed investments in an array of dynamic enterprises and industries. Hamilton's policies probably advanced America's economic development by at least a generation.

The Bank of the United States was the core of Hamilton's economic revolution. For two decades after it opened for business in 1791, the bank performed a crucial role in developing America's economy by acting as the lender of first resort for the government and lender of last resort for other banks and investors. The bank eventually had nine branches including Philadelphia, New York, Boston, Baltimore, Charleston, Norfolk, Washington, Savannah, and New Orleans. Each branch directly and indirectly developed the regional economy by collecting and lending money, along with the sheer example of its sound banking practices. It was required to keep a ratio of one to five between its assets and liabilities, or its money in the vault and its loans.

The bank at once regulated, lent money to, and competed with other banks. It lent money only to those with sound reputations and proposals. As such it restrained the irrational exuberance that could feed frenzied speculative bubbles that inevitably popped with disastrous economic results. It attracted foreign investments to the United States, both as investors in and borrowers from the bank. And all along, the bank made a steady profit.

During its twenty years, the bank led the development of a national financial market. In 1791, there were only four banks in the United States, with one each in its biggest cities, Philadelphia, New York, Boston, and Baltimore. That number expanded to twenty-nine by 1800 and then tripled to ninety by 1811. The financial system expanded and integrated as those banks and other financial institutions lent to and borrowed from one another. By encouraging sound investments rather than get-rich-quick speculations, the Bank of the United States attracted allies and provoked enemies. Investors loved and speculators hated the Bank of the United States. The "loose money" advocates eventually defeated those who promoted "sound money." It was the speculators allied with Republicans and their philosophy of states rights and antifederalism who killed the bank by blocking the renewal of its twenty-year charter in 1811.

The result was a double whammy to American power. The bank was forced to liquidate its assets. The private shareholders were paid their due, with about $7 million in gold going to the bank's foreign holders. The federal government's share was divvied among state banks by political rather than financial criteria. Those state banks mostly squandered the windfall either by mismanagement or corruption. As if that were not disastrous enough, the Republicans destroyed the Bank of the United States on the eve of the War of 1812. The nation's financial system imploded just as the government was in desperate need for money. The federal government was forced to borrow money at outrageous interest rates and discounts. Meanwhile by 1815, the state banks had issued $170 million of depreciated paper on $82 million of capital.[1]

After Congress killed the bank in 1811, the financial sector became more chaotic, unstable, and perilous. The number of incorporated banks exploded from 90 to 246 over the next five years, with the amount of money on their books more than doubling from $28 million to $68 million. There were hundreds of other moneylenders in the form of unincorporated banks, insurance companies, and merchant houses. Many of those businesses were fly-by-night operations or black holes that pocketed money from the greedy and gullible. That rapid growth was anything but healthy for the American economy. The result was soaring inflation and the crowding out of investments by speculation. Although a majority in Congress came to their senses and voted for the establishment of the Second Bank of the United States in 1816, the damage had been done. The Second Bank would need a generation to clean up the disaster inflicted on the economy by the Republican Party's destruction of the First Bank.[2]

The battle over the Bank of the United States was only the most prominent in a constant war over the fate of American wealth and power. In the tug-of-war between the two parties, the Federalists had a slight edge from 1789 to 1801. The Washington and Adams presidencies staved off Republican pressure to wage an economic war with Britain that would hurt America much more than its adversary. Yet, at the end, they had little to show for their efforts. The Jay Treaty with

Britain was excoriated by Republicans for failing to achieve reciprocity. Although Adams did take the nation into the Quasi-War with France over freedom of the seas and trade, he relegated himself and his party to the political wilderness by his administration's excesses, follies, and conceits, culminating with the unconstitutional repressive measures of the Sedition Act.

The Republicans took control over the Executive Mansion and Congress in 1801, and they and their ideological descendants would hold those institutions for most of the next half century. The American tendency to shoot itself in the economic foot dates from their tenure in power. The Jeffersonians believed in war by trade rather than arms; they thought that they could bend foreign opponents to their will by denying them American goods and markets.

Unfortunately, the Republican policy of wielding partial or complete trade embargoes as a diplomatic weapon repeatedly backfired, inflicting grievous damage on America's economy and resulting in an unnecessary and disastrous war. The reason was that the Republicans simply did not understand the nature of economic power any better than they did military power. They believed that economic isolation would strengthen the United States, when it actually deprived the nation of all the wealth that could be earned from international trade.

A key justification for the War of 1812 was to protect America's right of "freedom of the seas." Yet the worst enemy of that freedom was not Whitehall's policies that licensed its warships and privateers to confiscate certain American cargoes and crew members. America's international trade and thus economic growth soared when the federal government placed no restrictions on merchants, and withered when it did.

Merchants and shipowners were well aware of the risks they took in the destinations, cargoes, and crews of their vessels; they defied those risks amid a transatlantic naval war because they coldly calculated that the odds favored their profits even if they lost a cargo or more. As for impressment, it was certainly horrendous for those who were kidnapped from American to British service or, if they were British deserters, executed. But from a business point of view, the loss of time for the search and seizure was a minor inconvenience. The worst loss of time and money came when a shipowner tried to fight a confiscation order in the corrupt and lethargic British court system.

While Jefferson and Madison were clearly responsible for the era's two worst depressions and the killing of the Bank of the United States, they do receive high marks for their fiscal policies of imposing deep cuts on government spending. As a result, the national debt, which had fluctuated from a low of $75.4 million in 1791 to peak at $86.4 million in 1805, plunged to $45.2 million by 1813 before skyrocketing to $119.6 million by 1815 as the war bills came due and trade nearly vanished. Without "Mr. Madison's War" the national debt would have been eliminated by 1820 at the latest.[3]

Even more astonishing was the ability of Jefferson and Madison to reduce the debt while government revenues plummeted with the embargo. That took some mighty stringent belt-tightening by Albert Gallatin, who was the treasury secretary from 1801 to 1813, and was second only to Hamilton when it came to understanding and managing the economy in the early republic. The government's revenue included customs and miscellaneous sources, as well as a fleeting internal revenue from 1793 to 1803, and then again from 1814 to 1815. The surviving records reveal that the amount started at $4.4 million in 1791, dropped to $3.6 million the next year, and then fluctuated upward to peak at $17 million in 1808. Revenue dropped to $7.7 million and $9.3 million over the next two years as the economy suffered the embargo's full impact, rose to $14.4 million in 1811, dropped to $9.8 million in 1812, and then hit $14.3 million, $11.1 million, and $15.6 million during the three fiscal war years.[4]

Yet the Washington years matched or exceeded those of Jefferson and Madison in fiscal sanity. Although Hamilton's economic development program was expensive, it largely paid for itself with the greater revenues generated by an expanding, vigorous economy. The national budget doubled from $3.0 million in 1791, the first year for which records survive to $6.0 million in 1797, Washington's last budget. Yet the government actually enjoyed budget surpluses in four of those six fiscal years and was only slightly behind in the other two.

All along trade was the most powerful force shaping the fate of the federal budget and debt, as well as the national economy. For fifteen years from 1792 to 1807, the United States profited from Europe's wars. Trade nearly quadrupled during the Washington years, from $43.2 million in 1790 to $148.4 million in 1796. Trade fell slightly to $132.8 million as French along with Spanish and British seizures of American merchant vessels took a toll, but then actually rose to $162.1 million in 1800 as John Adams's naval Quasi-War against France made the seas safer. Trade soared to $205.1 million in 1801 as the Treaty of Mortefontaine with France took effect, rose steadily to peak at $246.8 million in 1807, but plunged to $111.8 million in 1809 during the worst of the embargo. The Madison years were no less a disaster to America's trade and the economy. After the embargo was revoked, trade jumped to $152.1 in 1810, followed by a decline to $115.5 in 1812. It then plummeted to $17.9 million in 1814, before skyrocketing to $165.5 in 1815, after the Treaty of Ghent was signed the previous Christmas Eve. The proportion of the nation's trade carried by American vessels ranged just as widely from a high of 96.6

percent in 1811 to a nadir of 52.0 percent in 1813. Nonetheless, overall the tonnage of American vessels engaged in international trade more than tripled from 564,000 to 1,732,000 from 1791 to 1815. American policy determined the volume, direction, and conveyors of trade during that era. American trade and shipping flourished when the United States allowed its merchants to sell freely and withered when it imposed restrictions.[5]

The total trade volume is only part of the story. Three other dimensions are vital to understanding the relationship between trade and American economic development. One is whether trade revenues roughly keep up with government expenditures, which has already been touched on. Then there are the questions of who is selling more than they are buying and what is being sold to whom.

The United States suffered trade deficits during twenty-four of the twenty-six years from 1790 through 1815. The deficits ranged from a low of $0.4 million in 1799 to $60.5 million in 1815. Ironically, America's only two trade surpluses—$7.9 million and $5.8 million—occurred when Madison was in the Executive Mansion.

The true Achilles' heel of America's trade and thus the economy during that era was its composition, which changed little. Americans mostly sold raw or semifinished materials like wheat, corn, tobacco, cotton, lumber, pig-iron, and livestock to others in return for a range of finished goods that they could not then make for themselves. That composition would have undoubtedly changed remarkably had Congress not killed Hamilton's 1792 plan to break the nation's dependence on British factory-made goods through myriad incentives to convince Americans to invest in mass production. Economic dependence directly translated into political and military weakness, with the severity of each linked to the others.

Territory and Power

The expanse and location of American territory was an essential facet of national power. From the 1776 Declaration of Independence through the 1814 Treaty of Ghent, American policy was to take, hold, and consolidate ever more territory into what would become a republican empire, or "empire of liberty" as Jefferson envisioned it. For nearly all Americans, this was not an oxymoron. The reality of "manifest destiny" preceded the coining of that phrase in 1845 by more than two centuries. From the founding of Jamestown in 1607, an expanding frontier was at once a place, a process, a necessity, and a state of mind.

The founders were in accord on America's destiny to eventually stretch across the continent and possibly beyond. Hamilton foresaw "the ascendancy of the United States in the system of American affairs." Standing in the way of that ambition were "the arrogant pretensions of the European." Eventually the United States would be able "to vindicate the honor of the human race, and to teach that assuming brother moderation." Likewise Jefferson envisioned the "distant times when our rapid multiplication will expand itself beyond those limits, and cover the whole northern, if not the southern continent, with a people speaking the same language, governed by similar laws." In his first inaugural address, he explained that America's imperial expansion would be peaceful because the nation was "separated by nature and a wide ocean from the exterminating havoc of one quarter of the globe; too high-minded to endure the degradations of the others; possessing a chosen country, with room enough for our descendants to the thousandth and thousandth generation."[6]

By the time Jefferson entered the Executive Mansion, the United States had already concluded most of the first phase of national expansion that began with the Declaration of Independence a quarter century earlier. The first step in that phase was for Britain to accept American independence and a specific expanse of territory. The British did so with the 1783 Treaty of Paris. But that was just the preliminary victory. The boundaries between the United States and the neighboring Spanish and British empires were illy defined. Power rather than law would ultimately determine where those lines would be drawn. The United States would not definitively settle those disputes until decades after 1815.

Those nagging boundary questions did not inhibit the United States from expanding elsewhere. The second phase involved one major and two minor acquisitions of American territory: Jefferson's purchase of the Louisiana Territory in 1803, and Madison's use of military rather than diplomatic power (twice) to assert an American claim to West Florida. Troops marched into the region around Baton Rouge in 1810 and into Mobile and all lands east to the Perdido River in 1813.

Of those three expansions, Jefferson's was the most controversial. The Louisiana Purchase doubled the nation's territory. Jefferson announced the Louisiana Purchase on July 4, 1803, thus pointedly drawing attention to the link between national expansion and independence. From the distance of more than two centuries, the Louisiana Purchase was beyond doubt the greatest achievement of Jefferson's presidency. However, that was not how most people saw it at the time. Even the majority in Congress that voted for annexation and appropriations recognized that the purchase could bring more problems than it was worth. Would the Louisiana Purchase exacerbate western separatist sentiments? And how would it affect the delicate balance between slave states and the lengthening list of states that had abolished slavery or were considering doing so? Those and related burning questions would not be resolved until sixty years later with the end of a civil war in which more than 750,000 men died and an immeasurable amount of national wealth was destroyed.

Arms and Power

War is history's ultimate catalyst, making or breaking the power of nations and governments, redrawing lines on maps, and robbing the lives and wealth of many while enriching the privileged few. To war or not to war is the most crucial question that a government can answer. Ideally, that choice comes only after a careful deliberation over what is at stake and whether it is worth fighting for. The answers depend on whether the nation has the appropriate power to defend or enhance vital national interests against its adversaries. One permanent national interest is power itself. Will the war expand or diminish a nation's ability to assert its other interests, however defined? A decision for war is just the first moral dilemma. Every decision that follows can affect the fate of countless lives and fortunes of those nations at war, as well as neutral nations that hope to profit from the violence by expanding their exports to the belligerents.

The question of whether or not to war may be more troubling when the nation is a liberal democracy committed to upholding individual rights and representative government. Does being a liberal democracy restrict one to fight only defensive wars? Are wars of aggression permitted if they spread liberal democracy to others? Is there a trade-off between democracy and imperialism or can they be compatible? Americans have debated those and related questions since the early republic.

After winning independence, America's leaders largely did what they could to avoid war until they believed they had no other choice. Hamilton was the most articulate in explaining that American national interests dictated that its leaders do whatever they could "to keep out of war as long it should be possible; to deter, to a state of manhood, a struggle to which infancy is ill adapted." He went so far as to insist that "it is not the interest of the United States to be engaged in any war whatsoever. . . . We have acted right hitherto in laying it down as a principle, not to suffer ourselves to be drawn into the wars of Europe."[7]

In a kind of circular reasoning, that aversion to war reflected both cold calculations that as a weak state the United States had little chance of winning and the fear that a military buildup might ultimately threaten American liberties and prosperity. Madison said that "war is the parent of armies; from these proceed debts and taxes; and armies and debts and taxes are the known instrument for bringing the many under the domination of the few."[8]

The Federalists and Republicans agreed that the United States had to avoid any unnecessary wars that dissipated or destroyed its wealth and power. As for what constituted the nation's proper defense and honor, they fiercely competed over who could beat the drum louder but had diametrically opposing visions for what that meant and how to realize it.

The Federalists understood that peace ultimately rested on the relationship among economic, diplomatic, and military power. The more dynamic and diverse a nation's economy, the more wealth is created and distributed across the population, and the more revenues flow into government coffers, of which some are diverted into a defense budget. That in turn gives diplomats the bargaining power necessary to assert American interests without violence. Hamilton explained that "the rights of neutrality will only be respected when they are defended by an adequate power. A nation, despicable by its weakness, forfeits even the privilege of being neutral. Under a vigorous national government, the natural strength and resources of the country, directed by a common interest, would baffle all the combinations of European jealousy to restrain our growth."[9]

For Hamilton, the statesman's duty was "to exhaust the expedient of negotiations, and at the same time to prepare vigorously for the worst. This is sound policy." Inevitably that involved giving to as well as trying to take from the other side: "Where one party is not powerful enough to dictate to the other, and where there is a mutual disposition to avoid war, the natural retreat for both is in compromise. . . . What sensible man, what humane man, will deny that a compromise which secures substantially the objects of interest, is always preferable to war." Hamilton identified one final barrier to cross before he would carry the nation into the abyss—war should always be with the "cheerful support of the people."[10]

Just what type and amount of military forces are enough to deter and if necessary defeat America's enemies? The answer involves another golden mean. History teaches the important lesson that a nation can spend too much as well as too little on the military and thus imperil itself. The more a military is larded with unnecessary forces, the more it can sap a nation's wealth and lead to decline relative to one's rivals. Yet investing too little in the military can invite the aggression of others. So ideally a military is tailor-made to deter or defeat genuine threats.

For a generation, the Federalists had insisted on establishing such a military. Hamilton laid the foundation for a small but professional army and blue-water navy when he was treasury secretary during the 1790s. Then, after 1800, the Republicans dismantled that legacy. Presidents Jefferson and Madison championed militia and gunboats as the best means of defending the United States. They partly justified the policy by citing classical political theory and English tradition.

The Roman Republic and the English constitutional monarchy spurned a large standing army for fear it would be a tool in the hands of tyrants. Thus defending the nation from enemies foreign and domestic could only rest on citizen-soldiers. To that, Jefferson and Madison added the Republican celebration of states' rights and hatred of taxes. Finally, to ensure that the officer corps reflected those values, they purged as many Federalist officers as possible and replaced them with loyal Republicans.[11]

Although the early republic's leaders were united in promoting peace and prosperity for the nation, war or the threat of war haunted Americans during the early republic. The United States fought five wars between 1775 and 1815, with those against Britain opening (1775–1783) and ending (1812–1815) the era, bookending wars against the northwest Indian confederation (1789–1795), Tripoli (1801–1805), and the Creek Red Sticks (1813–1814), along with the Quasi-War against France (1797–1800).

America's War of Independence ground on for eight years before the British bitterly accepted the sovereignty of the United States. Although that elated most Americans, ever more came to realize that their legal sovereignty was a practical fiction. The United States remained economically dependent on Britain, which rebuffed all American attempts to realign the relationship so that it was reciprocal.

America's new system of government was inaugurated during one of the world's most tumultuous periods of history. The Bastille fell the same year that Washington took the presidential oath in 1789. The French Revolution split Americans between those who were inspired by its ideals and those who were appalled by its savagery. After war broke out in Europe in 1792, the Atlantic Ocean could not shield the United States from those struggles. The United States was militarily incapable of preventing the confiscations of its merchant ships, cargoes, and sailors by the European powers, of which the British were by far the most voracious. More U.S. policies were reactions against the challenges posed by the struggle for power in Europe. Eventually the losses of wealth and honor were so great that the president and Congress declared a second war against Britain in 1812.

There is a dynamic between culture and war in which each can crucially affect the other. War powerfully shaped American culture during the colonial era and early republic.[12] Nearly from the moment the first colonists stepped ashore, they found themselves at times fighting for their lives against the natives. In a series of wars fifty years before Lexington, the colonists devastated the Indians and drove their remnants ever farther from the colonies mushrooming along the Atlantic seaboard. Although for most colonists the existential threat receded with the frontier, war did not.

As the British Empire expanded westward, more of its extensions ground against the French Empire stretching through the St. Lawrence, Great Lake, Mississippi, and Ohio valleys. Britain and France fought five wars for supremacy in North America, or about one each generation. Although the French posed no threat of actually conquering the British colonies, whose combined population was ten times larger than that of their own empire, they did make life miserable for many along the frontier. The French and their Indian allies launched devastating raids on the isolated settlements. The French threat ended with the 1763 Treaty of Paris, which transferred Canada and all lands east of the Mississippi River to the British Empire. The Indians, however, continued to defend their homelands from the Americans. Then, from 1775 to 1815, the British replaced the French as the worst threat to Americans. During both the Independence and 1812 wars, armies marched, pillaged, and occupied cities and entire regions along the Eastern Seaboard, the Royal Navy scoured the seas of merchant vessels, and British and Indian raiding parties ravaged the frontier.

That legacy of warfare shaped American culture in several ways. Frontier warfare was merciless as each side tried to devastate the other. The immediate goal, however, was not conquest. Instead, raiding parties and sometimes armies would stealthily snake through the wilderness and then launch a surprise attack, destroy as many of the enemy as possible along with their homes, crops, and livestock before slipping away.

With constant threats and frequent wars, men had to be ready to march and fight at short notice. Every village and neighborhood had its own militia company that could respond to an immediate attack. Most members had more than a nodding acquaintance with one another by attending the same church, tavern, or shops, and many were related by blood or marriage. So a company might comprise clusters of close friends and relatives. Thus was the preparation for and at times execution of war woven into the social fabric of each community.

It was this militia tradition that Republicans celebrated as the backbone of American military defense. By 1812, the militia certainly seemed a formidable force—there were over 600,000 inscribed on the muster rolls. But Federalists warned that relying on the militia to fight America's wars would be disastrous. There were few more glaring gaps in early America between an ideal and reality than its citizen-soldiers. Off the battlefield, the militia were notorious for their lack of hygiene, discipline, and cohesion. Not surprisingly, on the battlefield, militia tended to scatter at the first volleys and advancing glint of steel bayonets. On those rare times when they stood and fought, they mostly had something to hide behind such as the entrenchments at Bunker Hill and New Orleans. All those militia and gunboats did not stop the British from sacking Washington and burning the Executive Mansion and Capitol in 1814. It was regular American infantry relentlessly trained in European tactics that ultimately defeated the British and other enemies.

So why did Americans continue to rely so heavily on militia throughout the early republic? The literal as well as figurative deadweight of tradition was the most important reason. The American colonists retained the animus of those they left behind against standing armies that were seen as an enemy of liberty and source of tyranny. Thus armies should be raised only in wartime and dismissed as soon as the guns fall silent. In addition, a large standing army was practically unnecessary in the New World, whose warfare mostly consisted of small-scale Indian raids on frontiers that were at times leavened by Europeans. The scattered communities along the frontiers were best defended by their own men. Then there was the relatively low cost of militia, which supplied their own weapons and time, although they were often short of each. American nationalists somehow had to break down those sentiments against the army and for the militia. Their practical argument against militia was ironclad. From the standpoint of military effectiveness, the militia had been in steady decline from the seventeenth century and was an anachronism by the early republic. The founders who fought in the Revolutionary War were scathing in their contempt for the militia, which devoured vital supplies and tended to flee at the first shots.

There was yet another argument favoring a national army. In early America, the military experience best shaped a mass national outlook. Indeed, it can be argued that the army was potentially even more powerful than the federal government in assisting that transition. But those who supported the missions of defending the country and promoting national identity ran into a cultural and political obstacle. Ironically, the militia were never so politically and ideologically powerful as during the early republic. The Republicans enshrined the militia along with representation without taxation and states' rights in a near holy trinity of values.

The result of that tug-of-war between Federalists and Republicans was a hybrid military system. If a war were prolonged, the militia could be called into the field to join a campaign against the enemy. More often, volunteers were enlisted into provisional regiments and paid for service ranging from nine to twelve months. And then there were those who joined regular army regiments. Like today, those who enlisted tended to have few other employment options. Certainly, in times of war, patriotism and a desire for adventure animated many and perhaps most who joined the ranks. In peacetime, there was no want of young men without much to do.[13]

Whether they were militia, volunteers, or regulars, those men had a chance to widen their minds as their companies were merged into a regiment and then marched off to a distant front. Most had probably never before ventured a half-dozen or so miles from their homes. Suddenly they were mingling with men from other colonies or states. While they may have poked fun at one anothers' accents and mannerisms, they shared the same language, purpose, and, increasingly, national identity.

One of the best ways to develop and define an identity is to contrast it with something else. Before 1775, Britain's army, Parliament, and, eventually, the king became foils against which to forge American nationalism. For tens of thousands of Americans who served in militia or volunteer regiments on campaign with British regiments, their identity was bolstered by the disdain and discrimination with which redcoat officers and the ranks alike treated them. That experience was not confined to veterans. Frictions are inevitable wherever the lives of soldiers and civilians overlap. While those communities with garrisons did enjoy an economic windfall, they did so at the cost of being forced to accept a reviled standing army in their midst. That presence can be explosive if the soldiers are enforcing hated laws that deprive the populace of their liberties, rights, and income, as the redcoats did with the 1774 Intolerable Acts in Boston.

Culture can just as powerfully affect how a nation wages war. The Age of Enlightenment's values of reason and restraint shaped eighteenth-century warfare. The science rather than art of warfare was emphasized. War was mostly conducted like a chess game of slow, methodical moves and countermoves. Generals mapped out strategy and tactics through councils of war among their highest-ranking officers. Campaigns mostly consisted of a series of maneuvers punctuated by a battle or siege or two. Armies rarely strayed far from a chain of supply depots leading back to their homelands. "Winter quarters" might last half the year as the ministries and generals amassed all the necessary supplies and troops.

As if that process were not inimical enough to bold, vigorous action, the early American way of war imposed further burdens. America's wars during the early republic were fought by amateurs rather than professionals, by communities as well as committees, and by militia and volunteers who elected most of their officers, as well as regular regiments. Democracy and war mix poorly.

Culture intruded into military affairs even after the United States adopted a regular army. Although regular officers were appointed rather than elected, alas, for American power, politics rather than merit tended to prevail in that process. During the Revolutionary War, there was a continual tug-of-war between George Washington and Congress over filling the officer corps. Washington obviously desired the most competent. A state's delegates naturally wanted to hand out as many commissions as possible to their own people whether or not they were fit for command; many were not.

That conflict was only partly resolved after the Constitution designated the president the commander in chief. While George Washington solely used merit for his choices, his successors tended to pick officers who were ideologically correct but lacked the skills and character for command. Winfield Scott recalled that many officers had "very generally sunk into either sloth, ignorance, or habits of intemperate drinking."[14] Those officers would parade their varied depravities during the War of 1812.

Officers learned their trade on the job and often under fire. With time the demands of camp, march, and battle exposed those who were unfit for command. Unfortunately, courts-martial weeded out very few of the often murderously inept. Although West Point was established in 1802, only about seventy graduates fought in the War of 1812. That war would be the last in which amateur officers prevailed. Thereafter a professional officer corps of West Point graduates would command regular and volunteer regiments. When the United States fought its next large-scale war three decades later, the militia were never mustered in that conflict against faraway Mexico.

The winnowing process applied to generals too, but unfortunately not before they led their men into a military disaster or more. The list of these inept is as grim as it is long, with names like Benjamin Lincoln, Charles Lee, Horatio Gates, William Hull, James Wilkinson, and William Winder only a few of the most prominent. What is astonishing is that so many outstanding generals somehow fought their way to the top. Mercifully for American power, that list also is long, with top honors going to a cluster that includes, yes, George Washington, even though he lost more battles than he won; Nathaniel Greene; Benedict Arnold; Daniel Morgan; William Henry Harrison; Jacob Brown; and Andrew Jackson.

The navy's record at war far surpassed that of the army. The reason was simple. The United States only mustered armies in wartime and then dismissed them in peacetime. During the twenty-eight years between the two wars against Britain, the American "army" numbered only a thousand or so troops. During those two wars nearly all who served did so for the first time. In contrast, there was a vast peacetime fleet of thousands of merchant and fishing vessels manned by tens of thousands of sailors. In wartime, hundreds of those vessels would be fitted with cannons and sail as privateers against the enemy. Like the army, the navy was abolished after the Revolutionary War. It would be reborn in the 1790s in the Quasi-War against France and would later fight against the Barbary states and

Britain. Those frigates that the president and Congress eventually agreed to build were state-of-the-art and manned by officers and sailors with years of experience at sea. All they needed to master were gunnery skills, and they proved to be murderously adept at that.

Unfortunately, the problems plaguing America's power to wage war only began with leadership. A persistent value of American culture is to demand something for nothing. In politics that can ideally mean representation without taxation. Americans demanded that the government defend them from their enemies but resented having to pay for the service. As a result, early American armies suffered shortages of virtually everything, including pay, food, clothing, blankets, shelter, arms, ammunition, and medicine. Meanwhile, politically well-connected merchants and manufacturers, often enjoying no-bid contracts, made vast profits from supplying mostly shoddy good to the military, if they actually bothered to send anything at all. All these deficiencies naturally dampened morale and thus the ability to fight.

The era's art of power reached its nadir with the War of 1812. The war was at once a failure by the leadership properly to wield power and a sharp diminishment of that very power. America's humiliating defeats were self-inflicted, and not just from bad generalship. The decision of the president and Congress to declare war against Britain was as troubling. Whether Madison or his fellow War Hawks ever lost a night's sleep over their decision is lost to history. They appear to have mustered every psychological device to justify their actions and to deny how disastrous the war became for American power and wealth, if not honor.

The War of 1812, which has unfairly been called Mr. Madison's War, was collectively the logical outgrowth of the Republican Party's ideology. The Republican attitude toward violence, revolution, and war could be cavalier. Jefferson best expressed it when he wrote, "What signify a few lives lost in a century or two? The tree of liberty must be refreshed from time to time with the blood of patriots and tyrants. It is its natural manure."[15]

Given the glaring deficiencies of U.S. military power during the early republic, it is astonishing that America's armies and warships fought as well as they did. The United States defeated Britain in one war, with crucial help from France, and battled it to a standstill in a second. In its more limited wars, the United States defeated the Northwest and Red Stick Indians, and essentially fought France and Tripoli to draws.

Yet, overall, the military would remain the early republic's stepchild through 1815 and beyond. As a result, America's diplomatic initiatives were frequently thwarted because they were not grounded on credible military power.

If the military record was at best mixed, that was not how most Americans recalled it. An essential dimension of American culture is the belief in the nation's omnipotence, that Americans will ultimately prevail even if they suffered some early defeats. And to sustain that belief they must turn a blind eye to their actual history.

Revolution and Power

The American Revolution obviously affected everyone differently. There were winners and losers, and what was won or lost varied enormously among individuals and groups. The lives of most people decline during wartime. Nonetheless, in the two generations between the beginning of one war with Britain and the end of a second, the American Revolution benefited more people than not.

Some individuals and groups are better at leading or adapting to change than others. The transformation may be as swift for some as it is glacial for others. Change can inspire the greatest hopes or provoke the most dire anxiety. That in turn depends on some dynamic among one's temperament, values, interests, and skills. There is no question that the American Revolution created more opportunities for more people to rise higher economically, socially, and politically. Most importantly, the middle class expanded steadily in wealth and numbers. Yet those who emphasize class, race, and gender rightly point out that the American Revolution's immediate political, economic, and social opportunities extended only to less than half of the population—white men of property. Blacks, women, and those living hand-to-mouth were left out. In many ways, these groups are still struggling for what they believe is their fair share. However, since 1775, the proportion of the population that has gained has mostly expanded with each subsequent generation.

By 1815, the American Revolution had reached the end of an extraordinary beginning. John Adams expressed what the American Revolution most meant to him: "I must study politics and war, that my sons may have the liberty to study mathematics and philosophy. My sons ought to study mathematics and philosophy, geography, natural history and naval architecture, navigation, commerce and agriculture, in order to give their children a right to study painting, poetry, music, architecture, statuary, tapestry, and porcelain."[16]

If Adams and the other founders could have peered ahead across the ever widening chasm of time to today, they would have been relieved to discover that future generations have largely fulfilled their dreams. And whatever Americans have achieved over the centuries would have been impossible had the founders not mastered the art of power.

Abbreviations

Adams Works	John Adams, *The Works of John Adams, Second President of the United States*, ed. Charles Francis Adams, 10 vols. (Boston: Little, Brown, 1850–1856).
AECPEU	Archives des Affaires Étrangères, Correspondance Politique, Etats Unis, Archives Nationales, Paris, France.
Annals	*Debates and Proceedings in the Congress of the United States*, 42 vols. (Washington, DC: Gales and Seaton, 1834–1856), http://memory.loc.gov/ammem/amlaw/lwsp.html.
ASPFR	*American State Papers: Foreign Affairs*, 6 vols. (Washington, DC: Gales and Seaton, 1832–1859).
ASPMA	*American State Papers: Military Affairs*, 7 vols. (Washington, DC: Gales and Seaton, 1832–1838).
ASPNA	*American State Papers: Naval Affairs*, 4 vols. (Washington, DC: Gales and Seaton, 1834–1861).
British Instructions	Bernard Mayo, ed., *The Instructions to the Ministers to the United States, 1791–1812* (Washington, DC: Government Printing Office, 1941).
Clay Papers	Henry Clay, *The Papers of Henry Clay*, ed. James F. Hopkins et al., 11 vols. (Lexington: University Press of Kentucky, 1959–1992).

Federalist Papers	Alexander Hamilton, James Madison, and John Jay, *The Federalist: The Famous Papers on the Principles of American Government*, ed. Benjamin Wright (New York: Barnes and Noble, 1996).
Hamilton Works	Alexander Hamilton, *The Works of Alexander Hamilton*, ed. Henry Cabot Lodge, 12 vols. (New York: Putnam, 1904).
Jefferson Life and Writings	Thomas Jefferson, *The Life and Selected Writings of Thomas Jefferson*, eds. Adrienne Koch and William Peden (New York: Modern Library, 1998).
Jefferson Papers	Thomas Jefferson, *Papers*, ed. Julian P. Boyd et al., 33 vols. (Princeton, NJ: Princeton University Press, 1950–2006).
Jefferson Works	Thomas Jefferson, *The Works of Thomas Jefferson*, ed. Paul Leicester Ford, 12 vols. (New York: Putnam, 1904–1905).
Jefferson Writings	Thomas Jefferson, *The Writings of Thomas Jefferson*, ed. Andrew A. Lipscomb, 20 vols. (Washington, DC: Thomas Jefferson Memorial Association of the United States, 1905).
LC	Library of Congress, Washington, D.C.
Madison Papers	William T. Huchinson and William M. E. Rachal, eds., *The Papers of James Madison*, 17 vols. (Chicago: University of Chicago Press, 1962–1991).
Madison Writings	James Madison, *The Writings of James Madison*, ed. Gaillard Hunt, 9 vols. (New York: Putnam, 1900–1910).
Monroe Writings	James Monroe, *The Writings of James Monroe*, ed. Stanislaus Murray Hamilton, 7 vols. (New York: Putnam, 1898–1903).
Presidential Messages	James D. Richardson, *A Compilation of the Messages and Papers of the Presidents*, 10 vols. (Washington, DC: Government Printing Office, 1973).
PRO FO	Public Record Office, Foreign Office, National Archives, Kew, United Kingdom.

Notes

Introduction: The Inauguration

1. Unless otherwise noted, the following information on the inauguration comes from: Dumas Malone, *Jefferson the President, First Term, 1801–1805* (Boston: Little, Brown, 1970); Fawn Brodie, *Thomas Jefferson: An Intimate History* (New York: W. W. Norton, 1974); Bernard Weisberger, *America Afire: Jefferson, Adams, and the Revolutionary Election of 1800* (New York: William Morrow, 2000); David McCullough, *John Adams* (New York: Simon & Schuster, 2001). Unless otherwise noted, the information on Washington City comes from: Bob Arnebeck, *Through a Fiery Trial: Building Washington, 1790–1800* (New Haven, CT: Yale University Press, 1962); Constance M. Green, *Washington: Village and Capital, 1800–1876* (Princeton, NJ: Princeton University Press, 1962); Thomas Froncek, ed., *The City of Washington: An Illustrated History of the City of Washington, by the Junior League of Washington* (New York: Alfred A. Knopf, 1977).

2. Jefferson Life and Writings, 321–25.

3. Ibid.

4. Ibid.

Chapter 1. The Revolution of 1801

1. Alexander Hamilton to Rufus King, June 3, 1802, Hamilton Works, 8:601–2.

2. David H. Fischer, *The Revolution of American Conservatism: The Federalist Party in the Era of Jeffersonian Democracy* (New York: Harper & Row, 1965); Linda Kerber, *Federalists in Dissent: Imagery and Ideology in Jeffersonian America* (Ithaca, NY: Cornell University Press, 1970); Kenneth C. Martis, *The Historical Atlas of Political Parties in the United States Congress, 1789–1989* (New York: Macmillan, 1989).

3. For the most comprehensive analysis, see Malone, *First Term*; See also Leonard White, *The Jeffersonians: A Study in Administrative History, 1801–1829* (New York: Macmillan, 1951); Noble E. Cunningham, *The Jeffersonian Republicans in Power: Party Operations, 1801–1809* (Chapel Hill: University of North Carolina Press, 1963); Lance Banning, *The Jeffersonian Persuasion:*

Evolution of a Party Ideology (Ithaca, NY: Cornell University Press, 1978); Merrill Peterson, *Thomas Jefferson and the New Nation: A Biography* (New York: Oxford University Press, 1970); Forrest McDonald, *The Presidency of Thomas Jefferson* (Lawrence: University Press of Kansas, 1976); Noble E. Cunningham Jr., *The Process of Government under Jefferson* (Princeton, NJ: Princeton University Press, 1978); Robert W. T. Tucker and David C. Hendrickson, *Empire of Liberty: The Statecraft of Thomas Jefferson* (New York: Oxford University Press, 1990).

4. Malone, *First Term*, 51.

5. Ibid., 110.

6. Ibid., 112.

7. Brodie, *Thomas Jefferson*.

8. Malone, *First Term*, 367–92.

Chapter 2. The Battle for the Courts

1. Malone, *First Term*, 136–56.

Chapter 3. Thomas Jefferson and American Power

1. Stanley Elkins and Eric McKitrick, *The Age of Federalism: The Early American Republic, 1788–1800* (New York: Oxford University Press, 1993), 196–97.

2. Ibid.

3. Ibid., 197–98.

4. Jefferson Life and Writings, 321–25. For an excellent overview of Jefferson's economic ideas and policies, see Drew R. McCoy, *The Elusive Republic: Political Economy in Jeffersonian America* (Chapel Hill: University of North Carolina, 1980).

5. Burton Spivak, *Jefferson's English Crisis: Commerce, Embargo, and the Republican Revolution* (Charlottesville: University of Virginia Press, 1979), 6–7; Burton Spivak, "Republican Dreams and National Interest: The Jeffersonians and American Foreign Policy," *SHAFR Newsletter* 12 (1981): 1; McCoy, *Elusive Republic*.

6. "Second Annual Address," December 15, 1802, Jefferson Life and Writings, 308.

7. Thomas Jefferson to Albert Gallatin, October 11, 1809, Jefferson Writings, 9:264.

8. Thomas Jefferson to Governor Joseph Bloomfield of New Jersey, December 5, 1801, LC 20360.

9. Alexander Balinky, *Albert Gallatin: Fiscal Theories and Policies* (New Brunswick, NJ: Rutgers University Press, 1958), chaps. 3–5; Curtis P. Nettels, *The Emergence of a National Economy, 1775–1815* (New York: Holt, Rinehart & Winston, 1962), 330; Marshall Smelser, *The Democratic Republic, 1801–1815* (New York: Harper & Row, 1968), 230.

10. Thomas Jefferson to James Monroe, June 17, 1785, Jefferson Writings, 8:232.

11. Thomas Jefferson to David Rose, May 8, 1785, Jefferson Writings, 9:475.

12. Thomas Jefferson to Elbridge Gerry, May 13, 1797, Jefferson Writings, 7:121–22.

13. Nettels, *Emergence of a National Economy*, 396.

14. Ibid.

15. Thomas Jefferson, *Notes on the State of Virginia*, ed. by William Peden (Chapel Hill: University of North Carolina Press, 1955), 175.

16. Ibid.

17. Thomas Jefferson to James Monroe, October 16, 1813, Jefferson Writings, 9:492.

18. Jefferson, *Notes on the State of Virginia*, 175–76.

19. Balinky, *Albert Gallatin*, 9, 103, 118, 123.

20. For an in-depth exploration, see Theodore J. Crackel, Mr. *Jefferson's Army: Political and Social Reform of the Military Establishment, 1801–1809* (New York: New York University Press, 1987); James R. Jacobs, *The Beginning of the U.S. Army, 1783–1812* (Princeton, NJ: Princeton University Press, 1947).

21. Winfield Scott, *Memoirs of Lieutenant General Winfield Scott* (New York: Sheldon and Company, 1864), 1:35–36; Donald Jackson, "Jefferson, Meriwether Lewis, and the Reduction of the United States Army," *Proceedings of the American Philosophical Society* 124, no. 2 (April 29, 1980): 91–96; Theodore J. Crackel, "Jefferson, Politics, and the Army: An Examination of the Military Peace Act of 1802," *Journal of the Early Republic* 2, no. 1 (Spring 1982): 21–38.

22. Thomas Jefferson to Thomas Mann Randolph, June 16, 1801, LC 19483; Annals, 8 Cong., 2d Sess. 1804–1805, 1684; Harold and Margaret Sprout, *The Rise of American Naval Power, 1776–1918* (Princeton, NJ: Princeton University Press, 1966), 13–15, 25–53.

23. Thomas Jefferson to William Short, October 3, 1801, Jefferson Writings, 10:287; Donald R. Hickey, *The War of 1812: A Forgotten Conflict* (Chicago: University of Illinois Press, 1989). 13; Thomas Jefferson to Madame d'Enville, April 2, 1790, Jefferson Papers, 16:291.

24. Thomas Jefferson to John Jay, August 23, 1785, Jefferson Papers, 8:428.

25. Thomas Jefferson to James Madison, November 19, 1803, quoted in Malone, *First Term*, xviii.

Chapter 4. The Louisiana Dilemma

1. E. Wilson Lyon, *Louisiana in French Diplomacy, 1759–1804* (Norman: University of Oklahoma Press, 1934), 88–93; Alexander DeConde, *This Affair of Louisiana* (New York: Scribner, 1976), 75–90.

2. Thomas Pickering to Charles Pinckney, February 25, 1797, National Archives, Department of State, Diplomatic and Consular Instructions, http://history.state.gov.

3. DeConde, *This Affair of Louisiana*, 84.

4. Ibid., 85.

5. Rufus King to James Madison, March 29, ASPFR, 2:509; Thomas Jefferson to James Monroe, May 25, 1801, Jefferson Writings, 8:58.

6. Louis Andre Pichon to Charles Maurice de Talleyrand-Périgord, July 20, 1801, AECPEU, 53:171.

7. James Madison to Robert Livingston, September 28, 1801, ASPFR, 2:510–11.

8. Louis Andre Pichon to Talleyrand, October 25, 1801, AECPEU, 53:343–45.

9. Robert Livingston to James Madison, December 12, 1801, ASPFR, 2:512; Alexander DeConde, *The Quasi-War: The Politics and Diplomacy of the Undeclared War with France, 1797–1801* (New York: Scribner, 1966), 325.

10. Rufus King to James Madison, November 20, 1801, ASPFR, 2:511–12.

11. Thomas Jefferson to John Bacon, April 30, 1804, Jefferson Writings, 8:228.

12. Thomas Jefferson to Robert Livingston, April 18, 1802, Jefferson Writings, 9:363–68; Lawrence Kaplan, *Jefferson and France: An Essay on Politics and Political Ideas* (New Haven, CT: Yale University Press, 1967); Lawrence Kaplan, *Entangling Alliances with None: American Foreign Policy in the Age of Jefferson* (Kent, OH: Kent State University Press, 1987).

13. James Madison to Robert Livingston, May 1, 1802, ASPFR, 2:516; James Madison to Robert Livingston, August 10, 1802, ASPFR, 2:520–524.

14. Thomas Jefferson to Pierre Du Pont, April 25, 1802, in *The Correspondence of Thomas Jefferson and Du Pont de Nemours*, ed. Gilbert Chinard (Baltimore, MD: Johns Hopkins Press, 1931), 46–47; Thomas Jefferson to Pierre Du Pont, February 1, 1803, Jefferson Writings, 9:436–41.

15. Robert Livingston to James Madison, September 1, 1802, ASPFR, 2:525.

16. Robert Livingston to Thomas Jefferson, October 28, 1802, ASPFR, 2:525–26.

17. Louis Andre Pichon to Talleyrand, July 7, 31, 1802, January 3, 1803, quoted in Irving Brant, *James Madison: Secretary of State, 1800–1809* (Indianapolis: Bobbs-Merrill, 1953), 90–91, 105.

18. Thomas Jefferson to James Monroe, November 24, 1801, Jefferson Writings, 8:105; Louis Andre Pichon to Talleyrand, July 22, 1801, AECPEU, 53:178.

Chapter 5. Squaring Off with Spain

1. Arthur Preston Whitaker, *The Mississippi Question: 1795–1803, A Study in Trade, Politics, and Diplomacy* (New York: C. Appleton-Century, 1934).

2. James Madison to Charles Pinckney, November 27, 1802, Madison Writings, 6:462; DeConde, *This Affair of Louisiana*, 142.

3. William Claiborne to James Madison, January 3, 1803, in *The Official Letter Books of W. C. C. Claiborne, 1801–1816*, ed. Dunbar Rowland (Jackson, MS: State Department of Archives and History, 1917), 1:253.

4. Malone, *First Term*, 265.

Chapter 6. The Louisiana Purchase

1. Roger Griswold Resolution, January 4, 1803, John Randolph Resolution, House Committee Recommendations on Resolutions January 11, 1803, January 12, 1803, Annals, 7 Cong., 2d Sess., 1803–1804, 312–14, 338, 371–74.

2. Gouverneur Morris to James Parish, January 14, 1803, in *The Diary and Letters of Gouverneur Morris, Minister of the United States to France*, ed. Anne Cary Morris (New York: Da Capo Press, 1970), 2:431.

3. Alexander Hamilton to Charles Pinckney, December 29, 1802, Hamilton Works, 6:551–52.

4. Ibid.

5. Resolutions, Annals, 7 Cong., 2d Sess., 1801–1802, 83–88, 105–256.

6. Malone, *First Term*, 180.

7. William Claiborne to James Madison, January 3, 1803, in Rowland, *Official Letter Books*, 1:253.

8. Thomas Jefferson to James Monroe, January 10 and 13, 1803, Jefferson Writings, 8:188, 190–92; James Monroe to Thomas Jefferson, January 7, 1803, Monroe Writings, 4:1; James Madison to Robert Livingston and James Monroe, March 2, 1803, ASPFR, 2:540–44.

9. Pierre Samuel Du Pont de Nemours to Thomas Jefferson, October 4, 1802, in Thomas Jefferson, *Correspondence between Thomas Jefferson and Pierre Samuel du Pont de Nemours, 1798–1817*, ed. Dumas Malone (New York: Da Capo Press, 1970), 68–71; Robert Livingston to Thomas Jefferson, April 14, 1803, LC 22586.

10. Cabinet Memorandum, April 8, 1803, in Franklin B. Sawvel, ed., *The Complete Anas of Thomas Jefferson* (New York: Da Capo Press, 1970), 219; James Madison to Robert Livingston and James Monroe, April 18, 1803, ASPFR, 2:555–56.

11. DeConde, *This Affair of Louisiana*, 142–43.

12. Antoine Marie Roederer, ed., *Oeuvres du comte P. L. Roederer* (Paris: Firmin Didot Frères, 1855), 3:461.

13. James Madison to Robert Livingston, January 18, 1803, ASPFR, 2:529; Robert Livingston to Gouverneur Morris, April 18, 1803, in Brant, *Madison: Secretary of State*, 111–12.

14. François Barbé-Marbois, *The History of Louisiana, Particularly of the Cession of the Colony to the United States of America* (Philadelphia: Carey & Lea, 1830), 264–65, 270–71, 274–75.

15. Robert Livingston to James Madison, April 11, 1803, ASPFR, 2:552.

16. Thomas Jefferson to Robert Livingston, February 3, 1803, Jefferson Writings, 8:209; Louis Andre Pichon to Talleyrand, January 24 and 28, 1803, AECPEU, 55:192–98, 249–51.

17. Robert Livingston to James Madison, February 18, 1803, ASPFR, 2:533.

18. Michel Kerautret, ed., *Les Grands Traités du Consulat, 1799–1804: Documents Diplomatiques du Consulat et de l'Empire*, tome 1 (Paris: La Bibliothèque Napoléon, 2002), 278–89; Robert Livingston to James Madison, May 20, 1803, in *State Papers and Correspondence Bearing upon the Purchase of the Territory of Louisiana* (Washington, DC: Government Printing Office, 1903), 200.

19. Robert Livingston to Gouverneur Morris, May 7, 1803, in Robert R. Livingston, *The Original Letters of Robert R. Livingston, 1801–1803, Written during His Negotiations of the Purchase of Louisiana*, ed. Edward Alexander Parsons (New Orleans: Louisiana Historical Society, 1953), 60; Barbé-Marbois, *History of Louisiana*, 312.

20. James Monroe and Robert Livingston to James Madison, May 13, 1803, ASPFR, 2:558–60.

21. Albert Gallatin to Thomas Jefferson, January 13, 1803, Gallatin Writings, 1:111–14.

22. Thomas Jefferson to Albert Gallatin, January 1803, Gallatin Writings, 1:115.

23. Robert Livingston to Thomas Jefferson, June 2, 1803, LC 23173; Thomas Jefferson to Albert Gallatin, August 23, 1803, Gallatin Writings, 1:144–45; Thomas Jefferson to Wilson Nicolas, September 7, 1803, Jefferson Writings, 10:11.

24. Gouvion St. Cyr to Pedro Cevallos, July 12, 1802, ADPFR, 2:569; Irujo to James Madison, September 4 and 27, 1803, Carlos Martinez d'Irujo to Pedro Cevallos, September 12 and 30, 1803, in James A. Robertson, ed., *Louisiana under the Rule of Spain, France, and the United States, 1785–1807* (Freeport, NY: Books for Libraries Press, 1969), 2:77–79, 81–85.

25. Thomas Jefferson to James Madison, September 14, 1803, Jefferson Writings, 8:253; Memo of Meeting, October 4, 1803, Jefferson Writings, 1:300.

26. Thomas Jefferson to Robert Livingston, November 4, 1803, Jefferson Writings, 10:50.

27. James Madison to Irujo, October 4, 1803, ASPFR, 2:569–70; James Madison to Robert Livingston, October 6, 1803, and James Madison to Charles Pinckney, October 14, 1803, Madison Writings, 67–64; Thomas Jefferson to Robert Livingston, November 4, 1803, Jefferson Writings, 10:50; Carlos Martinez d'Irujo to Pedro Cevallos, November 5, 1803, in Robertson, *Louisiana under the Rule*, 2:121.

28. Ibid., 2:69–70.

29. Pedro Cevallos to Charles Pinckney, February 10, 1804, and Carlos Martinez d'Irujo to James Madison, May 15, 1804, ASPFR, 2:583.

30. Malone, *First Term*, 354.

31. James Madison to Robert Livingston, January 31, 1804, Madison Writings, 7:115–16.

32. Charles Francis Adams, ed., *The Memoirs of John Quincy Adams*, (Philadelphia: J. B. Lippincott, 1874), 5:364–65.

Chapter 7. Where to Draw the Line?

1. James Monroe to James Madison, July 1, 1804, Monroe Writings, 4:218–19.

2. James Monroe to James Madison, December 16, 1804, Monroe Writings, 4:280–82.

Chapter 8. Rising Tensions with Britain

1. Thomas Jefferson to John Langdon, September 11, 1785, Jefferson Writings, 8:512.

2. Samuel Flagg Bemis, *Jay's Treaty: A Study in Commerce and Diplomacy* (New York: Macmillan, 1923), 320.

3. Malone, *First Term*, 367–92.

4. James Madison to James Monroe, January 5, 1804, ASPFR, 3:81–89; See also James Monroe to James Madison, June 3, 1804, ASPFR, 3:92–94; James Monroe to James Madison, June 19 and July 20, 1803, Madison Writings, 4:19, 44–51.

Chapter 9. To the Shores of Tripoli

1. For good overviews, see Ray W. Irwin, *The Diplomatic Relations of the United States with the Barbary Powers, 1776–1816* (Chapel Hill: University of North Carolina Press, 1931); Joseph Wheelan, *Jefferson's War: America's First War on Terror, 1801–1805* (New York: Carroll & Graf Publishers, 2003); Joshua E. London, *Victory in Tripoli: How America's War with the Barbary Pirates Established the U.S. Navy and Built a Nation* (Hoboken, NJ: John Wiley & Sons, 2005); Richard Zacks, *The Pirate Coast: Thomas Jefferson, the First Marines, and the Secret Mission of 1805* (New York: Hyperion, 2005).

2. Irwin, *United States with the Barbary Powers*, 70.

3. Ibid.

4. Ibid., 77–81.

5. James Madison to William Eaton, August 22, 1802, *Naval Documents Related to the United States wars with the Barbary Powers: Naval Operations Including Diplomatic Background from 1785 Through 1807* (Washington, DC: Government Printing Office, 1940), 2:245.

6. Samuel Edwards, *Barbary General: The Life of William H. Eaton* (Englewood Cliffs, NJ: Prentice-Hall, 1968).

7. Wheelan, *Jefferson's War*, 282.

8. Ibid., 322, 367.

Chapter 10. To the Ends of the Earth

1. Donald Jackson, *Thomas Jefferson & the Stony Mountains: Exploring the West from Monticello* (Norman: University of Oklahoma Press, 1993); Stephen E. Ambrose, *Undaunted Courage: Meriwether Lewis, Thomas Jefferson, and the Opening of the American West* (New York: Simon & Schuster, 1996).

2. Thomas Jefferson to George Rogers Clark, December 4, 1783, and George Rogers Clark to Thomas Jefferson, February 8, 1784, in Donald Jackson, ed., *Letters of the Lewis and Clark Expedition, with Related Documents, 1783–1854* (Urbana: University of Illinois Press, 1978), 2:654–55, 655–56.

3. Confidential Message on Expedition to the Pacific, January 18, 1803, Jefferson Writings, 9:421–34.

4. Ambrose, *Undaunted Courage*; Richard Dillon, *Meriwether Lewis: A Biography* (Santa Cruz, CA: Western Tanager Press, 1988).

5. Thomas Jefferson to Paul Allen, August 18, 1813, quoted in Dumas Malone, *Jefferson the President: Second Term, 1805–1809* (Boston: Little, Brown, 1974), 174.

6. Thomas Jefferson to Meriwether Lewis, June 20, 1803, in Donald Jackson, ed., *Letters of the Lewis and Clark Expedition with Related Documents, 1783–1854* (Urbana: University of Illinois Press, 1978), 1:61.

7. Landon Y. Jones, *William Clark and the Shaping of the West* (New York: Hill and Wang, 2004).

Chapter 11. Faltering Steps

1. Thomas Jefferson Inaugural Address, March 4, 1805, Jefferson Works, 8:341–48.

2. John Quincy Adams Memoir, 1:330–31.

3. Malone, *First Term*; Malone, *Second Term*.

4. Thomas Jefferson to Thomas Lomax, January 11, 1806, LC 27225.

5. Annals, 9th Cong., 1st Sess., 1805–1806, 302, 842–48.

Chapter 12. The Fate of West Florida

1. James Monroe to James Madison, July 1 and 5, 1804, Monroe Writings, 4:218–19, 302; James Monroe and Charles Pinckney to James Madison, May 23, 1805, ASPFR, 2:667–69.

2. James Monroe to James Madison, May 25, 1805, in Hubert Bruce Fuller, *The Purchase of Florida: Its History and Diplomacy* (Gainesville: University of Florida Press, 1964), 146.

3. John Quincy Adams to Robert Smith, April 13, 1811, John Quincy Adams Writings, 4:51.

4. James Madison to John Armstrong, June 6, 1805, Madison Writings, 7:183.

5. John Armstrong to James Madison, July 3, 1805, in Malone, *Second Term*, 55.

6. Reginald Horsman, *The Causes of the War of 1812* (Philadelphia: University of Pennsylvania Press, 1962), 53.

7. John Armstrong to James Madison, September 14, 1805, in Clifford L. Egan, "The United States, France, and West Florida, 1803–1807," *Florida Historical Quarterly* 47 (January 1960): 238.

8. Sawvel, *Complete Anas*, 232–22; Thomas Jefferson to James Madison, October 23, 1805, Jefferson Writings, 8:380–82; Cabinet Memorandum, November 12, 1805, Jefferson Writings, 1:308–9; Cabinet Memorandum, November 19, 1805, Jefferson Writings, 1:309.

9. Jefferson address, December 6, 1805, ASPFR, 2:613.

10. Annals, 9th Cong., 1st Sess., 1805–1806, 333–34, 398–408, 946–93, 1226–27, 1265–66; Malone, *Second Term*, 72–75.

11. Madison-Irujo correspondence, January 15–19, 1806, Annals, 9th Cong., 1st Sess., 1805–1806, 1221–24.

Chapter 13. The Burr Conspiracy

1. David Robertson, *Trial of Aaron Burr for Treason: Printed from the Report Taken in Short Hand* (New York: J. Cockcroft, 1875); I. J. Cox, "General Wilkinson and His Later Intrigues with the Spaniards," *American History Review* (July 1914): 794–812; Malone, *Second Term*, 215–370; Buckner F. Melton, *Aaron Burr: Conspiracy to Treason* (New York: John Wiley & Sons, 2001); Nancy Isenberg, *Fallen Founder: The Life of Aaron Burr* (New York: Viking, 2007); Andro Linklater, *An Artist in Treason: The Extraordinary Double Life of General James Wilkinson* (New York: Walker, 2009).

2. John Adams to James Wilkinson, February 4, 1798, Adams Works, 8:563–64.

3. George Washington to Alexander Hamilton, June 25, 1799, Washington Papers.

4. Ron Chernow, *Alexander Hamilton* (New York: Penguin, 2004), 562.

5. Melton, *Aaron Burr*, 66.

6. Linklater, *An Artist in Treason*, 243–46.

7. Malone, *Second Term*, 238.

8. James Wilkinson to Thomas Jefferson, October 21, 1806, Letters in Relation to Burr's Conspiracy, LC.

9. Proclamation, November 27, 1806, Jefferson Writings, 8:481–82.

10. Annals, 9th Cong., 2d Sess., 1806–1807, 402–25.

11. Thomas Jefferson to James Wilkinson, February 3, 1807, Jefferson Works, 147–51.

12. Thomas Jefferson, [unaddressed, undated, unsent], Jefferson Writings, 9:62; See also Thomas Jefferson to George Hay, June 12, 17, 20, 1807, Jefferson Writings, 9:55–56, 56–57, 59–60; Marshall Opinion, June 13, 1807, in Robertson, *Trial of Aaron Burr*, 1:172–86; Thomas Jefferson to George Hay, June 17, 1807, Jefferson Writings, 9:56–57.

Chapter 14. The *Chesapeake* Atrocity

1. For excellent overviews, see Bradford Perkins, *Prologue to War: England and the United States, 1805–1812* (Berkeley: University of California Press, 1961); Bradford Perkins, *The First Rapprochement: The United States and England, 1795–1805* (Berkeley: University of California Press,1967); William S. Dudley and Michael J. Crawford, eds., *The Naval War of 1812: A Documentary History*, 3 vols. (Washington, DC: Naval Historical Society, 1985).

2. James Madison, Observations in Cabinet Meeting, February 2, 1807, Jefferson Papers, LC; Albert Gallatin to James Madison, April 13, 1807, Madison Papers, LC; James F. Zimmerman, *The Impressment of American Seamen* (Port Washington, NY: Kennikat Press, 1925), 272, 266–67.

3. Malone, *Second Term*, chap. 15.

4. James Monroe to James Madison February 12, 1805, ASPFR, 3:112–13; James Monroe to Charles Fox, February 25, 1806, ASPFR, 3:117.

5. James Madison to James Monroe, April 23, 1806, ASPFR, 3:117; Annals, 9th Cong., 1st Sess., 1805–1806, 1272–73.

6. Proclamation, May 3, 1806, Jefferson Writings, 8:445–46.

7. Thomas Jefferson to James Monroe, May 4, 1806, Jefferson Writings, 8:448; James Madison to James Monroe and William Pinkney, May 17, 1806, ASPFR, 3:119–24.

8. James Monroe and William Pinkney to James Madison, August 15, 1806, ASPFR, 3:132; Charles Fox to James Monroe, August 20, 1806, ASPFR, 3:132.

9. James Monroe and William Pinkney to Holland, September 10, 1806, ASPFR, 3:136–37; James Monroe and William Pinkney to James Madison, September 11, 1806, ASPFR, 3:133–35; Thomas Jefferson to Congress, December 3, 1806, Jefferson Writings, 8:496–97.

10. David Erskine to Earl Grey Howick, February 2, 1807, PRO FO 5:52; David Erskine to Canning, October 5, 1807, no. 25, PRO FO 5:52.

11. Treaty of 1806, ASPFR, 3:147–51; James Monroe and William Pinkney to James Madison, January 3 and April 22, 1807, ASPFR, 3:146, 160–61; James Monroe to James Madison, February 28, 1807, ASPFR, 3:174.

12. James Monroe and William Pinkney to James Madison, January 3, 1807, ASPFR, 3:142–47.

13. James Madison to James Monroe and William Pinkney, February 3, 1807, ASPFR, 3:153.

14. Herbert Heaton, "Non-Importation, 1806–1812," *Journal of Economic History* 1 (November 1941): 178–98; Louis Martin Sears, *Jefferson and the Embargo* (New York: Octagon Books, 1966).

15. ASPNA, 1:149; Malone, *Second Term*, 500.

16. Annals, 9th Cong., 2d Sess., 1806–1807, 609–19.

17. David Erskine to James Madison, March 12, 1807, ASPFR, 3:158; James Madison to David Erskine, March 25 and 29, 1807, ASPFR, 3:159, 210–13.

18. Jefferson declaration on treaty in Hickey, *War of 1812*, 16; James Madison to James Monroe and William Pinkney, May 20, 1807, ASPFR, 3:166–73.

19. Donald R. Hickey, "The Monroe-Pinkney Treaty of 1806: A Reappraisal," *William and Mary Quarterly*, 3rd ser., 44, no. 1 (January 1987): 65–88.

20. Henry Adams, *A History of the United States of America during the Administrations of Jefferson and Madison* (New York: Charles Scribners Sons, 1891): 6:279.

21. David Erskine to James Madison, January 4, PRO FO 5:52; James Madison to David Erskine, January 7, 1807, PRO FO 5:52; David Erskine to George Canning, July 17, 1807, no. 21, PRO FO 5:52.

22. Samuel Smith to Thomas Jefferson, June 30, 1807, LC 29610.

23. Meeting minutes, July 2, 4, 5, 7, 1807, Jefferson Writings, 1:324–25, 325; Jefferson Proclamation, July 7, 1807, Jefferson Writings, 9:93.

24. James Madison to James Monroe, July 6 and 17, 1807, Madison Papers, 7:454–60, 463–64; James Madison to John Armstrong and James Bowdoin, July 15, 1807, Madison Papers, 7:460–62; Thomas Jefferson to James Bowdoin, July 10, 1807, Jefferson Works, 11:269.

25. William Cabell to Thomas Jefferson, July 20, 1807, LC 29778.

26. Thomas Jefferson to William Cahill, July 24, 1807, Jefferson Writings, 12:89–90.

27. Thomas Jefferson to John Page, July 9, 1807, Jefferson Papers, LC.

28. Spivak, *Jefferson's English Crisis*, 77.

29. Malone, *Second Term*, 464.

30. For the militia muster, see Thomas Jefferson to Henry Dearborn, July 7, 1807, Jefferson Writings, 9:101; for the privateers and conquest of Canada, see Thomas Jefferson to John Page, July 17, 1807, and Thomas Jefferson to John Armstrong, July 17, 1807, Jefferson Papers, LC; for his belief that Napoleon's victories would restrain Britain from warring against the United States, see Thomas Jefferson to John Wayles Eppes, July 12, 1807, Jefferson Papers, LC; and for his belief in the "ruinous folly of a navy," see Thomas Jefferson to Thomas Paine, September 6, 1807, Jefferson Papers, LC.

31. Thomas Jefferson, notes on consultations, July 28, 1807, Jefferson Papers, LC.

32. Albert Gallatin to Samuel Smith, July 17, 1807, Gallatin Papers; Albert Gallatin to Hanna Gallatin, July 4, 1807, Gallatin Papers.

33. Thomas Jefferson to Thomas Leiper, August 21, 1807, Jefferson Writings, 9:130.

34. James Monroe to James Madison, August 4, 1807, ASPFR 3:186–88; James Monroe to George Canning, July 25, 29, September 7, 1807, ASPFR, 3:187, 189–191; George Canning to James Monroe, July 6, 25, August 3, 8, September 23, 1807, ASPFR, 3:183–85, 188, 199–201; George Canning to James Monroe and William Pinkney, October 22, 1807, ASPFR, 3:198–99; George Canning to William Pinkney, September 23, 1808, ASPFR, 3:231–32.

35. Malone, *Second Term*, 439–50.

36. Jefferson address to Congress, October 27, 1807, Annals, 10th Cong., 1st Sess., 1807–1808, 14–18.

37. John Quincy Adams to John Adams, November 30, 1807, John Quincy Adams Writings, 3:164.

38. George Canning to James Monroe, September 23, 1807, ASPFR 3:199–20; James Monroe to George Canning, September 29, 1807, ASPFR 3:200–21; Thomas Jefferson to Thomas Randolph, November 30, 1807, LC 30506.

Chapter 15. Within the Turtle Shell

1. Annals, 10th Cong., 1st Sess. 1807–1808 33–38, 40; ASPNA, 1:168; Annals, 10th Cong., 1st Sess. 1807–1808 32–33, 44, 1040, 1065–71.

2. Annals, 10th Cong., 1st Sess., 1807–1808, 1215–1223, 1240–41, 1244–57, 1271, 2815–17.

3. Malone, *Second Term*, 487–90.

4. James Madison to Thomas Jefferson, September 14, 1805, Jefferson Papers, LC.

5. Thomas Jefferson to John Taylor, January 6, 1808, LC 30732.

6. Jefferson Proclamation, December 20, 1806, Jefferson Writings, 8:499–501; Jennings, *American Embargo*, chaps. 7–9.

7. Thomas Jefferson to J. C. Cabell, February 2, 1816, Jefferson Works, 14:422; Thomas Jefferson to Maj. Joseph Eggleston, March 7, 1808, LC 31085.

8. Thomas Jefferson to Albert Gallatin, May 15, 17, 1808, Jefferson Works, 12:56, 66.

9. Albert Gallatin to Thomas Jefferson, July 19, 1808, Gallatin Writings, 1:398; Thomas Jefferson to Albert Gallatin, August 11, 1808, Jefferson Writings, 9:202.

10. Annals, 10th Cong., 1st Sess., 1807–1808, 2834–35.

11. Eli F. Heckscher, The *Continental System: An Economic Interpretation* (Oxford: Clarendon Press, 1922), 245.

12. George Rose to James Madison, January 26, 1808, ASPFR, 3:213–14.

13. James Madison to George Rose, March 5, 1808, ASPFR, 3:214–17.

14. James Madison to George Rose, March 5, 1808, and George Rose to James Madison, March 17, 1808, ASPFR, 3:213–20.

15. Account of unofficial conversation between Canning and Pinkney, January 18 and 22, 1809, ASPFR, 3:299–300; James Madison to William Pinkney, April 4, 1808, ASPFR, 3:221–222; William Pinkney to George Canning, August 23 and December 28, 1808, ASPFR, 3:228, 240; William Pinkney to James Madison, November 23, 1807, January 26, February 2, September 21, 1808, ASPFR, 3:203–6, 206–7, 207, 228–30.

16. Thomas Jefferson to William Short, July 6 and September 6, 1808, LC 31643, L & B, 12:159–60; William Short to Thomas Jefferson, September 4 and 28, 1808, LC 32012–13, 32143–46; Thomas Jefferson to James Madison, September 13, Jefferson Works, 12:165–66; Thomas Jefferson to Alexander, August 29, 1808, Jefferson Writings, 9:206–7.

17. James Madison to John Armstrong, July 21, 1808, ASPFR, 3:254; John Armstrong to Champagny, July 4 and August 6, 1808, ASPFR, 3:254, 255.

Chapter 16. Abolishing the Slave Trade

1. Jefferson Address to Congress, December 2, 1806, Jefferson Writings, 8:492.

2. Malone, *Second Term*, 546.

3. Ibid.

Chapter 17. Across the Wide Missouri

1. Bernard W. Sheehan, *The Seeds of Extinction: Jeffersonian Philanthropy and the American Indians* (New York: W. W. Norton, 1974); Thomas Jefferson to William Henry Harrison, February 27, 1803, LC 22410–22413.

2. Jefferson, *Notes on the State of Virginia*, 63, 101.

3. Thomas Jefferson to Osage Chiefs, January 7, 1802, Jefferson Works, 16:390.

4. Thomas Jefferson to William Henry Harrison, February 27, 1803, LC 22410–22413.

Chapter 18. Passing the Torch

1. Thomas Jefferson to John Taylor, January 6, 1805, in *Thomas Jefferson: Writings* (New York: Library of America, 1984).

Chapter 19. James Madison and American Power

1. Marshall Smelser, *The Democratic Republic, 1801–1815* (New York: Harper & Row, 1968), 181.

2. Irving Brant, *James Madison*, 6 vols. (Indianapolis, IN: Bobbs-Merrill, 1941–61); Ralph Ketcham, *James Madison: A Biography* (New York: Macmillan, 1971); Robert Allen Rutland, *James Madison: The Founding Father* (New York: Macmillan, 1987); Lance Banning, "The Moderate as Revolutionary: An Introduction to Madison's Life," *Quarterly Journal of the Library of Congress* 37 (1980): 162–75; Robert Allen Rutland, *The Presidency of James Madison* (Lawrence: University Press of Kansas, 1990).

3. Rutland, *Founding Father*, 21.

4. Brant, *James Madison*, 5:269.

5. Rutland, *Founding Father*, 1.

6. Federalist Papers, 383.

7. *Annals*, 1st Cong., 1st Sess., 1789–90, 235.

8. Banning, *Jeffersonian Persuasion*; McCoy, *Elusive Republic*.

9. For an especially scathing appraisal, see White, *The Jeffersonians*.

10. Memorandum on Robert Smith, Madison Writings, 8:138–44.

11. Albert Gallatin to Thomas Jefferson, November 8, 1809, Gallatin Writings, 1:465–66.

12. Rutland, *Founding Father*, 34.

13. Martis, *Historical Atlas of Political Parties*; Rudolph M. Bell, "Mr. Madison's War and Long-Term Congressional Voting Behavior," *William and Mary Quarterly*, 3 ser., 36, no. 3 (July 1979): 373–95; Hickey, *War of 1812*, 105.

14. Norman K. Risjord, *The Old Republicans: Southern Conservatism in the Age of Jefferson* (New York: Columbia University Press, 1965); James Sterling Young, *The Washington Community, 1800–1828* (New York: Columbia University Press, 1966); Robert E. Shalhope, "Toward a Republican Synthesis: The Emergence of an Understanding of Republicanism in American Historiography," *William and Mary Quarterly*, 3rd ser., 29, no. 1 (1972): 49–80.

15. Reginald Horsman, "Who Were the War Hawks?" *Indiana Magazine of History* 60, no. 2 (June 1964): 121–36; Ronald L. Hatzenbuehler, "The War Hawks and the Question of Congressional Leadership in 1812," *Pacific Historical Review* 45, no. 1 (February 1976): 1–22; Harry Fritz, "The War Hawks of 1812: Party Leadership in the Twelfth Congress," *Capitol Studies* 5 (1977): 25–42; J. C. A. Stagg, "James Madison and the 'Malcontents': The Political Origins of the War of 1812," *William and Mary Quarterly*, 3rd. ser., 33, no. 4 (October 1976): 557–85.

Chapter 20. From Embargo to Non-Intercourse

1. James Madison to Thomas Jefferson, Madison Writings, 12:269–70.

2. Brant, *James Madison*, 1:160–61.

3. Annals, 10 Cong., 2d Sess., 1808–1809, 343–85, 451–52, 1432, 1541, 1824–30.

4. George Canning to David Erskine, January 23, 1809, British Instructions (see list of abbreviations), 261.

5. David Erskine to Robert Smith, April 17 and 18, 1809, Robert Smith to David Erskine, April 17 and 19, 1809, ASPFR, 3:295–97; Madison proclamation, April 19, 1809, Madison Papers, 1:125–26.

6. Frances Jackson to Robert Smith, October 11 and 27, 1809, ASPFR, 3:308–11, 316; Robert Smith to Frances Jackson, October 19, 1809, ASPFR, 3:311–14.

7. Annals, 11th Cong., 2d Sess., 1810–1811, 1780.

8. Annals, 11th Cong., 2d Sess., 1810–1811, 2582–83.

9. Cadore to John Smith, August 5, 1810, ASPFR, 3:396–87; John Armstrong to James Madison, August 5, 1810, James Madison to John Armstrong, October 29, 1810, Madison Papers, LC.

10. Presidential Messages, 1:481–82.

11. Richard Wellesley to William Pinkney, August 31 and December 29, 1810, ASPFR, 3:366, 408–9; William Pinkney to Robert Smith, December 14, 1810, ASPFR, 3:375; Richard Wellesley to William Pinkney, February 11, 1811, ASPFR, 3:412.

12. Horsman, *Causes of the War of 1812*, 196–87.

Chapter 21. Florida Coups and Intrigues

1. Isaac Cox, *The West Florida Controversy 1798–1813: A Study in American Diplomacy* (Baltimore: Johns Hopkins Press, 1918); Hubert Bruce Fuller, *The Purchase of Florida: Its History and Diplomacy* (Gainesville: University of Florida Press, 1964); Charles D. Ameringer, *U.S. Foreign Intelligence: The Secret Side of American History* (Lexington, MA: Lexington Books, 1990); Frank Lawrence Owsley and Gene A. Smith, *Filibusters and Expansionists: Jeffersonian Manifest Destiny, 1800–1821* (Tuscaloosa: University of Alabama Press, 1997); John J. Carter, *Covert Operations as a Tool of Presidential Foreign Policy in American History from 1800 to 1920: Foreign Policy in the Shadows* (New York: Edwin Mellen Press, 2000).

2. James Madison to Thomas Jefferson, October 19, 1810, Madison Papers, LC.

3. Fuller, *Purchase of Florida*, 188.

4. Brant, *James Madison*, 5:442–43; Rembert W. Patrick, *Florida Fiasco: Rampant Rebels on the Georgia-Florida Border, 1810–1815* (Athens: University of Georgia Press, 1954).

Chapter 22. The Struggle for the Northwest Frontier

1. David R. Edmunds, *The Shawnee Prophet* (Lincoln: University of Nebraska Press, 1983); David R. Edmunds, *Tecumseh and the Quest for Indian Leadership* (Boston: Little, Brown, 1984); John Sugden, *Tecumseh: A Life* (New York: Henry Holt, 1998).

2. William Henry Harrison to William Eustis, August 7, 1811, in Logan Esarey, ed., *The Messages and Letters of William Henry Harrison* (Indianapolis, IN: Bobbs-Merrill, 1922), 1:548.

3. Sugden, *Tecumseh*, 235–36.

Chapter 23. Down the Slippery Slope

1. Memorandum as to Robert Smith, Madison Writings, 8:138–44; James Madison to Thomas Jefferson, July 8, 1811, Madison Papers, LC.

2. Augustus Foster to James Monroe, November 1, 1811, April 15 and June 1, 1812, ASPFR, 3:499–500, 454, 459–60; James Monroe to Augustus Foster, November 12, 1811, May 30 and June 8, 1812, ASPFR, 3:500, 343, 464.

3. August Foster to James Monroe, July 3, 1811, ASPFR, 3:435–37; James Madison to August Foster, July 23, 1811, ASPFR, 3:439–42.

4. Bassano to Jonathan Russell, May 4, 1811, ASPFR, 3:505–6.

5. Alfred Mahan, *Sea Power in Its Relations to the War of 1812* (Boston: Little, Brown, 1905), 1:268.

6. James Madison to Joel Barlow, November 17, 1811, Madison Papers, LC.

7. J. C. A. Stagg, *Mr. Madison's War: Politics, Diplomacy, and Warfare in the Early American Republic, 1783–1830* (Princeton, NJ: Princeton University Press, 1983), 78.

8. For overviews of the causes of the 1812 War, see Charles C. Hyneman, *The First American Neutrality: A Study of the American Understanding of Neutral Obligations during the Years 1792 to 1815* (Urbana: University of Illinois Press, 1934); A. L. Burt, *The United States, Great Britain, and British North America from the Revolution to the Establishment of Peace after the War of 1812* (New Haven, CT: Yale University Press, 1941); Warren H. Goodman, "The War of 1812: A Survey of Changing Interpretations," *Mississippi Valley Historical Review* 28 (September 1941): 171–86; Bradford Perkins, *Prologue to War: England and the United States, 1805–1812* (Berkeley: University of California Press, 1961); Reginald Horsman, *The Causes of the War of 1812* (Philadelphia: University of Pennsylvania Press, 1962); Clifford L. Egan, "The Origins of the War of 1812: Three Decades of Historical Writing," *Military Affairs* 38, no. 2 (April 1974): 72–75; Bradford Perkins, ed., *The Causes of the War of 1812: National Honor or National Interest?* (Huntington, NY: R. E. Krieger Publishings, 1976); Ronald L. Hatzenbuehler and Robert L. Ivie, *Congress Declares War: Rhetoric, Leadership, and Partisanship in the Early Republic* (Kent, OH: Kent State University Press, 1983).

For the view that the war reflected an emerging bipartisan consensus built partly on a common enemy and fear of a crumbling national unity, see Shalhope, "Toward a Republican Synthesis"; Robert E. Shalhope, *The Roots of Democracy: American Thought and Culture, 1760–1800* (Boston: Twayne, 2004).

For the view that partisanship was a primary cause, see Richard Hofstadter, *The Idea of a Party System: The Rise of Legitimate Opposition in the United States, 1780–1840* (Berkeley: University of California Press, 1969); Robert Allen Rutland, *Madison's Alternatives: The Jeffersonian Republicans and the Coming of War, 1805–1812* (Philadelphia: Lippincott, 1975); Ronald Hatzenbuehler, "Party Unity and the Decision for War in the House of Representatives, 1812," *William and Mary Quarterly*, 3rd ser., 29, no. 3 (July 1972): 367–90.

For the view that the war was mostly a reaction to the attacks on American interests caused by the wars in Europe, see Horsman, *Causes of the War of 1812*.

For the view that the War Hawks and national honor led America to war, see Margaret Kinard Latimer, "South Carolina—A Protagonist of the War of 1812," *American Historical Review* 61, no. 4 (July 1956): 914–29; Norman K. Risjord, "1812: Conservatives, War Hawks, and the Nation's Honor," *William and Mary Quarterly*, 3rd ser., 18, no. 2 (April 1961), 200, 294; Horsman, "Who Were the War Hawks?"; Roger Brown, *The Republic in Peril: 1812* (New York: Columbia University Press, 1964); Ronald L. Hatzenbuehler, "War Hawks"; Fritz, " War Hawks of 1812."

For the view that economic dislocations in the trans-Appalachian West were a primary cause of war, see George Rogers Taylor, "Prices in the Mississippi Valley Preceding the War of 1812," *Journal of Economic and Business History* 3 (1930): 148–63; George Rogers Taylor, "Agrarian Discontent in the Mississippi Valley Preceding the War of 1812," *Journal of Political Economy* 39 (August 1931): 471–505.

For the view that freedom of the sea and trade was the primary cause, see Perkins, *Prologue to War*.

For the view that an aggressive republicanism was a primary cause, see Richard Buel, *Securing the Revolution: Ideology in American Politics, 1789–1815* (Ithaca, NY: Cornell University Press, 1972).

9. Mahan, *Sea Power*, 1:74, 71–72.

10. Ketcham, *James Madison: A Biography*, 498.

11. Augustus John Foster, *Jeffersonian America: Notes on the United States of America, Collected in the Years 1805–6–7, and 11–12*, ed. Richard Beale Davis (Westport, CT: Greenwood Press, 1980), 97.

12. Merrill Peterson, *The Great Triumvirate: Webster, Clay, and Calhoun* (New York: Oxford University Press, 1987), 3.

13. Hickey, *War of 1812*, 29.

14. Annals, 12th Cong., 1st Sess. 1811–1812, 534, 441.

15. Annals, 12th Cong., 1st Sess. 1811–1812, 599.

16. For the definitive biography, see Robert V. Remini, *Henry Clay: Statesman for the Union* (New York: W. W. Norton, 1991).

17. Annals, 12th Cong., 1st Sess. 1811–1812, 599–601.

18. John Spencer Bassett, ed., *The Correspondence of Andrew Jackson*, 6 vols. Washington, DC: Carnegie Institute, 1926–33), 1:221–22.

19. Rutland, *Founding Father*, 95.

20. Ibid., 105.

21. Thomas Jefferson to William Duane, August 4, 1812, Jefferson Writings, 11:265.

22. Augustus Foster to James Monroe, November 1, 1811, and James Monroe to Augustus Foster, ASPFR, 3:499–500.

23. Presidential Messages, 1:494.

24. Alexander S. Balinky, "Gallatin's Theory of War Finance," *William and Mary Quarterly*, 3rd ser., 16, no. 1 (January 1959): 73–86; Robert D. Horwats, *The Price of Liberty: Paying for America's Wars from the Revolution to the War on Terror* (New York: Times Books, 2007); George C. Herring, *From Colony to Superpower: United States Foreign Relations Since 1776* (New York: Oxford University Press, 2008).

25. E. A. Cruikshank, *The Political Adventures of John Henry: The Record of an International Imbroglio* (Toronto: Macmillan, 1936).

26. Presidential Messages, 1:498.

27. Henry Clay to James Monroe, March 15, 1812, Clay Papers, 1:637.

28. Hickey, *War of 1812*, 39.

29. Isaac Cox, "The Border Missions of General George Mathews," *Mississippi Valley Historical Review* 12, no. 3 (December 1925), 309–33; Rembert W. Patrick, *Florida Fiasco: Rampant Rebels on the Georgia-Florida Border, 1810–1815* (Athens: University of Georgia Press, 1954), 120–22.

30. Horsman, *Cause of the War of 1812*, 15.

31. Hazenbuehler and Ivie, *Congress Declares War*, 21.

32. Stagg, *Mr. Madison's War*, 105.

Chapter 24. Into the Abyss

1. James Madison to Henry Wheaton, February 26–27, 1812, Madison Writings, 9:272–73; Castlereagh to Augustus Foster, March 19, 1812 (three letters), British Instructions, 350.

2. James Madison to Thomas Jefferson, May 25, 1812, Madison Papers, LC.

3. Presidential Messages, 2:484–490.

4. Ronald L. Hatzenbuehler, "Party Unity and the Decision for War in the House of Representatives, 1812," *William and Mary Quarterly*, 3rd ser., 29, no. 3 (July 1972): 367–90.

5. Stagg, *Mr. Madison's War*, 107; Hickey, *War of 1812*, 46.

6. Rutland, *Founding Father*, 103.

7. Presidential Messages, 1:512–13.

8. Adams, *History of the United States of America*, 2:440.

Chapter 25. Second Thoughts?

1. John Warren to James Monroe, September 30, 1812, ASPFR, 3:595–96; James Monroe to John Warren, October 27, 1812, ASPFR, 3:596–97.

2. Adams, *History of the United States*, 6:215–18; Report of the Foreign Relations Committee, June 3, 1812, ASPFR, 3:567–70.

Chapter 26. Mustering the Nation

1. Thomas Jefferson to James Madison, August 5, 1812, and James Madison to Thomas Jefferson, April 24, 1812, Madison Papers, LC.

2. Hickey, *War of 1812*, 49–50.

3. Brant, *Madison: Secretary of State*, 5:266–67.

4. Bray Hammond, *Banks and Politics in America: From the Revolution to the Civil War* (Princeton, NJ: Princeton University Press, 1957), 211–26.

5. Malone, *Second Term*, 515–16.

6. John R. Etling, *Amateurs to Arms!: A Military History of the War of 1812* (New York: Da Capo Press, 1995), 69; Navy Secretary Report, June 9, 1809, and December 3, 1811, ASPNA, 1:200, 249–50.

7. Adam Seybert, *Statistical Annals . . . of the United States of America* (New York: A. M. Kelly, 1970), 712. First printing 1818; Etling, *Amateurs to Arms!*, 6.

8. Hickey, *War of 1812*, 50, 342.

9. William Eustis to James Madison, April 9, 1812, Madison Papers, LC; Hickey, *War of 1812*, 75.

10. Royal Ornan Shreve, *The Finished Scoundrel: General James Wilkinson, Sometime Commander in Chief of the Army of the United States, Who Made Intrigue a Trade and Treason a Profession* (Indianapolis: Bobbs-Merrill, 1933), 256; Thomas R. Hay and M. R. Werner, *The Admirable Trumpeter: A Biography of General James Wilkinson* (Garden City, NY: Doubleday, Doran, & Company, 1941), 300–307.

11. Rutland, *Founding Father*, 57–59.

12. Stagg, *Mr. Madison's War*, 167.

13. Scott, *Memoirs*, 1:35; William B. Skelton, "High Army Leadership in the Era of the War of 1812: The Making and Remaking of the Officer Corps," *William and Mary Quarterly*, 3rd ser., 51, no. 2 (April 1994): 253–74.

14. Hickey, *War of 1812*, 76.

15. Scott, *Memoirs*, 1:31.

16. 1810 Census, www.censusrecords.com.

17. Stagg, *Mr. Madison's War*, 162–63.

18. Hickey, *War of 1812*, 77.

19. Ibid., 76–77.

20. Henry Clay to Thomas Bodley, December 18, 1812, Clay Papers, 1:842.

21. Hickey, *War of 1812*, 72–73.

22. Adams, *History of the United States*, 2:392; J. C. A. Stagg, "James Madison and the Coercion of Great Britain: Canada, the West Indies, and the War of 1812," *William and Mary Quarterly*, 3rd ser., 38, no. 1 (January 1981): 3–34.

Chapter 27. The Great Lakes Front

1. William Hull, *Memoirs of the Campaign of the Northwestern Army of the United States, A.D. 1812* (Boston: True and Green, 1824); Ernest A. Cruikshank, ed., *Documents Relating to the Invasion of Canada and the Surrender of Detroit, 1812* (Ottawa: Publications of the Public Archives of Canada, 1912).

2. Stagg, *Mr. Madison's War*, 215.

3. Ibid., 205–7.

Chapter 28. The War at Sea

1. Hickey, *War of 1812*, 92–93.

2. Ibid., 96.

3. Ibid., 93–99.

Chapter 29. Staying the Course

1. Hickey, *War of 1812*, 102.

Chapter 30. Paying the Piper

1. Stagg, *Mr. Madison's War*, 292.

2. John Jacob Astor to Albert Gallatin, February 6, 14, March 20, April 5, 1813, Albert Gallatin to Stephen Girard et al., February 24, 1813, Albert Gallatin to Alexander Dallas, March 19, 1813, David Parish and Stephen Girard to Albert Gallatin, April 5, 1813, Albert Gallatin to James Madison, March 5, 1813, Gallatin Papers; Donald R. Adams, *Finance and Enterprise in Early America: A Study of Stephen Girard's Bank, 1812–1831* (Philadelphia: University of Pennsylvania Press, 1978), 30–34.

3. Stagg, *Mr. Madison's War*, 298; Axel Madsen, *John Jacob Astor: America's First Multimillionaire* (New York: John Wiley & Sons, 2001), 141–42.

Chapter 31. Truth and Consequences

1. Stagg, Mr. Madison's War, 53.

2. James Monroe to Thomas Jefferson, November 11, 1812, Monroe Papers, LC.

3. Presidential Messages, 2:499–506.

Chapter 32. The Politics of War

1. James Madison to John Armstrong, January 14, 1813, John Armstrong to James Madison, January 17, 1813, Madison Papers, LC.

2. Unless otherwise noted, statistics come from either Etling, Amateurs to Arms!, or Hickey, War of 1812.

3. John Armstrong to William Henry Harrison, March 17, 1813, in Logan Esarey, Messages and Letters of William Henry Harrison (New York: Arno Press, 1975), 2:386.

Chapter 33. The Lake Ontario Deadlock

1. Scott, Memoirs, 1:94.

Chapter 34. "We Have Met the Enemy and They Are Ours!"

1. Hickey, War of 1812, 133.

2. William Henry Harrison to John Armstrong, May 11, 1814, Harrison Papers, LC.

Chapter 35. The Red Stick War

1. David S. Heidler and Jeanne T. Heidler, Old Hickory's War: Andrew Jackson and the Quest for Empire (Mechanicsburg, PA: Stackpole Books, 1996); John Buchanan, Jackson's War: Andrew Jackson and the People of the Western Waters (New York: John Wiley & Sons, 2001).

2. Hickey, War of 1812, 148; Buchanan, Jackson's War, 224.

Chapter 36. "Don't Give Up the Ship!"

1. Hickey, War of 1812, 151.

2. Journal of Charles Napier, August 12, 1813, in William F. P. Napier, The Life and Opinions of General Sir Charles James Napier (London: J. Murray, 1857), 1:221.

3. Hickey, War of 1812, 155.

4. Ibid., 157.

Chapter 37. Groping for a Way Out

1. Albert Gallatin to James Monroe, January 4, 1813, Monroe Papers, LC.

2. Nikolai Bolkhovitinov, The Beginnings of Russian-American Relations, 1775–1815, trans. Elena Levin (Cambridge, MA: Harvard University Press, 1975), 304–14; Nikolai Bolkhovitinov and S. I. Divil'kovskii, "Russian Diplomacy and the Anglo-American War of 1812–1814," Soviet Studies in History 1 (1962).

3. John Quincy Adams to James Monroe, September 30, October 17, December 11, 1812, ASPFR, 3:625, 625–26, 626–27; James Monroe to John Quincy Adams, April 26, 1813, Adams Family Papers, MHS; Dashkov to James Monroe, March 8, 1813, ASPFR, 3:624; James Monroe to Dashkov, March 11, 1813, ASPFR, 3:624–25.

4. Stagg, Mr. *Madison's War*, 300.

5. James Monroe to Commissioners, April 15, 1813, ASPFR, 3:695–700; James Monroe to Albert Gallatin, April 27, and May 5, 6, 1813, Gallatin Papers, LC.

6. James Monroe to Commissioners, April 27, 1813, Gallatin Writings, 1:539.

7. Ibid.; Albert Gallatin to James Monroe, May 2, 1813, Gallatin Writings, 1:539–40; James Monroe to Albert Gallatin, May 6, 1813, Gallatin Writings, 1:542–44.

8. Alexander Dallas to Albert Gallatin and Hannah Gallatin, July 22, 1813, Gallatin Papers.

9. Richardson, Presidential Messages, 1:526; Annals, 13th Cong., 1st Sess., 1813–1814, 98.

10. Harmunus Bleecker, January 7, 1813, Annals, 12th Cong., 2d Sess., 1814–1815, 621.

11. Felix Grundy speech, June 18, 1813, Annals, 13th Cong., 1st Sess., 1813–1814, 225–26.

12. Annals, 13th Cong., 1st Sess., 1813–1814, 302–10.

13. ASPFR, 3:608–18.

14. ASPFR, 3:606–8; Annals, 13th Cong., 1st Sess., 1813–1814, 99–101, 501–3.

15. Stagg, Mr. *Madison's War*, 319.

16. John Quincy Adams to James Monroe, June 26, 1813, ASPFR, 3:627.

17. James Madison to Congress, December 7, 1813, Annals, 13th Cong., 2d Sess., 1814–1815, 538–44.

18. Annals, 13th Cong., 2d Sess., 1814–1815, 2031–32.

19. Albert Gallatin to Alexander Baring, June 22 and August 27, 1813, Gallatin Writings, 5:545–46, 564–67; Alexander Baring to Albert Gallatin, July 22, 1813, Gallatin Writings, 1:546–52, 584–87.

Chapter 38. Politics as Usual

1. Hickey, *War of 1812*, 161–62.

2. Stagg, Mr. *Madison's War*, 375.

3. Hickey, *War of 1812*, 164.

4. Annals, 13th Cong., 2d Sess., 1814–1815, 1374.

5. George Campbell to James Madison, May 4, 1814, James Madison to George Campbell, May 7, 1814, Madison Papers, LC; John Jacob Astor to James Monroe, April 30 and June 1, 1814, Monroe Papers, LC; Treasury Secretary report, September 23, 1814, ASPFR, 2:845–46; Adams, *Finance and Enterprise*, 36, 37, 44.

Chapter 39. First the Good News

1. Castlereagh to James Monroe, November 4, 1813, ASPFR, 3:621.

2. James Monroe to Castlereagh, January 5, 1814, ASPFR, 3:622–23.

3. James Monroe to Commissioners, January 28, February 10, April 15, 1814, ASPFR, 3:701–2, 703, 695–700.

4. John Bayard and Albert Gallatin to James Monroe, May 6, 1814, Gallatin Writings, 1:611–13.

5. Annals, 13th Cong., 2d Sess., 1814–1815: 694, 731–41, 1946, 1962–77, 1986–2001, 2001–2, 2839.

Chapter 40. The Rock of Sisyphus

1. John Armstrong to James Madison, June 4, 1814, Madison Papers, LC.
2. Ibid.
3. Hickey, *War of 1812*, 177–80.
4. James Madison to James Monroe, May 23, 1814, Monroe Papers, LC.

Chapter 41. Moral and Diplomatic Dilemmas

1. Cabinet Memorandum, June 23 and 24, 1814, Madison Papers, LC.
2. Albert Gallatin and James Bayard to James Monroe, May 5, 1814, Monroe Papers, LC.
3. Cabinet Memorandum, June 27, 1814, Madison Papers, LC; James Monroe to Commissioners, June 29, 1814, Gallatin Papers, LC.
4. *Daily National Intelligencer*, June 20, 1814, NYPL.

Chapter 42. Indian Summer Campaigns

1. John Mahon, *The War of 1812* (New York: Da Capo Press, 1991), 269.

Chapter 43. Is Washington Burning?

1. John Armstrong to Richard Johnston, October 17, 1814, ASPMA, 1:539.
2. George Dangerfield, *The Awakening of American Nationalism, 1815–1828* (New York: Harper & Row, 1965), 5.
3. ASPMA, 2:524–99; Stagg, *Mr. Madison's War*, 429.
4. ASPFR, 2:840–843.
5. Hammond, *Banks and Politics in America*, 209–50.

Chapter 44. Conformists and Dissidents

1. David H. Fischer, *The Revolution of American Conservatism: The Federalist Party in the Era of Jeffersonian Democracy* (New York: Harper & Row, 1965); Linda K. Kerber, *The Federalists in Dissent: Imagery and Ideology in Jeffersonian America* (Ithaca, NY: Cornell University Press, 1980).
2. Russell Kirk, *John Randolph of Roanoke* (Chicago: University of Chicago Press, 1951); John S. Pancake, "The 'Invisibles': A Chapter in the Opposition to President Madison," *Journal of Southern History* 21, no. 1 (February 1955): 17–37; Risjord, *Old Republicans*.
3. Henry Clay to Caesar Rodney, December 29, 1812, Clay Papers, 1:750.
4. Stagg, *Mr. Madison's War*, 254.
5. Henry Clay to Caesar Rodney, December 29, 1812, Clay Papers, 1:750.
6. John C. Calhoun to James McBride, December 25, 1812, in Robert L. Meriwether, ed., *The Papers of John C. Calhoun* (Columbia: University of South Carolina Press, 1959).
7. Theodore Dwight, *History of the Hartford Convention: With a Review of the Policy of the United States Government Which Led to the War of 1812* (Boston: Russell, Odiorne, & Company, 1833), 352–79.
8. James Madison to Wilson Cary Nicholas, November 25, 1814, Madison Papers, LC.

Chapter 45. The Treaty of Ghent

1. Frank A. Updyke, *The Diplomacy of the War of 1812* (Baltimore: Johns Hopkins Press, 1915), 194–95.

2. Commissioners to James Monroe, August 12 and 19, 1814, ASPFR, 3:705–7, 708–9; James Monroe to Commissioners, June 27 and October 19, 1814, ASPFR, 3:704–5, 732; British to American Ministers, August 19, September 4, 19, October 8, 31, December 22, 1814, ASPFR, 3:710, 713–15, 717–18, 721–23, 726, 744–45; American to British Ministers, August 24, September 9, 26, October 13, 24, November 10, December 14, 1814, ASPFR, 3:711–13, 715–17, 719–21, 723–24, 725, 733–34, 743–44.

3. British to American Ministers, October 8, 1814, ASPFR, 3:721–23.

4. American to British Ministers, October 13, 1814, ASPFR, 3:723–24; Commissioners to James Monroe, October 25, 1814, ASPFR, 3:710–11.

5. Commissioners to James Monroe, December 25, 1814, ASPFR, 3:732–33.

Chapter 46. The Battle of New Orleans

1. Robert Remini, *Andrew Jackson and the Course of the American Empire, 1767–1821* (New York: Harper & Row, 1977); Heidler and Heidler, *Old Hickory's War.*

2. Frank Owsley Jr., *The Struggle for the Gulf Borderlands: The Creek War and the Battle of New Orleans, 1812–1815* (Gainesville: University Press of Florida, 1981).

3. Andrew Jackson to James Monroe, October 27 and 31, 1814, Andrew Jackson to Manrique Gonzales, November 6 and 7, 1814, Jackson Papers, LC.

4. James Monroe to Andrew Jackson, October 21, 1814, Jackson Papers, LC.

5. Andrew Jackson to James Monroe, November 14, 1814, Jackson Papers, LC.

6. General Orders of December 16, 1814, in Niles Register 7, January 14, 1815, 316–17.

7. Hickey, *War of 1812*, 212.

Chapter 47. A Distant Mirror?

1. For the best overviews of the war, see Glenn Tucker, *Poltroons and Patriots: A Popular Account of the War of 1812*, 2 vols. (Indianapolis: Bobbs-Merrill Company, 1954); Reginald Horsman, *The War of 1812* (New York: Knopf, 1969); Stagg, *Mr. Madison's War*; and Hickey, *War of 1812.*

2. Nettels, *Emergence of a National Economy*, 385, 396, 399; Rutland, *Founding Father*, 196; Edwin J. Perkins, *American Public Finance and Financial Services, 1700–1815* (Columbus: Ohio State University Press, 1994); and Hormats, *Price of Liberty.*

3. Hickey, *War of 1812*, 302. As for veterans' payments, the last veteran died in 1905 and the last pensioner, a veteran's daughter, in 1946!

4. Stagg, *Mr. Madison's War*, 376.

5. Annals, 14th Cong., 1st Sess., 1815–1816, 783.

6. J. C. A. Stagg, "Enlisted Men in the United States Army, 1813–1815: A Preliminary Survey," *William and Mary Quarterly*, 3rd ser., 43, no. 4 (October 1986): 615–45; William B. Skelton, "High Army Leadership in the Era of the War of 1812: The Making and Remaking of the Officer Corps," *William and Mary Quarterly*, 3rd ser., 51, no. 2 (April 1994): 253–274.

7. Etling, *Amateurs to Arms!*, 325–26; Hickey, *War of 1812*, 302.

8. Skelton, "High Army Leadership," 271–72.

9. Donald R. Hickey, "The War of 1812: Still a Forgotten Conflict?" *Journal of Military History* 65, no. 3 (July 2001): 748; Ian W. Toll, *Six Frigates: The Epic History of the Founding of the U.S. Navy* (New York: W. W. Norton, 2006), 408.

10. Updyke, *Diplomacy of the War*, 373; Michael Smelser, *The Democratic Republic, 1801–1815* (New York: Harper & Row, 1968), 250. The best naval studies include Theodore Roosevelt, *The Naval War of 1812* (New York: G. P. Putnam's Sons, 1882); Mahan, *Sea Power*; and Toll, *Six Frigates*.

The Art of American Power in the Early Republic

1. Hammond, *Banks and Politics*, 242.

2. Ibid., 227.

3. Nettels, *Emergence of a National Economy*, 384.

4. Ibid., 385.

5. Ibid., 396, 399; Ben Wattenberg, ed., *The Statistical History of the United States from Colonial Times to the Present* (New York: Basic Books, 1976), 750–51, 760–61.

6. Federalist Papers, 136–42; Thomas Jefferson to James Monroe, November 24, 1801, Jefferson Writings, 9:317; Jefferson's Inaugural Address, March 4, 1801, Jefferson Writings, 494.

7. Camillus, 1795, Hamilton Works, 5:207; "The Answer," 1796, Hamilton Works, 7:228.

8. "Political Observations," 1795, *Letters and Other Writings of James Madison* (Philadelphia: J. B. Lippincott, 1867), 4:491–92.

9. Federalist Papers, 11:139.

10. Alexander Hamilton to Oliver Wolcott, March 30, 1797, in George Gibbs, ed., *Memoirs of the Administrations of Washington and John Adams, Edited from the Papers of Oliver Wolcott, Secretary of the Treasury* (New York: William Van Norden, 1846), 1:485; Camillus, Hamilton Works, 5:213; Alexander Hamilton to George Washington, September 15, 1790, Hamilton Works, 4:335.

11. Richard Kohn, *Eagle and Sword: The Federalists and the Creation of the Military Establishment in America, 1783–1802* (New York: Free Press, 1975); Craig Symonds, *Navalists and Antinavalists: The Naval Policy Debate in the United States, 1785–1827* (Newark: University of Delaware Press, 1980); Crackel, "Jefferson, Politics, and the Army," 21–38.

12. John Shy, "The American Military Experience: History and Learning," *Journal of Interdisciplinary History* 1, no. 2 (Winter 1971): 205–28; Charles Royster, *A Revolutionary People at War: The Continental Army and American Character, 1775–1783* (Chapel Hill: University of North Carolina Press, 1979); E. Wayne Carp, *To Starve the Army at Pleasure: Continental Army Administration and American Political Culture, 1775–1783* (Chapel Hill: University of North Carolina Press, 1984); Don Higginbotham, "The Early American Way of War: Reconnaissance and Appraisal," *William and Mary Quarterly*, 3rd. ser., 44, no. 2 (April 1987): 230–73; Kohn, *Eagle and Sword*; Russell F. Weigley, *The American Way of War: A History of United States Military Strategy and Policy* (New York: Macmillan, 1973).

13. J. C. A. Stagg, "Soldiers in Peace and War: Comparative Perspective on the Recruitment of the United States Army, 1802–1815," *William and Mary Quarterly*, 3rd ser., 57, no. 1 (January 2000): 79–120.

14. Scott, *Memoirs*, 1:31.

15. Jefferson to William Stephens Smith, November 13, 1787, Jefferson Papers, 12:356–57.

16. McCullough, *John Adams*, 236–37.

Index

About the Author

William Nester is the author of thirty books on international relations, national development, and the nature of power. He is a professor in the Department of Government and Politics at St. John's University in New York City.